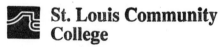 **St. Louis Community College**

Forest Park
Florissant Valley
Meramec

Instructional Resources
St. Louis, Missouri

GAYLORD

Sport and Society

Series Editors

Benjamin G. Rader

Randy Roberts

A list of books in the series appears at the end of this book.

Making the Team

Making the Team

*The Cultural Work
of Baseball Fiction*

Timothy Morris

University of Illinois Press
Urbana and Chicago

© 1997 by the Board of Trustees of the University of Illinois
Manufactured in the United States of America
1 2 3 4 5 C P 5 4 3 2 1

This book is printed on acid-free paper.

Library of Congress Cataloging-in-Publication Data
Morris, Timothy, 1959–
Making the team : the cultural work of baseball fiction
/ Timothy Morris.
    p.   cm. — (Sport and society)
Includes bibliographical references and index.
ISBN 0-252-02294-7 (alk. paper).
ISBN 0-252-06597-2 (pbk. : alk. paper)
1. Baseball stories, American—History and criticism.
2. Literature and society—United States—History
—20th century. 3. American fiction—20th century—History
and criticism. 4. Children's stories, American—History and
criticism. 5. National characteristics, American, in literature.
6. Assimilation (Sociology) in literature.
7. Maturation (Psychology) in literature. 8. Elite (Social
Sciences) in literature. 9. Heterosexuality in literature.
10. Social status in literature. 11. Bildungsroman. I. Title.
II. Series
PS374.B37M35   1997
813.009′355—dc20   96-10131
                                          CIP

For Margaret

nisi vero adprobat quisquam bonus rerum arbiter vapulasse me, quia ludebam pila puer et eo ludo inpediebar, quominus celeriter discerem litteras, quibus maior deformius luderem. aut aliud faciebat idem ipse, a quo vapulabam, qui si in aliqua quaestiuncula a condoctore suo victus esset, magis bile atque invidia torqueretur quam ego, cum in certamine pilae a conlusore meo superabar?

[But perhaps some indifferent judge might account me to be justly beaten for playing at ball, being yet a boy, because by that sport I was hindered in my learning, by which, when I came to be a man, I was to play the fool more unbeseemingly; or did my master, who now beat me, anything else? who, if in any trifling question he were foiled by another schoolmaster, he was presently more racked with choler and envy at him, than I was, when at a match at tennis-ball, I lost the game to my play-fellow.]

Augustine, *Confessions*

Baseball is a game that boys play for fun and men play for keeps.

Martin Quigley, *Today's Game*

Contents

Acknowledgments

I want to thank the students in my "Baseball and Writing" course at the University of Texas at Arlington (UTA). I also thank the Association of American Colleges and Universities for sponsoring the Boundaries and Borderlands Institute at Williams College in July 1995.

Part of chapter 3 was presented to the Sport Literature Association and appeared, in an earlier version, as "'Forget It Means Fuck It': Hispanic Stereotypes in Baseball Fiction," *Aethlon* 12, no. 2 (Spring 1995): 63–70. Part of chapter 5 was presented in a Hermann colloquium at UTA, and part of chapter 2 was read to the Gorgias Society there. Part of chapter 4 was presented to the Group for Early Modern Cultural Studies. For giving me these chances to share my ideas, I thank David Vanderwerken, Don Johnson, Carolyn Barros, Alan Taylor, and Rajani Sudan.

Michael Oriard critiqued the manuscript with great care and helped to tighten and clarify its language. Bruce Bethell continued this process with attentive and thoughtful editing. Ann Lowry gave this book thorough reading, wondrous help through technicalities, and the faith of a lifelong Cubs fan. I am also grateful for the interest and support of Stacy Alaimo, Nannette Manalo Brenner, Douglas Brown, Barbara Chiarello, Curtis Fukuchi, Mark Johnson, Dallas and Jo Lacy, Lori Lebow, Lisa Rathert, Ken Roemer, Deeanne Westbrook, Nancy Wood, and David Schoem's 1995 seminar group.

Very special thanks go to Donna Oliver, who challenged me to think more critically about baseball—and literature too—in terms of race, gender, and economics. Margaret Morris read the book in its earliest stages and helped me throughout its composition. Fran Morris helped with the index. Johanna Smith gave encouragement; also, this book would not have been written had she not given me a copy of *The Strike-Out King*. Thanks, Johanna.

Introduction

The few critical studies of baseball fiction that have been published deal with serious, literary adult novels. Cordelia Candelaria's *Seeking the Perfect Game* and Deeanne Westbrook's *Ground Rules* construct and discuss an emerging canon for the genre: *Bang the Drum Slowly*, by Mark Harris; *The Natural*, by Bernard Malamud; *The Great American Novel*, by Philip Roth; *The Universal Baseball Association*, by Robert Coover; *Shoeless Joe* and *The Iowa Baseball Confederacy*, by W. P. Kinsella; and *The Celebrant*, by Eric Rolfe Greenberg. These studies and other more general treatments of sport literature, such as Michael Oriard's *Dreaming of Heroes* and Christian K. Messenger's *Sport and the Spirit of Play in Contemporary American Fiction*, also talk about other baseball novels, but this is the core of their common canon: six or seven texts whose literary status is well respected.

There is, of course, a flourishing genre of far less respectable juvenile baseball fiction. The most valid generalization that can be made about adult baseball fiction and the scholarship on it is that it sets itself apart from that juvenile fiction. As Jerry Klinkowitz says of Earl Wasserman's early championing of *The Natural* as high literature, "Without the famous Romanticist's interpretation of Malamud's work it is doubtful Major League Baseball could parade all those quotations from Jacques Barzun and the like . . . it is the Malamud-Wasserman combination that clears the page of John Tunis-like drivel and prepares readers for the lines that have now—for better or for worse—taken their place as writerly monuments to the game" (33). Readers of *Making the Team* will need to prepare themselves for the reverse, however, for this book takes John Tunis —and many other writers working in the juvenile baseball genre— very seriously indeed. Moreover, it argues that to clear this "drivel" from the page is to deny a vital part of a genre, just as to clear genre fiction from the larger page of "literature" is to impoverish cultural understanding.

No other popular genre is so continually concerned with putting away childish things as is the baseball novel. Children's and teen mysteries, young adult romances, and juvenile science fiction, adventure, horror, and Western novels foster reading tastes that provide a bridge to adult genre fiction, but the reader of boys' or girls' baseball stories pauses on the threshold of adult reading with no easy way into a genre that is determined to rebuff its childhood fans.

Alternatively one could say that the genre is determined to disillusion them. It seems almost absurd to say this, but adult baseball fiction, and adult sports fiction in general, is darker, more disturbing, and more sinister than is other adult genre fiction—the more so because of sports fiction's determination to distance itself from its adolescent origins. Adult genre fiction is full of sex, violence, and sudden death, which are the stock-in-trade of escapism. Adult baseball fiction is full of sex and violence and death, but it presents all three as violations of a childhood world of play. The grown-up baseball novel is not for kids and never could be. It seems to want to say to its readers: "*This* is what your youth did not prepare you for; *this* is what it is really all about. The books of your childhood lied to you."

Baseball fiction employs the passing of time in a way that other genre fiction usually does not. Athletes have life trajectories. They are children; grow and mature; master some skills and fail others; and age, retire, and die, as the heroes of baseball books inevitably do as well. But heroes in other genre fictions do *not* age. Maigret was two years from retirement in about sixty-five consecutive novels by Georges Simenon, just as the Hardy Boys have been seventeen and eighteen for seventy straight summer vacations. Captain Kirk has been in space, with nothing but the suggestion of a different waistline to mark his aging, for what seems like centuries. Neither Nero Wolfe nor Archie ever aged or upset the initial balance of the generational dynamic between them. Philip Marlowe indeed ages in the Raymond Chandler novels, but only in the strange way that he descends deeper and more centrally into his original *middle age*. In genre fiction as in ancient mythic cycles, the hero's lifespan is like an accordion: we can expand it as needed to insert an infinitely great number of stories about him.

In contrast the baseball hero is, like the characters of realistic bourgeois fiction generally, of a specific age and aging at the usual rate. If young, he is learning his trade; if older, his body is forgetting what his mind is beginning to comprehend. He is more like Anna Karenina than like Miss Marple. He has a history and he has (ominously) a future; from the moment that he has no future, he *is* history.

What makes the split between adult and children's baseball fiction harder to understand is that there is no essential difference between adult and juvenile series heroes. Roy Tucker in John R. Tunis's juvenile Dodgers series learns, matures, earns stardom, goes to war, gets too old, and makes a last comeback; Henry Wiggen in Mark Harris's adult Mammoths series learns, matures, earns stardom, avoids the war, gets too old, and makes a last comeback. Novels for the young and old alike are committed to the realistic course of an athlete's existence. Nonetheless, baseball novels for the old are never for the young—not even for the young who may learn most of what they know about aging from baseball.

My argument in this book is that despite this well-policed boundary, the cultural work and ideological constructions of adult baseball fiction are continuous with those of juvenile baseball fiction. The continuity between the juvenile and the adult in baseball fiction and the rhetoric that denies and conceals this continuity can in turn provide a model for insights into the cultural construction of other kinds of literature, both "genre" and "serious," and into the functions of the literary as a cultural value.

I examine this often-denied, often-resisted continuity in baseball fiction in four thematic areas, followed by a chapter that considers the implications of a text's being "literary." The four themes—assimilation, heterosexuality, language, and meritocracy—do not exhaust the things that baseball fiction means or does. I choose them from the many possibilities because they are particularly problematic issues for America and Americanists in the mid-1990s.

Baseball fiction, and more generally the whole culture of baseball, is about assimilation to an American way of life. Baseball is a uniquely American game of tag in origin, recognizably a cousin of cricket and of various forms of rounders and dodgeball but idiosyncratic to the early nineteenth-century United States. Although originally American, the game has been exported to other countries, always maintaining its archetypal American form and rules. When rugby traveled abroad in the British Empire, it fragmented into as many different versions as there were Anglo-settled nations. American, Canadian, Australian, and Gaelic versions of "football" are its descendants. Baseball has remained an invariant window on American metropolitan culture for the neocolonial world, however. It flourishes in those nations where the United States has had a dominant economic or military presence: Japan, Korea, the Philippines, Taiwan, the Dominican Republic, Mexico, Puerto Rico, Cuba, and Venezuela.

Assimilation works at home, too. The classic locus for assimilation via baseball is the Jewish immigrant community. Baseball fiction is also concerned with a general dynamics of assimilation of which Jewish experience is the type example. In baseball novels players join to and meld with their teams, assimilating from the country to the city, from the experiences of the second-generation immigrant to those of the unmarked "American," from the south to the north, from black to white experience, from speaking Spanish to speaking English, and from the insular regional culture to cosmopolitanism. The nature of "American" experience is never straightforward, however. Assimilation is a dialectic, and America thus changes as groups from the margin join the center. Moreover the center itself has certain imperative reasons for asserting that it does not really exist, that it is always open, original, and new.

Actually the center claims only to be partially open. One ideology to which the assimilant must subscribe is that of heterosexuality. The literature of baseball is continuously about male heterosexuality; its characters are straight men in the process of reinforcing their straightness. They nevertheless are locked dangerously into all-male workplaces, where the primary vehicle for their individual success must be the professional and personal relationships they form with other men.

All these young men aim to construct a normative heterosexuality (which is more complicated an idea than is that of America), yet that heterosexuality must be won in the context of intense emotional bonding with other men, carried on far from the presence of women. Baseball players must find paths to manhood in a clubhouse stocked with twenty-four other naked young men. It should not be surprising that they find themselves in territories of plot and theme first explored in *The Picture of Dorian Gray* or in the paranoid Gothic.

The language in which the problems of assimilation and heterosexuality are worked out is not neutral, even if it aspires to be "plain American which cats and dogs can read" (Moore 46). The teams that unite to win the pennant or the "Big Game" are as much linguistic communities as they are ball clubs. The common language uniting the team members is threatened by jargons and dialects of all kinds, especially by the jargons of privileged social strata. Hence comes an attempt to find a common ground, an intranational vernacular that unites their linguistic communities of origin. Immigrants learn English through baseball and join the larger national community. That community is continually defended, in the rhetorics of baseball, from the pressure of Spanish, both in the United States and in the neoimperial territories that draw so many Spanish speakers into the game.

Baseball fiction is frequently convinced that Spanish does not really exist, that its speakers are subhuman, incapable of rational language. This conviction is balanced by an equally crazy suspicion that Spanish speakers can understand English and that their incomprehension is only a front for passive aggression or insidious eavesdropping: "I believe George can read," says Henry Wiggen of his Cuban teammate in *Bang the Drum Slowly* (205). Such suspicions help to construct the English-language community in baseball fiction and for the general culture that the genre addresses.

Of course all but the fairest-skinned Hispanics were kept out of organized American baseball until the 1950s. Legalized segregation was finally eroded, however, in part by the powerful ideology of meritocracy—the belief that in any sphere of endeavor, people who perform better than other people deserve more rewards, a better quality of life, more security, and more power. The rewards of meritocracy can be local or global, but they are invoked everywhere in American culture. They range from a private room on the road if you are a star ballplayer to a salary many times that of the highest-paid ballplayer if you are perceived as selling movies, soda pop, or cigarettes better than other CEOs do. Babe Ruth was perceived as having many better years than Herbert Hoover did, and he earned more than Hoover did during them.

The evil of meritocracy is that it rationalizes inequality. This central injustice of meritocracy was recognized when the word was coined, in Michael Young's satire *The Rise of the Meritocracy* (1958). Evil inheres in the most innocuous uses of merit to determine reward; from the moment a teacher lets the most obedient kindergartners go home first, it is used in the service of surveillance and control.

The apparent good of meritocracy is that it can erode other rationalizations of inequality, most notably racism and sexism. It is stretching a point only a little to say that when Jackie Robinson hit .342 to lead the National League in 1949, any rationale for legal segregation based on supposed black incompetence was shattered—the more so because baseball is a team sport, encoding in its formula for success social and intellectual abilities that individual sports do not require. Joe Louis and Jesse Owens became heroes to white Americans only because they were strong and fast; whites could discount their intellect. Robinson was *smart*, however, and to deny his brains would have been to dismantle the long-standing constructions of baseball as a "thinking man's" sport.

Nonetheless, although meritocracy may be used to erase an inequity based on one cultural category, it reinforces other inequities. It may even strengthen new inequities that mimic previous ones. Previously most engineers were men because only men were hired as engineers. Now most engineers are men because men have higher SAT scores than women do. The reification of aptitude in the abstract and seemingly objective form of test scores is difficult to dislodge from people's consciousness. Nor does this reliance on objective measures of merit do anything to change the fact that engineers make more money and have more power in society than most other people do. In Michael Young's fantasia of the perfect meritocracy, lines of class become even more strictly drawn than they were in the days of caste rule and nepotism.

American functionalist meritocracy could not survive without the batteries of statistical support that standardized testing provides. Baseball offers a spectacle of the pure work of statistical meritocracy. For any manager in business, it would be a dream come true to have the same kind of performance data at hand that a manager in baseball has. But even the unassailable numbers—batting average, ERA—provoke their own counter-rhetoric. "The things you do to win games don't show up in the box score," goes the old cliché. The numbers do not tell the whole story. The part of the story they do not tell is the region of social charisma, work ethic, and moral self-presentation, the (for want of a better term) *whiteness* of the player whose contribution to winning cannot be measured conventionally. This suspect "quality statistic" provokes deeper dreams of the perfect statistical reckoning, a reckoning surreally portrayed in Coover's *Universal Baseball Association.*

Baseball's lessons of meritocracy take many classic parabolic forms: steady effort and determination (the tortoise and the hare), teamwork and division of labor (the stomach and the hands, a parable dear to those who supported the owners during the 1994–95 baseball strike), and neglected merit revealed (the ugly duckling). Ultimately numbers are not enough for rhetorical purposes. We need narratives of merit, interpretations of merit, whole hermeneutics of merit. "The holders and possessors of wealth need, in all societies, to have the assurance of the best of moral titles to their fortune" (M. Young 130–31).

It may seem strange that I have chosen baseball and its fiction as the context for a critique of some centrally capitalist values in America, because many of the game's recent celebrants see it as our ultimate pre- and anticapitalist game. A critique of the ideologies of patriarchal functionalism seems to be more properly directed at football. Nevertheless baseball's power to employ pastoral perfectionism is exactly what motivates me to challenge the game's cultural work. The pastoral self-presentation of the sport is only the final layer of patina on the sport as spectacle—a spectacle that the 1994–95 strike awoke many fans to perceiving.

In addition baseball is like football in the most crucial respect: it is a zero-sum game. Public spectacles do not have to be zero-sum games, where there are as many winners as losers. The spectacles we watch, identify with, and learn from do not have to be contests of merit. Literature might be one of them—although we should remember that much of our sense of the literary in the West comes from the Peisistratan contests of Homeric recitation and the Athenian dramatic competitions. There continue to be other kinds of important public spectacles where the results are not contested (plays), where the conclusion is foregone (the Mass), or where the spectacle lacks rules (improvisational theater or performance art). Pastoral rhetoric about the cleanly competitive space of baseball, dear to both liberals and conservatives, seizes on an object central to corporate competition: team sport as pedagogic spectacle.

Baseball pastoralism typically conceives of a golden age of baseball: the 1920s or 1930s, the time of day baseball, played (supposedly) for the love of it in old cozy ballparks (and by segregated teams, in an era of oppressive labor conditions and chattel-like players bound by the reserve clause). Memorabilia that evoke the days of segregated baseball, either of the white teams or of the Negro leagues, are among the hottest marketing items of the 1990s. Negro league memorabilia and facsimiles are aimed at and sold to young white people who cannot remember segregation times. People are certainly trying to sell them to me, and my delight in learning about this era, my joy in reading about the careers of Turkey Stearnes or Biz Mackey, is tempered by an ironic realization that social injustice is being marketed as innocent nostalgia, as if there were something worth recapturing about the conditions that made segregation possible.

Baseball pastoralism celebrates the ballparks of the past and mourns their departure. It tries to re-create them in new stadiums such as the ones in Cleveland, Baltimore, and Arlington, Texas. The visual imagery of segregation times is invoked in a kind of perverse re-sculpturing of the blank suburb or the blasted center city into a time machine that will serve, at increasingly exclusionary prices, the self-congratulatory nostalgia of white liberals and white conservatives alike. The city gutted by white flight is reinvented under imaginary glass as an urban utopia. Alternatively (as in Arlington) it is simply posited as a completely imaginary space: outside the Ballpark one feels that one is on an urban street of the 1920s, when one is in fact in the middle of an enormous theme park on a suburban prairie; inside the Ballpark one feels that one is in a vital city center—till one looks up and out at nothing but the featureless blue Texas sky, broken only by small planes towing advertisements for topless bars.

I should not be talking like this. I am a baseball fan. I am a white liberal. I live, work, and go to ball games in Arlington, Texas. It took me many years, but I too finally fled the city. I spent my childhood in inner-city Chicago, where my father took me to my first baseball game in Wrigley Field, long before the lights. It was Ernie Banks Day, August 15, 1964, the year of the Civil Rights Act; in some ways that day was a celebration of integration. I realize now that it was also the Feast of the Assumption and that we should have been at mass instead. We were on our lapsing routes from ethnic urban Catholicism to the featureless civil religion of sport. I should now be defending the faith of day baseball and the El line to Cubs' Park, should be congratulating myself that my first hero in life was my father's hero too, a black Texan who became the most beloved person on Chicago's white North Side. I should be, and maybe in a way I am. But the instincts of someone born just on the waning edge of the Baby Boom impel me to critique what I have been raised to accept.

. . . . .

This book is unusual in several respects, and some comments on organization and procedure are appropriate.

First, as will seem evident, this is a resister's reading of baseball fiction, to use a term introduced by Judith Fetterley in *The Resisting Reader: A Feminist Approach to American Fiction.* Most studies of sports literature are so hesitant about asserting the importance of their subject, and so eager to defend and promote that subject, that resistance has till now seemed premature at best and disastrous at worst. Why write a book resisting something that other scholars are inclined to resist anyway? I do so because I think that sports literature as a genre and as a subject for academic study is now robust enough to support a dissenting approach. If that dissenting approach can clarify criticism on the genre and challenge others to develop the conversation, so much the better.

There will be almost no treatment of authors in this study. I talk instead about what texts do. Much of what I have to say concerns the cultural implications of texts that the authors, especially authors of juvenile books, never intended. I wish to make absolutely clear at the start that when I discuss the racial, sexual, and political implications of juvenile texts, I am not considering such implications to be part of the actual intentions of the authors of those texts. In fact most of the time I am almost certainly misreading these texts, in the sense of proposing significances that run counter to, or are merely tangential to, the main express themes of the works.

I misread in this way because I believe that juvenile texts—indeed, any texts—do cultural work that their authors do not intend. Academic criticism routinely proposes that adult texts do unintentional cultural work; most readers and authors of scholarly books agree that it is all right to see multiple meanings in the serious text.

Kids' books are usually not fair game for such critical practices, but I intend to treat them no differently than I would any serious text. I do not propose that the author of any text discussed here intended my reading of that text. In fact I do not know what any author meant, and I do not want to substitute stories about authors' lives for readings of their books. I think that what they actually write, and how people read it, is far more culturally significant.

Making the Team treats only fiction, and within fiction only novels. The great majority of baseball texts therefore lie outside its scope: short stories, poetry, drama, and film,[1] of course, but also game stories, features, columns, yearbooks, memoirs, oral histories, reference books, biographies, nonfiction accounts of every imaginable form, and books of statistical, scientific, and sociological analysis—frankly, almost all baseball writing is absent here. A comprehensive study of the rhetorics of baseball would be truly massive and require knowledge that I do not possess. I have decided to stick to what I know, and what I know is novels.

There is also an intrinsic reason for sticking to novels, however. Baseball novels tend to follow a seasonal rhythm—the majority, in fact, are about a single baseball season. The coming-together of a team, its conflicts and vicissitudes, the problems it solves, and its distractions off the field all funnel toward the "Big Game" that decides the pennant. The baseball novel is the story of the Big Game and what led up to it. The novel is an overgrown game story, that basic unit of sportswriting. The persistence of this pattern, as I will show, is all the more intriguing when one considers the insistence with which literary baseball novels are said to escape cliché.

It may seem at times that I treat all baseball novels as a single novel. I drop into the corpus of baseball fiction for supporting examples much as one might dip into one play of Shakespeare to explain the language of another. Treating all baseball novels as manifestations of a single textual impulse may seem unfair and even antiliterary, but the convergent evolution of baseball novels, the way they resemble and explain one another, does not make them less valid for study. It may make them all the more important as cultural artifacts.

Where it is possible, I try to see these texts not through their authors but through their readers—through reviewing and reception. The reception of most of these books is obscure, however. Few of them sustain any kind of critical tradition. The baseball novel is ephemeral; as the title of one of them remarks, it happens every spring: two or three get published, are briefly reviewed, and pass quickly out of print. Some of the best have been out of print for years, and some good recent ones have passed directly out of print, never even reaching paperback.

The situation is slightly different for juvenile baseball novels. Thanks to the power of series publication and its brand loyalties and to other publishing mechanisms such as school marketing and book-fairs, as well as low production and retail costs, some juvenile books have stayed in print for decades—you can buy the Tunis novels in paperback anywhere, for instance. Old copies of out-of-print juvenile novels are scarce, however. Records of the effects they may have had on readers are even scarcer. Kids leave home and their parents throw their books away. Many libraries hold copies of scarce adult novels like *Man on Spikes* or *The Seventh Babe*. If you own any titles in Lester Chadwick's "Baseball Joe" series, however, you have some-thing that few libraries have bothered to collect.

The academic reception of baseball fiction is largely limited to the small canon I presented at the beginning of this introduction. There is now a fair amount of criticism on those works, and in a pattern familiar from all literary criticism, most of the scholarship focuses on a tiny selection—I estimate that the majority of all baseball fiction criticism is on *The Natural* and *The Universal Baseball Association.* I discuss the latter of those two texts in chapter 4; the former appears only as deep background. I cite many books, but I have inevitably left out many that readers (for better or worse) might want me to discuss. I have not felt constrained to "cover" any possible canon or to con-struct one. As will soon become apparent, one of my aims is to ques-tion the construction not only of canons but of "literature" itself.

My final chapter is on just that issue: what it means to be literary. For those with a main interest in baseball or in cultural studies, that last chapter is on a narrower topic than is the rest of the book; for those (like me) in literary studies, the last chapter is on a wider issue, one crucial to our profession. In a sense we cannot separate books into literary and nonliterary; we simply read them. We read them, I argue, in pretty much the same way, and they are all culturally significant. Although the separation of books into literary and non-literary, serious and shallow, "good" and garbage, is a false distinc-tion, it is a distinction almost everyone makes anyway. This status distinction has increasingly greater cultural and social importance, as debates over the canon and education invest more and more energy into upholding—or attacking—the value that we pour into literature.

Note

1. Now and then I adduce a baseball film to elaborate my illustration of a point. "You are in the same world no matter what the medium," as Jane Tompkins says of the Western (7), but there are almost as many baseball films as baseball books, and my background is as a literary critic, not as a film scholar.

1

Everybody Wants to Play for the Yankees

. . . .

If you want to understand America, goes the saying by Jacques Barzun, you had better learn baseball. Barzun's legendary assertion is the most cherished comment on the game for American baseball writers, the ratification of their interests by a genuine Continental intellectual. The statement is a curious tautology, however. It is really nothing more than a slogan that tries to make the listener feel good about both baseball and America. How would one test Barzun's assertion? How "American" is baseball? To answer that, one would have to define America, but here one is perilously close to starting with attributes like mom and apple pie, and . . . baseball. Baseball is American because America is baseball because baseball is American.

Baseball is a route into assimilation to American identity, as this chapter shows, but that route into American identity goes both ways. If baseball teaches Americanism, then the America to which it provides entry is constructed in turn by the dynamics, logics, and rhetorics of baseball. To define a nation's essence in terms of a competitive sport makes it a nation of and for sport, one where the (unexamined) values of sport come to constitute national character. The examples of assimilation via baseball in this chapter are literary, but they constitute a cultural work that goes far beyond any bounds of the literary and affects how ideologies of sport dominate the way we think about the nature of the United States.

It is a common observation that immigrants to the United States are intrigued and, as it were, naturalized by baseball. George Freeman tells this anecdote:

> In 1948 my parents came over from Hungary. They had just got off
> Ellis Island and they were proud that they knew all about American
> politics. They had studied hard. They knew about Washington and
> Jefferson and the election coming up with Truman and Dewey. And
> then they see on the newsstands every paper has this story on page
> one—"Durocher Quits," and here's a name they never heard of. Dur-
> ocher. They were so upset because they had never heard of him and
> they had never studied about him. And they thought they were
> Americans. (quoted in Eskenazi 230)

Apparently one cannot become an American without coming to
terms with Leo Durocher. Of course one must also replace Jefferson's "All men are created equal" with Durocher's "Nice guys
finish last." Sport offers ways to understand America, but sport was
not waiting innocently devoid of meaning until it was grasped for its
interpretive usefulness by Barzun or by George Freeman's parents.
Sport and the rhetorics of sport that are crystallized in sports fiction
are competitors for the construction of American meaning. The
more that sport argues that it molds the individual and provides
exemplars for the molding of the American individual, the more it
justifies the amount of time, energy, and money that Americans
spend on it. In terms of another uninnocent American symbolism,
sport and sports fiction are players in the marketplace of ideas.

Scholars have asserted that sports literature is a natural part of the
larger field of American literature and hence of American studies. In
Seeking the Perfect Game Cordelia Candelaria "applies the elusive
(and controversial) ideal of the sport's concept of the 'perfect game'
to the literary and philosophical search for truth about America's
fundamental soul and substance" (15). For Candelaria, baseball literature offers a perfect entry into the study of American culture because baseball has served to produce myths for American ideologies.
She sees the history of the sport as proceeding from an infancy of
pagan ritual and folk play through an adolescence of organized club
sport into a disillusioning adulthood of professionalism and corruption centered on the 1919 Black Sox scandal (13-14). The social
history and in turn the literary history of baseball parallel that of the
United States "as a consequence of its deeply ingrained place within
the country's history, culture, and lore" (14).

As Candelaria's title indicates, her analysis of baseball fiction
centers on the way texts employ the game's possibility of perfection
as a site for talking about ideologies of perfectibility in American

literary and political culture. In taking this approach Candelaria echoes a more general assertion by Michael Oriard that "the athlete represents one case of the American belief in the possibility of perfection . . . Americans need heroes who represent the attainability of perfection" (*Dreaming of Heroes* 55). Perfectibility has been present in American intellectual history from Puritans to Transcendentalists to utopians, socialists, New Leftists, Christian Coalitioners, and Third Wavers, and it finds a mirror in the pure, circumscribed arenas of sports. "No human activity is more thoroughly regulated and ordered than sport" (*Dreaming of Heroes* 8), and only in baseball is the acme of regulation—perfection—attainable. Although one could conceive of a shutout in basketball, or a football game where the opponent does not gain a single yard, only baseball allows for the truly perfect game (twenty-seven up and twenty-seven down) or for smaller icons of perfection such as the triple play (all the outs of an inning on one ball in play). In baseball fiction the perfect game and the triple play occur far more frequently than they do in reality.

Perfection, purity, origin, and order give baseball its centripetal magnetism in American ideology and for American literature. Oriard argues that "sport solves a persistent problem for the American author by providing a center . . . an ordered universe like Melville's *Pequod* or Twain's Mississippi River . . . that can comprehend all the varieties of American people and ideas" (*Dreaming of Heroes* 7). The problem of American literature, as framed by Oriard here, is that of finding a center that comprehends varieties, the problem of *e pluribus unum*. I will argue that in baseball novels it is primarily the team as unit that provides a metaphor for solutions to this tendentiously conceived American problem.

I call it tendentiously conceived (although certainly Oriard is not alone in this tendentiousness) because if the nature of America is to be various, then a pure and original center is an artificial imposition— just as if the nature of America is urban (in another common confrontation of the same problem), then baseball, as the most natural and pastoral of sports, is also the most artificial, its park lands set down with surreal unnaturalness in the urban landscape. In the common formulations of fiction, baseball teams, which coalesce as organic families of men within larger communities of disparate, diverse, alienated individuals, are an analogous kind of artificially natural solution to America conceived of as problematically disparate.

"Baseball is *the* country game" (*Dreaming of Heroes* 77), says Oriard; hence the protagonist of the baseball novel is often the "natural" or "rube" come from the country to play ball in the town or city: Jack Keefe, Roy Tucker, Roy Hobbs, Henry Wiggen. As the rube learns to be streetwise, he is assimilated into a milieu that is least rustic of all, into the City, Chicago or New York. There his destiny converges with that of other immigrants to the city, foreigners or the descendants of foreigners. The rube meets the foreigner in a place antithetical to the heartland—the urban cityscape—and there they merge their talents to reimagine a perfect America on artificial grounds (if not artificial turf).

The baseball novel is often therefore a collision of two bildungsroman plots, stories about a young man's moral and spiritual development. The plot of the young rural quester in the city meets the plot of the immigrant making his way in that city by swearing allegiance to adopted ideologies. Whereas the young protagonist of canonical literary American fiction, for better or worse (Huck Finn or Clyde Griffiths), can be unproblematically "American," the hero of baseball fiction begins as an Other and is given the puzzle of fusing into a group identity with teammates who are themselves Others. The center is never assumed but emerges from struggles both intrasquad and interteam.

It is surprisingly rare for a fictional baseball team to be homogeneous. When Alfred Slote's Paul Mather joins new teammates in Michigan, he thinks, "As far as I was concerned, everyone looked alike: chewing gum, freckles . . . they looked like the kids in Texas and California" (78). The text may be opting for a wholly Anglo social milieu in order not to detract from its main theme of how parents and children live with cancer—or young Paul may just be indulging the propensity of all Mathers to hammer a regulated America out of wild materials. But it is an exceptional case. The baseball team in fiction more often resembles what Melville would have called an "Anacharsis Cloots deputation": Jews, Italians, Poles, Appalachian whites, southern blacks, American Indians (out of all realistic proportion), Asians, Latinos, and in nearly every group the obligatory alcoholic Jewish Indian (K. Baker 60) or black Hispanic/Dutch creole (Carkeet). In texts where historical veracity requires some exclusions (like novels about organized ball before the color line was broken), the multiculturalism reflects other dynamics of diversity, splintering the team along lines of class, education, region, or religion. Thus jigsawed by the need of the text to set itself a problem to solve, the ball club remains in bits till the plot nudges it into pattern. Melville is not just a stray analogue; as Oriard notes, the sports team is more like the crew of the *Pequod* than like anything else in literature.

Making a baseball team out of this mess of material becomes a possible (and necessary) solution to America conceived of *as* a problem; the datum for most baseball novels is a fractious mess of different subjects. The mechanism for making the team is assimilation, but there is rarely a distinct central model to which the diverse subjects must assimilate. Instead the team coheres not in terms of common identity but in terms of corporate function (with all its implications of division of labor rather than common abilities and styles). America defined in terms of a baseball team is always an emergent identity, defined only by rules of play that have nothing to do with politics or even with culture: geometric dimensions, angles, numerologies.

The America of the fictional baseball team must be emergent for the same reasons that literature itself must be emergent. The American identity defines itself as new, ahistorical, fresh. It is the place where it is always the first inning and the count is always 0 and 0. This emergent place is optimistic and elastic, the kind of nation least bound by stereotype and by convention. If we claim that we have to learn baseball to understand America, we are saying at the same time that America is child's play.

I am not suggesting that baseball fiction portrays free play as the American essence, however. Even at its most free, play is bound to be serious. As Terry Eagleton states, "'Game' in the positive sense— the ludic disportings of disruption and desire—plays itself out in the crevices of 'game' in the negative sense—game theory, the techno-scientific system—in an endless conflict and collusion" (389). (The positive and negative value markers here are Eagleton's own and not a natural feature of the landscape of games.) Baseball, highly regulated even when apparently clearing a space that is most free, hardly qualifies as play in any positive poststructural sense. Baseball is a game in Jacques Derrida's sense of centered structure: "The concept of centered structure is in fact the concept of a play based on a fundamental ground, a play constituted on the basis of a fundamental immobility and a reassuring certitude, which itself is beyond the reach of play. And on the basis of this certitude anxiety can be mastered, for anxiety is invariably the result of a certain mode of being implicated in the game, of being caught by the game, of being as it were at stake in the game from the outset" ("Structure, Sign and Play" 109). Derrida is thinking here of the languages of the *sciences humaines*, not of baseball—of Fernand Braudel, not Frenchy Bordagaray—but he can lend insight into sport's centrality to American experience. The fully constituted team is multiethnic, multicultural, and multifarious. It is the multiculturalism of external competition, however, not the multiculturalism of carnival. The multiculturalism of the made team is that of Maya Angelou reading at the Clinton inaugural, celebrating a bland and indiscriminately tolerant multiplicity of American identities as being central to an America that is moving in some positive direction: forward, upward, onward. The functional benefit of such multiculturalism is that it helps America as a team to be the best team it can be; let everybody play, and we can beat Japan.

In at least one of the texts I discuss, the rhetoric of the team is implicitly directed toward beating Japan: John R. Tunis's wartime novel *Keystone Kids* (1943). Outside of the imperatives of actual wars, however, the rhetoric of America moving up together as a team is centrally empty—the fact (or the fiction) of competition becomes an end in itself. Play as centered structure becomes the regulating monitor of an entire culture unable (in these texts) to define itself in any freer terms. The rules of baseball require opponents, scores, and no fraternizing with the enemy. We frequently see the parklike spaces of baseball as oases from postmodern life, so that we are frequently blind to the way that baseball literally as well as metaphorically is "constituted on the basis of a fundamental immobility." Every inning the players return to their positions, and it is the eternal return: they were standing in the same places when Lincoln was shot, and they will be standing there when the glaciers of the next Ice Age reach the green Fenway wall.

Play that functions solely to function, that has as its cultural work the control of anarchy, is always a zero-sum game, where there must be a winner and a loser. It is also a game where, as I will show, the assumptions of meritocracy seem most natural and in this camouflage are least noticed. One makes the team not because of one's personal identity or natural, organic relation to its other members but solely because of a merit that can be defined strictly within the order of the game. The game is an antiseptically cleansed nondiscriminatory milieu, as clean as the theoretical spaces of classical liberal rights theory or of a literary canon conceived of purely as an objective gauge of the greatness of books.

It is therefore no ordinary pea patch that the young slugger enters when he makes the bigs. Far more is at stake than his batting average or even his paycheck. He learns not so much baseball skills —he is usually a "natural" in that other Hobbsian sense—as skills for survival in the American metropolis. A rookie adapts to the metropolitan milieu by learning a set of references that constitutes almost a language. (Sometimes, of course, assimilation *does* involve learning a language, as in the examples in chapter 3.) When Roy Tucker first gets to Brooklyn, he admires the veteran Dodgers for "the way they could glance at a menu as long as your arm and order immediately what they wanted, strange dishes of which the kid had never heard. Their talk was of strange names and strange places too" (Tunis, *The Kid from Tomkinsville* 47).

They speak of Anthropophagi and men whose heads do grow beneath their shoulders, no doubt, but more intriguing than the banality of impressing gullible rookies is the milieu of the major league, a territory at the edges of the places that host it but central to them precisely because it is at their edges. The Pullman cars and train stations, the hotels and restaurants, cabs and nightclubs, and clubhouses and dugouts of St. Louis, Cincinnati, Pittsburgh, and Boston blend together into an amalgam that constitutes the local color of nowhere at all and becomes simply The American City. The rookies, who are distinctly from a locality—Nashville, Tomkins-ville, Perkinsville (Somewheresville, at any rate)—lose their local identity in the transition from busher to Pullman traveler and be-come temporarily men without a country. In that limbo of the City, they meet similar men and work to reconstitute a culture.

This is the transition faced by the Russell brothers in Tunis's *Keystone Kids*. When they are called up from Nashville, where they are playing their minor-league ball, they enter bewilderingly un-charted territory:

> The station in New York was a cavern, not a station. It was bigger far than anything they could imagine, yet jammed with Sunday evening travelers. In the confusion they became separated from the team. Some bad moments followed. Whichever way they looked were strange faces, everywhere strange faces, people hurrying for trains or from trains, no one they had ever seen.

> Say! Suppose we lost the club for good, suppose we missed the train! Why, we'd get shot back to Nashville pronto. (21)

The City is marked not just by its featureless magnitude but by the anxiety of those who, if they fail to master its ways, will be expelled.

Spike (the shortstop) and Bob (the second baseman) are quick learners, however. They learn that they are overdressed (the Dodgers wear casual clothes to travel) and overladen (big leaguers do not carry their own bags). They do not need tickets. They master the Pullman compartment and its infinite riches ("like nothing they had ever seen; a small room, compact and complete in every detail" [24]); they tip the porter, but far too little at first. They eat on the train and discover, too late, that they do not have to pay. They find a panel of buttons that looks to them like the controls of a Martian vessel and, omigosh, summon the porter again. The whole world around them presents opposites to the coordinates they have learned during their rough-and-tumble adolescence, forcing them to unlearn their past by performing arbitrary acts of psychic readjustment.

Disorientation is the method, but what is the content of what the Russells learn? They know how to play the game on the field, but what are the larger structures that will determine individual and team success and the balance between individual and team? The brothers quickly find that the ethics and attitudes of the big leaguers are like their travel arrangements in being opposite to the local-color world they have left. "On teams he [Spike] had played with before no one criticized a teammate openly" (47–48); on the Dodgers Raz Nugent mordantly ridicules outfielder Karl Case, saying that he runs "like a mob dispersing" (47). The image is uncomfortably central, or uncomfortably Grand Central; the Dodgers, like the stations through which they travel, are a "mob dispersing," atoms in motion with no gravitational center.

In Nashville the brothers' team had played ball for an avuncular manager, Grouchy Devine. They had wanted to win for their immediate tribal connection to home, the fans being their extended family. They were morally amateurs. The big-league professionals are paid as individuals, however, and lack incentives to form a virtual family. Fortunately Bob and Spike constitute a biological family, with parents conveniently absent, so that they are available as the nucleus of an extended, pseudobiological Dodgerdom.

This nucleus is immediately under threat. The Dodgers' management wants to demote Bob Russell and keep Spike with the big club. The prospect devastates them both. Spike thinks of not being able to hear Bob's voice: "Those yells, so natural to his ears, sounded almost schoolboyish on this team of veterans who talked about their golf scores, to whom baseball was not excitement and romance but business and nothing else" (58). The ideologies of these texts can seem like a set of circular equations: baseball is life, and therefore life is business but should be romance. Romance—here the Russells' fraternal romance—is central to the team, but the team is a business. Then, when a chance injury to another Dodgers player keeps Bob in Brooklyn, the businesslike coaching staff decides that Bob's function on the team should be that of "holler guy," so that his business role will be the romantic one of encouraging his elders in his schoolboyish way (66-68). Romance and business, starting as putative poles, wrap around and meet in the person of Bob Russell.

Spike and Bob must figure out the arbitrarily shifting definitions of romance and business before they can catalyze the Dodgers' teamwork. The focus of their first off-season is all business: they stage a protracted mutual holdout. Back in Nashville working on the railroad, the brothers hold out for a combined salary of $15,000. In the heyday of the reserve clause, the only recourse that this embryo Drysdale and Koufax have if the Dodgers decline is not to play at all; their safety net is their winter job with the L&N. As Spike (the thinking brother) negotiates over the phone with manager Ginger Crane, "the boss and three helpers were able to listen with interest. . . . [Spike] answered in baseball terminology, hoping the railway men around wouldn't get it" (76-77). The "baseball terminology" Spike uses is the phrase "forty-two five" for "$42,500," the sum another player has signed for, and both his idea of what will be impenetrable to the railway mentality and his reasons for encoding his conversation are of interest. Even the $6,000 a year that the Dodgers are offering him is a fortune to his fellow workers, but he must disguise the riches he is refusing in order to retain their sympathy—because if the Dodgers do not relent, Spike must continue to work with them on the railroad.

Of course there is not the remotest chance that *Keystone Kids* is going to leave its heroes in Nashville. The inevitability of the plot entails an implicit sympathy from the railway workers no matter what sum the Russells accept; when they ultimately do get $7,500 apiece (87), the text, by presenting no censure of their holdout or their high salaries, creates a tacit space of approbation for their success in business. This space is intriguing in the 1990s, when ballplayers who bargain for more money are anything but the nation's favorite role models. But is the holdout in the end a matter of business or of romance? When owner Jack MacManus meets the Russells face to face, he presents a complicated brief on the poverty of the Dodgers organization (82-84), detailing all the expenses that prevent him from paying the brothers more than $11,000 all told. The presentation nearly convinces Bob to sign, but when MacManus moves to sign Bob independently from Spike, the Russell bloodlines tighten and the boys refuse to sign anything. MacManus then hurls previously prepared contracts at them—for $7,500 each.

In other words, money has never been an object to the owner of the Dodgers. When his callousness is stripped away by the brothers' solidarity, what lies beneath is entirely sentimental. He would never let them go back to Nashville or anywhere else; under the cynical exterior of business, and ultimately inextricable from it, is a core of pure romance. One by one, the Dodgers—coaches, players, clubhouse attendants—are found to be hypocrites in reverse, surrounding little-kid-like Bob Russelly interiors with shows of jadedness that are perhaps mere defense mechanisms against losing the love of their teammates. As the Dodgers discover their childlike inner nature, they begin to play together as a team.

The Dodgers do not get in touch with those inner children without vicissitudes, however, and they certainly do not do it through psychotherapy. "MacManus hired and sent on from New York an Austrian psychiatrist to travel with the team and straighten them out" (104), but the boys do not take kindly to analysis. Whatever their neuroses, they prefer to deal with them unreflectively. The threat the analyst poses is more than merely psychological; he is typed as a "stranger," an alien, a New Yorker (although the club plays in New York, it is never *of* New York), and—dare we presume?—a Jew.

Assimilating Jewishness to the demands of the team is the subplot of *Keystone Kids*. In Spike and Bob's second year up, the Dodgers promote a rookie catcher named Jocko Klein, "with jet black hair and a prominent nose" (116). The opinion of the veteran Swanson is that "these Jewish boys can't take it. Haven't any guts" (118). Although Spike admires the catcher's hard work, he is troubled when

Klein answers to the name "Buglenose" on the practice field (119). The incident is troubling because Jocko does not at once resent the slur, but there is an underlying trouble as well; by letting a teammate call him "Buglenose," Jocko has assented to being an exception: a Jew. In the romantic business of baseball, the dissolution of individuality in the team goals is an imperative. Even as he watches Jocko, Spike is distractedly reflecting on Karl Case's selfishness in thinking about his batting average. Therefore, to let one's self be made into an Other as Jocko does is a kind of individualism; it undermines the entire club.

Jocko enters the novel lacking "guts" in some sense. Just which sense becomes a severe problem for the team's nucleus, the Russell brothers. Nascent social theorists as well as a fine double-play combination, Spike and Bob debate whether Jocko's gutlessness is socially constructed or immanent. Bob's position is that gutlessness is inherent in the Jewish nature. Jewish players are "'yellow. No guts,' announced [Bob] with the finality of a radio announcer" (127). Without reflecting on the larger connections of Bob's rhetoric to that of anti-Semitic radio announcers all over Europe in the 1940s, Spike proposes that various structural issues stemming from Jocko's roles as catcher, rookie, and hot hitter are why he is nervous on the ballfield. It is natural to throw at rookies and good hitters, he has been taking heat from opponents, and he does not yet know the voices of his teammates when they shout encouragement or warnings (128). To all these propositions Bob has the impassive answer "Everyone knows it": Jews are inferior in fortitude. This disagreement over race threatens to tear the team apart from its very center.

In a few pages Spike Russell becomes more than just the emotional center of the ball club; he is named manager.[1] Spike is a player-manager, that most democratic of leadership positions. He is one of the team but at the same time not one of them. It affects his grammar, and he begins his first pep talk to the team by saying, "Now we all know some of us haven't been keeping in shape the way you should" (144), melding the physician's inclusive *we* with the boss's accusing *you.* "Want you to realize one thing: when you do this, you're hurting all the other men on the club. It isn't just MacManus or the stockholders you hurt when you go out at night. It's us, all of us. That's what I mean when I say in the future we must be a team that pulls together, not an individual record team" (144). Spike's rhetoric is banal, but it is specific to the provisional constructions of America that *Keystone Kids* establishes. Spike is talking about more than how to win a few ball games; at stake in 1943 in the nation as well as in the National League is an ethic of incorporation vital to the survival of a polity in crisis. Especially important in Spike's role as player-manager is the way in which his democratically inclusive *we* conceals a necessary power relation. During the rest of the novel Spike imposes a degree of unity on the disparate material of the team like the benevolent despot he is (or like the Roosevelt for whom all such contemporary images of benevolent despots really stand). Spike starts to create unity from the moment he faces down Raz Nugent's plea for special favors at this first meeting (148–49). But it is a unity in tension with his equality with the others on the field.

To underscore Spike's rhetoric of teamwork, the first thing that the Dodgers do after he takes the reins is to turn a triple play, that miniature icon of perfection that requires maximum teamwork.[2] Involved in the triple play are (naturally) Spike, Bob, and Jocko. Three runs down in the ninth, with the count 2 and 2, no outs, and runners on first and third, the Cubs' manager calls for a double steal (ours not to reason why; presumably he represents the Platonic ideal of the clueless Cubs manager). The batter swings, striking out; Jocko sees the runners breaking and throws to Spike, who whips it back to him to get the runner from third; Jocko throws to Bob to catch the trail runner rounding second. "They had made a triple play. The game was won" (154). And they win "as a unit, something they hadn't been lately" (150).

The perfectibility of these Dodgers runs into a fatal flaw: Jocko Klein's nose, the emblem of his Jewishness. The Cubs have been riding him mercilessly as "Buglenose," using his teammates' own slur as ammunition against them. Even after the triple play, the Dodgers' appreciation of Jocko's alertness is couched in terms of his race: "'That's heads-up ball there, Buglenose,' said old Fat Stuff affectionately . . . 'Nice work, Buglenose, nice work there!'" (154). As far as intragroup loyalties are concerned, Jocko has been accepted by the team, with a kind of warm and fuzzy anti-Semitism as their peculiar mechanism for assimilating him. When the Cubs call him "Buglenose," it is an insult; when Fat Stuff does it, well, who can be offended by the doughy old politically incorrect Fat Stuff? In this dynamic the insultee learns which insulters to value by sorting them into the essentially charitable and the essentially vicious.

Rejoicing in the intimacy of a suffered insult is a pattern for many of white America's multicultural tolerances.

When Jocko is called a Jew from outside the team, his Jewishness threatens to expose the Dodgers' newly won unity as a fiction. To integrate fully as a fighting machine, the Dodgers have a much more fundamental need than mere tolerance. They need to erase Jocko's ethnic identity altogether, to make him no more and no less than the functional role "Brooklyn Dodger" or its subsets "catcher" and "batsman." Although their opponents' racism is officially excused by the narrative voice of the text—"Coaches make it their business to use every available weapon," the narrator apologizes at one point (160)—the appropriate response from the team and individual player under attack is to fight back as a unit that denies the cultural typing, to defend Jocko as one of the Dodgers, never as a Jew.

When the Pirates call Jocko "Jew-boy" and "kike" and he suffers silently (161), his affectionate teammates are quick to back away from him. Bob Russell again takes the theoretical lead, filling in the gaps in his earlier formulations with deadly logic: if Jocko is a Jew and does not resent being called one, then "He ain't an American" (167). Spike explodes: "He was born in K.C. and raised there, went to school there. . . . He's just as much an American as you are" (167-68). Spike makes no headway against Bob's racialist theorizing, however, and the Keystone Kids go to bed angry for the first time in the novel.

The space that has opened between Bob and Spike (an opening space is the text's metaphor for their dispute) must be sutured if the team is ever going to win. No amount of rhetoric can convince Bob that a Jew is an American; what Spike must do instead to remake the team is to convince Jocko that he is not a Jew. Jocko's identity must be replaced wholesale with the default value "American," the subject who exists without "being" anything particular at all. Spike confronts the problem of remolding Jocko's identity head on in chapter 17, one of the oddest and most telling passages in juvenile baseball fiction.

"When did this hit you first?" asks Spike (176); that is, when did you first suspect you were Jewish? After he was called "kike" by neighborhood kids, nine-year-old Jocko asked his mother what the word meant, and she answered with a history of the Jews and their persecution. Seeing that Spike cannot relate to Jewish history, however, Jocko presents his ethnic consciousness in terms of a baseball metaphor—Jews stick together just as teammates do when one is threatened (179; Jocko is apparently unconscious here that this is precisely what the Dodgers have been unwilling to do for him). Figures of speech do not get through to Spike either, and Jocko reaches for his last resort:

> "Wait a minute. Look, d'ja ever read poetry?"
> Read poetry! Oh, migosh! The question made Spike uncomfortable, and he was uncomfortable enough as it was. . . . Then for the first time he noticed a half-opened volume on the dresser. A catcher reading poetry, that's awful bad. . . . Lucky he's rooming with old Fat Stuff, a gent that keeps his trap closed. (179–80)

One hesitates to ask just what Spike might fear when he hears the word *poetry*. The sources of fear feed in from several directions, including surely the homophobic (for which see chapter 2) and the anti-intellectual (see chapter 3). Nevertheless the immediate fear is that Jocko will come out not as queer or as book-learned but as Jewish, and when Jocko opens the book and starts to read, it gets far worse: "Gosh, this was terrible. Suppose Fat Stuff opened the door with that kidder, Rats Doyle, right at this minute! Perhaps the poor guy is nuts. Say, maybe we drove him nuts, like what's-his-name, that catcher on the Reds[3] who committed suicide several years ago" (181). Jocko, in a dithyrambic ecstasy, shouts: "Look! I'm a Jew. It's in my blood" (181), and Spike has heard enough. He leaps down the catcher's throat. As Spike begins to chew out Jocko Klein for asserting a specifically racial identity, he shows the ideological underpinnings of the rhetoric he has employed in his debates with Bob. It is unthinkable and unsayable for Spike that Jocko's Jewishness could be hereditary. If Jocko is not malleable, he can never make the team. Spike will have to ship him back to Elmira. Spike's antiessentialism is based on the same axiom to which Bob subscribes: a Jew cannot be an American. Spike will never admit that Jocko cannot help being a Jew; there is always hope for him. "If you ever pull this-here Jew stuff on me again . . . I'll break every bone in your body . . . so help me, Hannah, I will" (181) says Spike, invoking Samuel's mother apparently to underscore his Gentile appropriation of the function of deciding and denying Jewish identities. One of the most deliberately inspirational moments in the novel's rhetoric becomes its closest approach to a coerced conversion.

"They'd have been prejudiced against you if you'd been a Hottentot or a Turk or a Texas boy who acted same as you did," says Spike illogically (182), blaming prejudice on postjudicial assessments (and on Jocko himself). What must Jocko do to resist prejudice? He must stop reading poetry, for a start, and then fight for himself. But Spike still fails to find the right verbal formula to spur Jocko to the necessary therapeutic action: purgation of all identities except that of his corporate function in the team.

Starting on Jocko is only half the battle. Spike must take to the Dodgers clubhouse generally a didactic message about race and team unity. He faces the club in a general meeting and defines their anti-Semitism as a matter of "murder" (194)—ignoring the fact that he has just threatened to beat Jocko out of his Jewishness but connecting perhaps for the first time, although in a deeply unconscious way, American corporate anti-Semitism with Nazism. The Dodgers, forced to think about it, proffer some of the favorite rhetorical ploys of American racism. "We couldn't do it if he didn't let us" (196) is Bob Russell's argument, one half-accepted by Spike himself: blame the victim for letting the persecution happen. Roy Tucker, like Bob and Spike a recent assimilant, is more subtly disputatious; he wishes that "they could explain that the boys aren't on him because he's Jewish but because they think he's yellow" (198)—in other words, that the Dodgers truly are judging Jocko not by the cut of his foreskin but by the content of his character. Roy sees nothing wrong with hazing Jocko, but he has a lot invested in suppressing any possible racial context for that hazing.

While Roy and Bob are exquisitely calibrating their racism over dinner, Spike and Jocko are out on the town themselves "in a small restaurant" (198; apparently none of the Dodgers can find better dates than each other). They talk about their mothers, and suddenly Spike Russell finds the key:

> "Look, Jocko-boy, tell me something. You don't ever think of yer ma as a Jew, do you?"
> The boy was startled. No one had ever asked him such a question. "Why no, of course not." (200)

The reader cannot help recalling—although is evidently supposed *not* to—that just twenty-two pages before, Jocko confessed to Spike that his mother was the original source of his entire race consciousness (as well as being the source of both his Jewishness and his life). Spike leaps into the opening provided by these readerly and catcherly amnesias:

"Fine. That's what you must do then, that's what you must do all the time. You gotta think of yourself as a catcher, not as a Jew. Get me? You gotta quit this thinking of yourself as a Jew first and a catcher on this-here team second. The last two thousand years, they don't matter. See, this is today, it's now. It's not even when you were nine years old; it's right now. You're a ballplayer, first and all the time . . . you're the catcher of the Dodgers."

The catcher of the Dodgers! The catcher of the Dodgers, he thought. (200)

That is all it takes. The next day at batting practice, when Karl Case (the ultimate selfish ballplayer) calls Jocko a kike, the catcher replies, "That stuff's over. I'm the catcher of the Dodgers, get it? If you wanna slug it out, O.K." (202). Case backs down. Jocko steps in to take his practice swing "and caught it squarely. It was high, very high, and very deep. In fact it was clearing the fence; it was over in Bedford Avenue" (203).

The rhetoric of *Keystone Kids* clears the fence in two senses with Jocko's batting-practice home run. It clears the playing field of all accumulated historical identities, those of centuries, years, or hours; everyone starts over as ballplaying equals. It clears the fence also by proposing a model for other corporate American endeavors, military, political, and economic. Perhaps deepest of all, Jocko's response to Spike Russell's bizarre question "You don't ever think of yer ma as a Jew?" means that "Ma" too is not a personal identity but a functional role in this cleansed version of America. The role of "Mom" precludes any other identities: maternity cannot be splintered into many pieces along the fault lines of class, race, or religion. For the purposes of *Keystone Kids*, and the baseball novel generally, the female is a sex that *is* one. Women are denied access to analyzed identities, to the pride or the persecution that they entail. The body of Ma Klein has become the level playing field that unites the Brooklyn Dodgers. This is fitting, because Mom is another of the tautological attributes of emergent America. If Spike were a little more puckish, she might as well have been the apple pie.

The climax of *Keystone Kids* is a fight between the Dodgers and some Philadelphia hecklers (217–20), where the Dodgers literally take their cultural work off the field and start to beat it into their enemies. Naturally Jocko hits a home run to beat the Phillies; the text clears fences to all fields. The Dodgers become much more than just a baseball team. They become all America seen as a ball club.

They are an America conceived of as deeply and ideally opaque to its history. It is a nation that has come together by erasing the conditions of history.

The nation conceived in *Keystone Kids* depends on its average workers' unconsciousness of the historical dimensions of their ancestries and names. One by one the other players are revealed as having mastered, much earlier in their racial pasts, the same sinking of ethnic into corporate identities that has made Jocko Klein a member of the Dodgers. As Spike meditates on the naked bodies of his winning ball club, he is explicitly denied knowledge of historical circumstances that the narrating voice in the novel explains to the reader. The Dodgers have a history, of course, but their history dates from Opening Day. "What was a team? It was everything in sport and in life, yet nothing you could touch or see or feel or even explain to someone else. A team was like an individual, a character, fashioned by work and suffering and disappointment and sympathy and understanding, perhaps not least of all by defeat" (222-23). The essence of the individuals is defined totally by their corporate function as a National League franchise. Spike, as manager, "knew them even better than their parents, better than their wives and children would ever know them . . . yet there were things about them that even Spike Russell did not know and could never know" (223). He cannot know these even more essential things about the Dodgers because the Dodgers do not know them themselves. Only the world-historical consciousness of the narrator has access to them.

The essential secrets embodied in Spike's Dodgers are above all race secrets; the text of *Keystone Kids,* and by extension its imagination of America, conceives of race as a scandalous but vital part of the identity of both, manageable as long as it is hidden by the ignorances of assimilation and visible only to an analysis that is given to the reader as a type of initiatory rite. This initiation contains an implicit directive that the tools of racial analysis not be shared with their primary subjects. The text makes a pact with its potentially elite reader not to reveal to working Americans the secrets of their racial origins. The essence of American identity, for *Keystone Kids,* is a deep race memory that is understood only by the guardians of an ideology that does its strenuous best to deny race altogether.

As the narrating voice reveals the race origins of the Dodgers, they turn out to be avatars of sundry archetypal pioneering white ethnicities: third baseman Harry Street is revealed as the Calvinist Pilgrim Herald van Stirnum; Elmer McCaffrey, as a Catholic English royalist; Swanson, as a Swede who fought with Gustavus II. The Russells and the Tuckers turn out to have been in opposite lines in the Civil War (224–25). One by one the Dodgers are peeled away and their proto-American ancestors revealed in their stead; one by one the history of these ancestors is shown as a hidden history of wars and battles that have been rendered meaningless by the fact of America itself. That the Swansons, Streets, and McCaffreys enclose a potential religious war within the clubhouse walls is made irrelevant, even laughable, by their assimilation to an American type and the consequent veiling of their racial antagonism. Persisting in race memory is only an abstract, depoliticized violence.

It does not matter whom these primeval Dodgers fought, whether earlier versions of each other or beings still outside the community but potentially integrable in turn. The center of the American corporate race memory is the motiveless teamwork of military violence. The causes and ideologies that the ancestral Dodgers fought for have become a shapeless catalog of atrocities (a McCaffrey expires with Gordon at Khartoum), yet they can be told *as* history because they are seen as generic martial violence. In this way a historyless racial potential for violence is seen as the foundation for an American character that can meet the violent and teamwork-demanding challenges of sport. Their racial compasses aligned with the central imperative of organized mayhem, the Dodgers can finally accomplish their own American Revolution in (where else?) Philadelphia.

Of course, for all the invocation of violence, there is one member of the polity whose racial antecedents are not offensively violent: Jocko Klein himself, the son of generations of merchants and businessmen (not usurers, surely?) who become perpetual emigrants in the wake of one disaster after another, "until one day in the ghetto of Vienna, a descendant of old Israel Klein of Marrakesh heard of a new land, a land where persecutions did not exist, or banishments or pogroms, where children were not sold into slavery or families destroyed" (227). One's first inclination on reading this is to retort that the descendant of old Israel Klein heard wrong about the children not being sold into slavery, but possibly he was a post-1865 immigrant. He and his ancestors are at any rate the only nonviolent precursors of the current Brooklyn ball club. One cannot argue that they lack "guts"; their narrative is filled with stick-to-itiveness. In the process, however, Jocko is revealed as initially true to racial type; when attacked, the Kleins have historically headed back to the high minors. Despite Spike's theories, Jews are the sole non-fighters in his unit.

At any rate the Jews would be the sole nonfighters if their history ever became visible to them. The point of this peroration to *Keystone Kids* is to ensure that these individual race histories never do. Even Jews can become fighters if they forget their Jewishness. By means of amnesia and protective coloration, they can be grafted onto the feisty body politic of America and thrive there just like anybody else. The ideal body politic, like the ideal baseball team, is externally but not internally feisty; it projects its deeply rooted violence outward and is therefore doubly indiscriminate: anyone can be a member as long as he has no identity (beyond a maleness that is taken for granted), and anyone can be an enemy if he makes the mistake of attacking. The only ideology is competition. "Calvinist and Covenanter, Catholic and Lutheran, Puritan and Jew, these were the elements that, fighting, clashing and jarring at first, then slowly mixing, blending, refining, made up a team. Made up America" (227). The phrase "made up" is used in the sense of "constituted," of course, but also at least as much in the sense of "being a necessary fiction."

A text whose principal style is the bizarre afterthought ("You don't ever think of yer ma as a Jew") would not be complete without a bizarre footnote to this making of the team. As Spike walks from the Ebbets Field clubhouse to the diamond, unconscious of what the narrator has been talking about, the clubhouse attendant, Old Chiselbeak, gives him "an affectionate shove" (228). "Chisel was part of the team, too; and, though Spike didn't realize it as he followed his team along the concrete runway, part of America also. He was the millions and millions who never have their names in the line-up, who never play before the crowd, who never hit home runs and get the fans' applause; who work all over the United States, underpaid, unknown, unrewarded. The Chiselbeaks are part of the team, too" (228). Is Chiselbeak black? The thought is transient, because these Dodgers are so unspeakably white that for any other color to be acknowledged is unthinkable. (Just as they are automatically male; there are no women in this clubhouse.) The only black character to have been associated with the Dodgers so far in this series of novels has been their mascot "little Snow White, the pickaninny" (*The Kid from Tomkinsville* 202). These Dodgers are not ready for integration—ironically enough, because after the real Dodgers integrated their organization in 1946, the fictional team proceeded through four more novels, remaining all-white even after Jackie Robinson had retired and the real club departed for Los Angeles. The first black player named in the series is "Carrington, the Redlegs' Negro slugger" (66), in *Schoolboy Johnson* (1958).

Nevertheless, although they may talk around color, the narrator's ideologies do not sign off without a final reemphasis of class. The front-line players, cozy in their functionalist democracy, are shown as depending on a vast horde of equally functional, equally well-assimilated, fundamentally content (white) proletarians. The Dodgers players constitute in this analysis a sort of virtual aristocracy (although as a bunch of guys afraid to quit their winter jobs on the L&N, they are hardly even bourgeois). They are an aristocracy created by the media. The novel ends with a scene of such creation: the media snapping publicity photos of the newly successful Brooklyn Dodgers.

The extent of the team's success can be measured from book to book. In the Dodgers novels that follow in the series, Jocko Klein never shows signs of slipping back into Jewishness again. In *Highpockets* (1948) we see him briefly and powerfully "on the edge of the rubdown table" (44) taking stock of Highpockets, the newest candidate for assimilation to Dodgerdom. Never after he faces down Karl Case in *Keystone Kids* is Jocko tentative about his primary identity as catcher of "this-here team."

. . . . .

The adult novel that provides the best parallel to *Keystone Kids* is Eric Rolfe Greenberg's *Celebrant*. It is a "natural" choice on two counts: it is frequently invoked as the best literary baseball novel, and it is focused on the problem of Jewish assimilation into America through the medium of baseball.[4] In a pattern common to consciously literary adult baseball fictions, the dominant mode of *The Celebrant* is tragic, not festive. It celebrates the disillusionment and decay of an American ideal, not its triumphant reiteration. *The Celebrant* never discards the values that it disappoints, however; it examines shortfalls in American ideals without imagining an alternative set of possibilities. Unlike *Keystone Kids*, *The Celebrant* is a text that acknowledges history. Whereas *Keystone Kids* comically erases history, however, *The Celebrant* thinks of history as a regrettable deflection of an ideal American destiny. In this pair of texts, the most campily chipper of kids' baseball stories meets and meshes with the ideologies of the most serious and historically sensitive of its adult tragedies. As so often happens, the child has been put away more rhetorically than effectively.

Assimilation in *Keystone Kids* is achieved through a simple erasure of individual ethnicities. Assimilation in *The Celebrant* is a complex system involving dynamics of impersonation, passing, and conversion. In the novel's ideological economy, these three dynamics are respectively playful, false, and true ways of becoming American. Nonetheless even the true method of assimilation, that of conversion, is treated ironically in the text. Those who pass for American may be detected and possibly forgiven; those who play at being American need no forgiveness. Those who convert, however, and are baptized in a new nationality are in deep trouble if the nation to which they swear allegiance is revealed as corrupt. Corruption is coded in *The Celebrant* as a product of formulaic behavior, indeed of addiction. The true America is coded here as a type of receding ideal, a place that never becomes fully realized and hence to which the assimilant swears allegiance only as an emergent system of values. This true America is corrupted by people who surrender to old addictions, who fossilize into old ways of behavior. The idea of an emergent America is (paradoxically) reaffirmed in *The Celebrant*. The pathos of the novel lies in its ironic questioning of ideals it deeply wishes were achievable.

The Celebrant is narrated by Jack Kapp—born Yakov Kapinski—a designer for his uncle's jewelry firm and former star amateur pitcher until an injury ended his baseball career. Jack is a Jew who came to New York with his family in 1889 at the age of eight. From the start of his narrative, he displays a self-consciousness about the role that baseball plays in his assimilation to the United States that would be unheard of in a juvenile novel; the racial issues that *Keystone Kids* tries so hard to erase move here to the front and center of the novel's rhetoric. The first sentence of the text ends "in the spring I saw my first game of baseball" (11); the first plot element is a misunderstanding between Jack's father and a German-speaking Brooklyner who hears the word *nine*—that most central of baseball numbers and the number of children in the Kapp family—as *nein*, "no." To become American is to learn the English terms of baseball, evidently; to misunderstand the nature of a nine-member team is to negate everything.

"We learned the game and the ways of the boys who played it," the narrator recalls; the children's accents disappear, and his own name changes from Yakov to Jackie (12). A key dynamic in this becoming American through baseball is impersonation, taking on the characteristics of the major-league hero one admires and using him literally, if playfully, as a role model for one's own persona. Jack "becomes" a New York Giants pitcher for the purposes of sandlot games (12)—just as, a few years later, he will "become" Giants pitcher Christy Mathewson sympathetically as he watches Mathewson pitch a no-hit ball game in St. Louis.

"He was everything I was not," says Jack of Mathewson (29), and one can run down the list of things Jack is not: blond, Gentile, college-educated, physically whole, famous, adored. Mathewson is the ideal that accentuates the many ways in which almost any man falls short of that ideal; specifically, he is the ideal American that the immigrant Jew can approach but never become. Here again is the sense that such an American identity is not definite but emergent. Mathewson, for all the distinctiveness of his parts, is no simple mark to emulate. He is more than their sum.

Jack Kapp, dark, Jewish, and self-educated, cannot become Mathewson, but he can construct an American identity that begins in the childish playacting of impersonating Mathewson and proceeds into genuine adult conversion. The conversion must always be a partial, marked conversion. The immigrant who truly assumes an assimilated identity must always bear the markers of his preconverted self—he cannot, in the literal or the symbolic sense, become uncircumcised again. The completely disintegrated identity is suspect in *The Celebrant*—although not in *Keystone Kids*—as an identity assumed in bad faith, an identity passed for rather than lived. In this way the ideal assimilant is one who continues to bear witness to the performative value of his or her conversion by continuing to make active homage, *as* a convert, to the principles of the new group. No other balance would as fully reinforce the continuous centripetal power of the assimilating national identity.

The true assimilants' dilemma is that this balancing point offers little secure foothold. Assimilants must not slip into the falsehood of the passer-for or retreat into the stubbornness of the unassimilated.

They must change their names, but it must be clear that the name is a changeling; "Jack Kapp" presents exactly the open-secret quality that is needed, the glass-closet identity that can be a comfortable social fiction without presuming too much. The difficulty of maintaining such a balance can be driven home by the first member of the in-group who breaks the surface of the fiction and outs its inhabitant. Jack meets such a person in Sammy Strang, a Giants infielder who at first cannot recognize Jack's Jewishness when his teammate Jack Warner introduces them to each other. Jack wants to show Mathewson a sketch of a ring he has designed to commemorate the pitcher's no-hitter; Strang, once Warner tells him that Jack is a Jew, suspects a confidence game and says, "Listen, Jew . . . stay away from Matty, you hear me?" (35)

The scene, on one level a representation of Jack's precarious and semitransparent status as a Jewish American, is on another level a deep interrogation of the status of passing. Although he is Strang's friend, the catcher Warner does not share Strang's anti-Semitism. In fact he has welcomed Jack's approach, remembering a banquet where the two once shared "Jew food" (33). They are both Lower East Siders, although Warner has escaped and lives "up on the Heights now" (32). Is Warner originally Jewish? His first name is the same as Kapp's, his neighborhood was the same, and they recognize each other. (Warner also prophetically bears the name of a later Jewish-American cultural figure, film producer Jack Warner.) Yet Warner is quick to "out" Jack Kapp as a Jew when Strang suspects him—almost preemptively quick. The mechanisms of blackmailability and paranoia that I examine in more detail in chapter 2 come into play here as Warner performs maintenance on his own tenuous ethnic identity.

Warner, possibly passing, is a broken, shabby character. His leitmotif is his after-dinner speech, the one he gives when he eats "Jew food" with Jack: "analogizing baseball and life. Practice, dedication, clean living, and fair play—these guaranteed success on and off the field" (13). Much later, when Jack has gotten to know Christy Mathewson, the pitcher remarks: "I know the speech . . . Jack offered it to me for five dollars when I joined the club. All the fellows use it, or something close. 'Baseball is a lot like life,' followed by ten pages of analogy. Is that the one?" (86). Mathewson proceeds to read the Warner speech by deftly exposing its clichés. In Mathewson's reading baseball is nothing like life. Life is contingent and messy, whereas baseball is stylized and artificial. Or, in the familiar pattern, baseball—and Warner's acceptance of its analogy to life—is childish, addictive, and ahistorical, perhaps Jewish in the overall map that these binarisms construct. Mathewson's values are adult, voluntary, contingent, and Christian. To convert to them is to put away childish things. To go a step further, baseball—extolled by Kapp's father-in-law, Sonnheim, as the American game (as opposed to foreign contests of brute force)—becomes oddly foreign on Mathewson's map. Life, by contrast, becomes American. If Jack ever thought (but he does not) that baseball was the ideal bridge to Mathewson and to America, he is thwarted as Mathewson himself constructs another conceptual moat around his centrally unreachable identity.

In a deep sense Jack Warner, if he is passing, has never put away childish things. He has changed merely his name; his addictive behaviors both literal (he drinks) and lingual (he gives the same speech over and over when he drinks) signal that he has never converted to the new dispensation that Mathewson offers and that his presence at the altar is ultimately a reflection of his bad faith.

Conversion is openly invoked as the primary dynamic for being a baseball fan (and hence an American) in *The Celebrant*. When his brother Eli asks whether Jack intends to worship Mathewson from afar, Jack answers,

> "Isn't that the proper distance for worship? You don't crawl into the ark to worship *torah*. . . . Eli, you don't really think I worship Mathewson, do you? In the religious sense? That's heresy."
> "Yes. I mean it would be heresy, wouldn't it?"
> I considered the thought. "A very American heresy, Mister Kapp."
> (42)

Only an American heretic would worship a baseball player, but only an assimilated American heretic would worship him from afar. The center of the American heresy is an object of worship that remains central yet unapproachable, that one can aspire to celebrate but not to emulate. Acknowledgment that one can never truly become the central worship object is a necessary part of the assimilant's religion. The real American is always behind the veil.

Even when he is allowed to glimpse behind the veil, Jack is not vouchsafed a simple approach to Mathewson's essence. In the same scene where Mathewson picks apart Warner's addictive rhetoric, he offers his own counter-rhetorics of sport and life. When Jack's father-

in-law refers to card games as a type of gambling, Mathewson demurs—and the demurral is crucial. "The man who thinks of poker,
or any card game, as a matter of blind fate will surely end a beggar.
The play of cards is a matter of continual calculation, and he who
best judges the odds will win the stakes. So also chess, or checkers.
So also a professional baseball game, for that matter. We play for
championship stakes, after all" (88). To Jack, listening, Mathewson's
distinction seems so subtle as to require almost a leap of faith.
Gambling, in the commonsense meaning of the term, is a risk of
money on an outcome. For Mathewson, however, gambling is the
risk of money only on outcomes over which the risker has no immediate control. A voluntary wager of money on a contest of skill is
not gambling; only the addictive impulse to bet money on contests
one cannot control—or can control only unfairly, by fixing them and
so reducing them to theater instead of level competition—constitutes gambling. The introduction of gambling tends "to reduce the
competition to the gain or loss of money. Exercise, honor, fair play,
achievement—all go by the board" (88). In working around to the
values destroyed by gambling, Mathewson thus returns, in a fine
self-contradictory way, to extolling the same values that figure as
boilerplate text in Warner's dinner speeches.

To assent to Christy Mathewson's analyses as to a creed requires
a leap of faith into the embrace of paradox as profound as that of the
original Jewish converts to Christ. The next passage in the gospel of
Mathewson takes place, appropriately, on a Saturday; there is no
Sunday game in the 1905 World Series (and Mathewson would not
pitch if there were). Jack must go directly from temple services to
the Polo Grounds, "that secular house of worship" (95). The game
turns out to be the decisive one that wins the series for the Giants.
Although the novel is not half-over, this will be the only series that
Mathewson wins and therefore the high-water mark of his career, as
well as the moment of Jack's supreme identification with him.

The course that *The Celebrant* takes downward from its climax
in the 1905 World Series is one of disillusionment and betrayal. The
disillusionment is both Jack's and Mathewson's. It is a disillusionment with the nature of America and of baseball as it reflects that
America. The betrayal comes from within baseball and from without. The plot of *The Celebrant* is a particular case of a larger disillusionment with American ideals that I study more closely in chapter 4, on meritocracy. Jack comes to perceive baseball itself as a

system far too much like the corporate world where he labors increasingly as an alienated functional role rather than as a self-integrated artist.

The Celebrant works itself out as family tragedy, a tragedy of different immigrant brothers assimilating at different rates and to different possible Americas. Jack is above all the artist, and for him Mathewson uses the ballfield, and therefore America, as an artistic medium. Eli, his brother, gambles; he is the type of addict who cannot break old habits and seize the open potentials of the future. Their younger brother Arthur is the functionalist, a manager who sees not people but roles and work. (Ominously Arthur has changed his name from Avram; typologically he should become Abraham, but he declines the patriarchal resonances of such a change in favor of the corporate managerial resonances of the head of the Round Table.)

The interlinked resonances of work and assimilation are crystallized into a brief meditation that Jack makes during the historic "Merkle Game" in 1908. Watching the aging Giants manager John McGraw come onto the field, Jack says, "I watched the players rehearse under his baton, and I thought of them and their actions as pieces of a great and intricate design. In isolation each of their skills signified nothing, like the separate parts that spilled out of the dumb machines at the shop. The game was the process that welded them into a meaningful form, and the pitcher was the gemstone" (129–30). Jack's rhetoric of production ultimately cannot hold in the novel's progress toward the 1919 World Series. He analyzes the process that a master manager like McGraw uses, the functional alignment of distinct, alienated parts to create a product, and he comes to the theory that the pitcher, as the central element, is exceptional. He therefore sees himself as exceptional, as the artist who designs the rings that represent the spirit of the ball club. The game is his central authority for this analogy and for the exceptions it involves. The game of baseball is the guarantee that the disparate elements of production will continue to cohere.

Nonetheless the game can be as much the functional zero-sum competition of the corporate world as the perfect art form of Jack's imagination. The Merkle game proves this point to him. Won by the Giants in spirit but disputed by the Cubs in letter after runner Fred Merkle makes the mistake of not touching second base, the game proves that even the most artistic of competitions can be forced into functionalism by invoking pedantic literalism, by managing a competition that only speciously exists in a world of free play. Of course Christy Mathewson pitches the game; of course he pitches brilliantly, near perfectly, but fails to win. (The game is ruled a tie and in fact never ends, since Arthur retrieves the game ball while it is still in play and presents it to Jack as a memento mori for his idealism.)

In the years after the Merkle game Arthur rationalizes the family business, changing its name from "Pincus" to "Collegiate" and replacing his uncle Sid's patriarchal touch with the latest in time-study management. As Jack is squeezed out of the intimate artistic connection that had once obtained between his designs and their execution, Mathewson undergoes a parallel descent into ineffective pitching and the decline of his artistic career. The faith that both men have had in baseball as a model for an ideal America finally runs aground on the 1919 World Series, as the corruption of the fixed competition engulfs Eli, who must commit suicide when he cannot cover his debts—and Jack, warned by Mathewson, refuses to cover them for him.

The scene in which Mathewson warns Jack not to follow his brother in being drawn into the Black Sox scandal is also his apotheosis as a type of Christ. "I rose from that death, I walked among the people as of old, and finally, finally, I came to sit in judgment of those I'd walked among, to root out their sin and damn them for it. . . . I damn the filth that corrupted them, the dicers and the high rollers. They will pay. They will pay in time. I shall not rouse them now, for I will allow them their full portion of loss, and when the corrupters are counting their gains I shall spring upon them and drive them from the temple" (262). As Mathewson reveals himself to Jack Kapp all but literally as the risen Christ, the scene becomes ever more one of disillusion and defeat. Spurned by baseball, the Christlike Mathewson has been spurned as well by America. His anathema on the gamblers is a larger anathema on the American allegiance to a sport whose ideals have been exposed as utterly hollow.

For Jack Kapp, the betrayal is double. He has believed in America as a perfect game of baseball, his idealism confirmed by watching Christy Mathewson pitch no-hitters. The America that he has believed in has been fatally emergent for him, however; as he was free to place Mathewson at the receding center of his assimilative quest, so his younger brother Arthur has been free to place a faceless functionalism at the heart of his becoming American. Jack Kapp is betrayed by his ideal America and by his Jewish-American family as well. The central lack of American definition has proved to be a space that invites men (all the major characters are male) to seize it for their own interested purposes.

This disillusion does not mean that *The Celebrant* discards the ideal of an undefined America or even the central project of assimilation. It simply means that the historical America of the fiction has fallen away from its ideals. *The Celebrant* is a hyper-realistic historical novel, one whose spaces are meticulously documented and aligned (and whose many symbolic coincidences merely make one all the more aware, as in much postmodern fiction, of how interpretation itself creates meaning out of raw experience). Yet it is a historical novel that regrets the history it writes. The abandonment of art by Pincus Jewelers when it becomes Collegiate and the abandonment of Mathewson by baseball when he sees through its corruptions become metaphors for how history betrays an original American promise. In *The Celebrant* that ideal ultimately is of a piece with the ideal of *Keystone Kids:* that of an uninscribed, indiscriminate America where men meet as liberal subjects on the field of play, shorn of their history and realigned along the lines of aesthetic categories.

The difference is that in *Keystone Kids* such an America is possible; indeed, it becomes perpetually possible at the climax of every Dodgers novel as the team puts aside its differences and drives to another pennant. In *The Celebrant* we, the narrator and the readers, know better. Adult life is like that; we see through our illusions and we give up our dreams. In return we write or read literature. The projective hopefulness of the child and the nostalgic retrospect of the adult are sides of the same coin, a coin whose currency, in specifically American terms, is that of the perpetual emergence of American identity—and the perpetual emergency of American writing as it struggles to keep the territory open. Everybody wants to play for the Yankees—but only in a perpetual spring training, where slates are clear, the year is young, and everyone is always batting zero for zero.

Notes

1. For the text to put the twentysomething Spike in charge of the whole club is melodramatic but not as unrealistic as it seems; in 1941 twenty-four-year-old Lou Boudreau, also a shortstop, was named manager of the Cleveland Indians.

2. Although it is possible for a single player to turn a triple play unassisted, such plays are even rarer than perfect games—and not as morally instructive.

3. The reference is to the real-life Cincinnati catcher Willard Hershberger, who committed suicide in August 1940.

4. For the best overview of this subject, see Eric Solomon's "Jews, Baseball, and the American Novel." For another parallel, in a children's picture book, see Mindy Avra Portnoy's *Matzah Ball*, where the prophet Elijah shows up at Camden Yards to console a boy who is sulking because it is Passover and he is not allowed to eat the usual ballpark food. When Cal Ripken hits a home run and shatters his matzah, the boy is elated. He has been made one with the American body politic despite the external signs of his difference.

2

"I Do Not Mean Fairy Love"

· ·

At the moment of maximum plot entanglement in Mark Harris's *It Looked Like For Ever* (1979), Henry Wiggen thinks aloud to his wife, Holly, about a houseful of family and guests:

> "There are 13 women in this house," I said to Holly.
> "Why are you counting women?" she inquired.
> "To get asleep," I said.
> "Why not count sheep?" she inquired.
> "I do not fuck sheep," I replied. (188-89)

In many ways this exchange serves as Henry Wiggen's character note throughout the four novels in which he appears. He is heterosexual to a fault; he fucks *women*—or rather, one woman, because in the four Wiggen novels Henry is never even prospectively unfaithful to Holly, although he lusts after Thedabara Brown in *The Southpaw*; an unnamed stewardess in *Bang the Drum Slowly*; the unmet "seam-stitch" in *A Ticket for a Seamstitch*; his lawyer, his broadcasting partner, his manager's wife, and his daughter's psychotherapist in *It Looked Like For Ever*; and Patricia Moors (the owner of his ball club) in all four books. Henry never lusts after sheep, however, and more significantly (what is surely concealed behind his ovine disclaimer) he never lusts after men.

When does Henry Wiggen first come to terms with his heterosexuality? The question seems pointless. Like most male heterosexual characters in fiction, he does not have to; his context is one where all men are presumed to be straight. It never occurs to Henry that he may desire men sexually. Although that possibility never occurs to Henry, however, it certainly occurs to other characters in the novels that he narrates. The tension between the subjective purity of Henry's straightness and the objective ambiguity of some of his actions is a matter for comment in *Bang the Drum Slowly,* and this tension reveals an often unexpressed dynamic: for the construction of normal heterosexuality, a deviant homosexuality must be invoked as the Other from which straight men are defended and against which they are guaranteed.

In *Bang the Drum Slowly* Henry holds out for a contract clause that will forbid his club, the Mammoths, from trading or releasing his roommate, Bruce Pearson. In the economics of baseball, where every individual player must bargain for his own labor contract and where the value of one's labor is based not on interpersonal relationships but on one's batting average, this request is very strange. "This is telling me who I must keep and who not, which nobody ever told me before, Author, and nobody will ever tell me again as long as I am upright" (69), says manager Dutch Schnell, and then it crosses Dutch's mind that sex may be behind the request. He dismisses that possibility, however: "Are you a couple fairies, Author? That can not be. It been a long time since I run across fairies in baseball, not since Will Miller and another lad that I forget his name, a shortstop, that for Christ sake when they split they went and found another friend" (70). Central to Dutch's reasoning is the idea that homosexuals are antimonogamous, making it impossible to construe Henry's fidelity to Bruce as a kind of homosexual pact. Dutch's consequent paranoia is the driving force behind the plot of the central section of the novel, where he makes good on a promise to "run it down to the end of the earth" (70); of immediate interest for the background of the problem is Dutch's contention that "it been a long time since I run across fairies in baseball." For Dutch, the possibility that a professional athlete can be a homosexual is just that—possible, but fraught with so many absurdities and internal contradictions that it is on the far margins of the possible. "That can not be."

The baseball novel, as part of a larger ideology of sport itself, gives us teams of young men who live together, spend much of their time more or less undressed together, and focus their attention on bodies— their own and one another's—while requiring these men to develop as normal heterosexuals, in a cultural atmosphere of compulsory heterosexuality where their own profession is the epitome of male heterosexual activity. Norman Mailer speaks of sexual prowess being the second-most admired athletic ability after "a good straight right," and it goes without saying, for Mailer and for American culture generally, that this prowess is heterosexual.

The athlete is the essential straight male, but his straightness is inherently suspect. It inhabits the thin boundary between homosocial bonding—social networks among people of the same sex—as the highest form of friendship and homosexual intercourse as the lowest form of perversion. To be melded into the American unit and "make the team," the male athlete must make the strongest interpersonal bonds with other men while maintaining the strongest watch on any homosexual tendencies. In this respect team sports resemble other milieus—the church, the military—that are typed single sex and heterosexual; the extent to which homosexuality in team sports goes beyond being individual scandal to become a threat to the integrity of society itself can be seen in the far less scandalous (though still scandalous) impact of homosexuality on individual sports such as tennis or golf. Although little may separate touring tennis pros from professional ballplayers in terms of facilities, interpersonal relations, and group cohesion, the tennis player is ultimately out for him- or herself, and perceived deviant sexuality threatens only the individual. Deviant sexuality on a ball club threatens the integrity of the unit, a unit much like a military unit in its aggressive heterosexist profile. Few things, muses manager Lou Phipps in Eliot Asinof's *Man on Spikes* (1955), can "screw up a ball club faster than a fag on a rainy road trip" (42).

Although heterosexuality is imperative, the ultimate focus of the athlete-character's life is his relationship with other men—athletes, coaches, managers, and the usually male sportswriters and administrators who populate the margins of these novels. Nothing is more important than one's homosocial networks, so the function of heterosexual relationships in baseball novels is predominantly to cement and extend homosocial bonds. Heterosexuality is more than a guarantee of being masculine or a guarantee against homosexuality; it is a way of putting together the homosocial hierarchies of teams and their larger "families." What is ultimately most important emotionally for these characters is their attachment to other men, an attachment they cannot qualify as love, though it appears as love plainly enough to a female observer. Dutch Schnell again:

> "Christ Almighty, I seen you on days when you hated Pearson, when you ate him out as bad as I myself ever ate him out. I seen you about

to kill him for his stupidity. I seen you once get up from the table and walk away."

"Because he laughed without knowing why," I said.

"Such a thing can be not only hate but also love," said Patricia.

"It is not love," said I.

"I do not mean fairy love," she said. (70)

That is the central dilemma of sexuality in the baseball novel. Love between men is the main theme, and it must indeed not "tell its name" but instead be continuously deflected and refracted through heterosexual relationships that themselves can threaten the homosocial community. When Henry is young, in *The Southpaw,* he thinks that "your *real* ballplayer steered clear of girls. This makes me laugh when I think of it now" (25), says the grown-up Henry, but his early insight is instinctively correct. The real ballplayer steers clear of becoming like a woman and becomes a real man and real athlete by treating women as objects. Henry also clearly sees heterosexuality as an issue more of gender than of genital sex. Men become friends in baseball novels over, through, and around the bodies of women—as Henry and Bruce notably do through Bruce's infatuation with Holly Wiggen and Henry's resistance to the team-destroying manipulations of Bruce's gold-digging girlfriend, Katie. When the novels are done, it is not any heterosexual bond but the success or failure of bonds between men that determines the success or failure of these men *as* men.

The phrase "between men" invokes the work of Eve Kosofsky Sedgwick, who pioneered analysis of homosocial bonding and homosexual panic in her study *Between Men: English Literature and Male Homosocial Desire* (1985). Sedgwick's work is a basic theoretical context for my analyses in this chapter. I argue that baseball novels construct the heterosexual through homophobia. If this homophobia were incidental to the cultural work of baseball fiction, its presence might be trivial. Homophobia in baseball stories then could be perceived as simple prejudice against a silenced minority and chalked up as a minor symptom of larger American ignorances. Sedgwick's work, notable among that of other queer theorists for its strong engagement with the way that stories are told, shows how homophobic narratives are more about the construction of heterosexuality than about the suppression of homosexuals. In particular I argue that the plot type Sedgwick defines as "paranoid Gothic" is crucial to many baseball novels. Of this genre Sedgwick argues that "the paranoid Gothic is specifically not about homosexuals or the homosexual; instead, heterosexuality is by definition its subject" (*Between Men* 116).

Patricia Moors presents Henry Wiggen with a theory of homosocial relationships: men's interest in other men can express itself as hate, love, or some unresolvable mixture of the two, but it is an expression of deep (and not necessarily sexual) desire for other men. Henry objects, and his objection is the same one encountered by Sedgwick when she asks, "Doesn't the continuum between 'men-loving-men' and 'men-promoting-the-interests-of-men' have the same intuitive force that it has for women?" (3) When Henry answers Patricia "It is not love," he raises this obstacle: "However convenient it might be to group together all the bonds that link males to males, and by which males enhance the status of males—usefully symmetrical as it would be, that grouping meets with a prohibitive structural obstacle" (*Between Men* 3). Love between men is seen as homosexual in a way that love between women can avoid. The result, for men who (like Henry) try to promote the interests of other men (like Bruce) in a compassionate way, is a double bind.

> The fact that what goes on at football games, in fraternities, at the Bohemian Grove, and at climactic moments in war novels can look, with only a slight shift of optic, quite startlingly "homosexual," is not most importantly an expression of the psychic origin of these institutions in a repressed or sublimated homosexual genitality. Instead, it is the coming to visibility of the normally implicit terms of a coercive double bind. . . . For a man to be a man's man is separated only by an invisible, carefully blurred, always-already-crossed line from being "interested in men." (*Between Men* 89)

When considering *Bang the Drum Slowly* in particular or the baseball novel in general, it is important to note that these fictions neither posit nor uncover homosexual bonds between their male characters. Henry and Bruce are not a Fiedleresque couple. Leslie Fiedler's detection, in his essay "Come Back to the Raft Ag'in, Huck Honey" (1948), of the unconsciously homosexual pairs who populate canonical American fictions made it possible for post-1948 fictions to achieve a Fiedler-like self-consciousness about male bonding. In a superficial sense Henry and Bruce are like Fiedler's famous pairs of whites and savages: Huck and Jim, Ishmael and Queequeg, Dana and Hope, Hawkeye and Chingachgook. They are both white, but they mix regional identities, the Yankee liberal and the southern redneck. They move together in a milieu, the ballfield, that excludes women, if only for nine innings at a time. And as in Fiedler's examples the non-Yankee of the pair sickens and dies. In these earlier American fictions (like the early British fictions discussed by Sedgwick), the text maintains a strict self-censorship with regard to its homosexual tendencies (if one might call them that). Ishmael may squeeze Queequeg's hand through the membranes in a bucket of sperm, but it is unthinkable that he would want to squeeze the sperm out of Queequeg's *membrum virile*. The open suspicion directed at Henry and Bruce's relationship marks *Bang the Drum Slowly* as a post-Fiedler text, one that openly represents homophobia—and in so doing marks as its true subject the construction of the heterosexual against a backdrop of homophobic suspicion.

Henry Wiggen and Bruce Pearson are heterosexual. Henry is monogamous and Bruce is indiscriminate, but *Bang the Drum Slowly* is at pains to construct them as subjectively straight from the start. Although Henry leaves Holly's marriage bed to visit Bruce's hospital bed at the novel's opening, he contemplates a quickie with a stewardess along the way and later defends his pursuit of Bruce by characterizing it to Dutch Schnell as the cover for his pursuit of a girlfriend. Bruce clearly desires Holly (although his primary loyalty to Henry prevents him from acting on the desire), and Henry appreciates Katie, the whore who is trying to marry Bruce, for her professionalism—although his primary loyalty to Bruce influences him even more than his monogamy in turning down her offer of a lifetime free pass to her whorehouse.

In other words, *they're not gay.* Nevertheless the prime cultural work of homophobia is accomplished by a dynamic in which "no man must be able to ascertain that he is not (that his bonds are not) homosexual" (Sedgwick, *Between Men* 88–89). The more his loyalty to Bruce draws Henry into preserving the secret of Bruce's Hodgkin's disease, the more he cannot be sure that his relationship with Bruce is social, not sexual. The secret of Bruce's medical vulnerability throws the background of Henry's entire sexual identity into relief. As a straight man Henry is always at risk, in his central relationships with other straight men, for the suspicion, internal or external, of homosexuality. The relationship between Henry and Bruce is an epitome of ways in which, especially in the homosocial world of sports fiction, "nonhomosexual-identified men" are "subject to control through homophobic blackmailability" (*Between Men* 90).

Blackmailability consists of quite a bit more than men's literal vulnerability to having their arrest records revealed to their wives; when it comes to that, most "blackmailable" heterosexuals have no arrest records to be revealed. The quality of blackmailability comes from the location of crucial homosocial bonds at the fuzzy boundary between the social and the sexual. An internalized, self-directed homophobia makes a man an "excruciatingly *responsive* creature and instrument" (*Between Men* 114), forcing him to perform acts of self-censorship that result in overt demonstrations of how straight he is. As Joseph Litvak says, "Heterosexual masculinity is not an identity that one simply has, but an identification that one must be terrorized into" (21). Blackmailability in turn is the key power dynamic in giving heterosexual patriarchy a domination "over the bonds that structure all social form" (Sedgwick, *Between Men* 87).

"Paranoia is the psychosis which makes graphic the mechanisms of homophobia" (*Between Men* 91), asserts Sedgwick, and it is easy to see why paranoia is the mental illness of choice when men must keep perpetual surveillance over their own erotic tendencies and the construction of their erotic identities by those who surround them (and who, since they are men, may be indistinguishably blackmailers, bait for blackmail, or both at once). For Sedgwick, the literary distillation of the mechanisms of homophobia comes in the early nineteenth-century paranoid Gothic, her central example being James Hogg's *Confessions of a Justified Sinner.* In these novels a man is shadowed, doubled, and tormented by a male persecutor, who combines the threats posed by a vampiric homosexual on the make, a doppelgänger, a blackmailer, and an Oedipal rival for the affections of a (frequently not specifically realized) father. A line of filiation (if that is the right word) clearly connects these British examples, from the dawn of homosexual panic in Europe, with twentieth-century avatars such as Dashiell Hammett's *Maltese Falcon,* Patricia Highsmith's *Strangers on a Train,* and the film renderings of both of those novels; the line extends just as clearly into the genre of baseball fiction.

Bang the Drum Slowly is not ultimately a paranoid Gothic; it is in fact a novel that confronts its own tendencies toward Gothic paranoia and resolves them in moves that reinforce, in ways peculiar to baseball fiction, the assimilative and meritocratic aspects of the special brand of American patriarchy on offer in the genre. For the paranoid Gothic in its pure diamond form, we must look slightly earlier, to Julian De Vries's young adult novel *The Strike-Out King*, published in the Fiedler year of 1948. Before discussing these novels in depth, I want to illustrate some of the archetypes of the construction of male heterosexuality in the baseball genre at large.

Key features of how baseball novels construct the male heterosexual (indeed, *teams of* male heterosexuals) include paranoid doubling, with pairs of men in relations that cycle from love to hate and continually spiral back to the forbidden category of "interest" in a way that amounts to obsession; blackmailability and homosexual panic; sudden irruptions of violence (a standard Gothic feature) that serve the purpose sometimes of eliminating a double but more often of erasing boundaries and suspicions in a celebration of masculine potential for violence, where the "good straight right" overrides obsessions with sexual prowess; and then (moving toward the construction of normative heterosexuality) establishment of homosocial bonds between men through the bodies of women in sexual and economic exchanges and a transference (sometimes symbolic) of the individual male hero's sexual direction toward female objects that, constrained in patriarchal systems, have no power to feminize him. The middle section of this chapter, treating individual texts as components of a larger genre text, establishes these archetypes of heterosexuality in baseball fiction.

Paranoid doubles in baseball novels take various forms, either appearing front and center or functioning more as warning signs in the margin of the text. In the second category is the homophobic manager Lou Phipps in *Man on Spikes*, already invoked here for his dislike of queers on rainy road trips. Phipps (an ephemeral character in the novel) thinks of the queer threat in the context on his musings on his own rivalry with scout Durkin Fain, the man who has discovered the novel's hero, Mike Kutner, and signed him to a pro contract. "Fain, the wise sonofabitch, always trying to squeeze some little squirt into the system with his so-called 'smart baseball.' . . . 'Durkin Fain can shove his friggen prospects up his butt'" (Asinof 42). Ostensibly the Phipps/Fain conflict is over access to power in the patriarchy of baseball management, where the credibility of manager or scout depends on patronizing the right prospects. By suggesting that Fain should make room anally for the prospects he signs, Phipps is implying that he may already be taking it anally from the "little squirts"—that his patronage of smart, underathletic players may be a cover for personal pederasty. Phipps himself begins to understand that he protests too much, however. "Phipps was too much aroused. His feeling for Durkin Fain was like a fever" (43). Rivalry, as much as love, is a potential site for subjective panic over sexuality; it will never do, no matter how much one's livelihood depends on it, to become *too* interested in the doings of other men.

The old man in the coach's box eying the young trade, the talent hawk who is incipiently a chicken hawk, is the most common marginal double for a younger ballplayer, as in the Phipps episode from *Man on Spikes* where Mike becomes briefly a pawn in the jealous rivalry between Phipps and Fain. This rivalry moves closer to the center in *The Celebrant*, where the evil that John McGraw poses to the idol of Americanism that Christy Mathewson consti- tutes for Jack Kapp is realized increasingly in the form of a specific- ally homosexual evil. McGraw is more central to *The Celebrant* than Phipps is to *Man on Spikes*, but he forms only an intrusion into the central homosocial triangle of Mathewson and the Kapp broth- ers. That he forms *only* an intrusion and not a main axis of the plot is because *The Celebrant* types McGraw as the older partner in a series of quasi-homosexual relationships with younger, less powerful men. As the eternal chicken hawk, McGraw never truly develops as a character; his archetypal invariability is stressed by a tableau of scenes spanning years of his managerial career.[1]

The first of McGraw's suspect doublings is with Mathewson, only seven years younger than McGraw but one of the first players he manages who is too young to have been his peer as a player and who is always potentially his neophyte. The McGraw/Mathewson rela- tionship is complicated and made doubly suspect by their social relation; in an implausible but historically true move, the text has McGraw and Mathewson (with their wives) sharing a Manhattan apartment. Jack first meets Mathewson in this apartment, in an extraordinary scene nested inside the story of Jack's plans for his own heterosexual and decidedly homosocial wedding, which will connect him to a wealthy and prominent father-in-law. McGraw, showing off his domestic intimacy with the pitcher while uttering strings of obscenities that (like Phipps's) center mostly on anal pen- etration ("Byron Bancroft fucking Johnson . . . can take his Western League and his National Commission and his World's Series and shove them all up his big brown asshole" [Greenberg 73]), introduces Jack to a gloriously, desirably nude Mathewson. When the conversation between Jack and Mathewson is pointedly nonobscene, McGraw feminizes them both: "You two sound like Mistress Mary's School for Girls" (74).

In this initial meeting Jack is too much blinded by gazing on Mathewson's naked beauty to register the presence of McGraw, who nonetheless has much of the dialogue, recorded by Jack's narrator's ear if not by his immediate consciousness. The social relation of mutual interest, as both Mathewson and Jack Kapp admire the other's artistry (in fields where they do not compete), is set against John McGraw's abusive homophobic taunts. At this point Jack can blot out McGraw or bracket him as humorous counterpoint to a homosocial bond that might exist beyond the reach of McGraw's blackmailing potential. Moreover, as if to underscore the delicate potential for a homosocial yet heterosexual connection, the Mathewsons send the Kapps a quilt as a wedding present (74-75), a feminine gift that also recognizes the Kapps' heterosexual congress and therefore Jack's straightness. The queerness of the threat posed by Mathewson's leering roommate nevertheless becomes an engine for Jack's disillusion with baseball as a route to American heterosexual identity.

"'Give me a body like that,' said McGraw, 'and I'd have been twice the player I was" (71). McGraw explores the boundaries of envy and desire. His desiring gaze is outshone by Mathewson's brilliance when Jack meets the pitcher for the first time. Later in the novel we see McGraw's unchanging attitude toward young male bodies, frozen in youth and perfection while he ages like the baseball card of Dorian Gray. The central heartbreak in the novel is the 1908 pennant lost to the Cubs when Fred Merkle—eight years younger than Mathewson and fifteen younger than McGraw—fails to touch second base, annulling the winning run. McGraw attacks chief umpire O'Day, bat in hand, apoplectic in his illogic, abusing O'Day as a "bog-crawling Mick" (141). The umpire calmly outlines the rules of the game that decree that Merkle is out and that his innocent conformity with the customs of the game (wherein runners, at that time, often left the field when the winning run had scored) has been turned into a historic blunder by sheer technicality—has been turned into the gruesomely named "Merkle Boner." O'Day taunts the tiny McGraw, calls him Muggsy, and gets in a pointed final comment.

When the manager says, "Nobody fucks with John McGraw!" the umpire replies, "Especially Mrs. McGraw, you randy rat-faced turd" (141). Almost lost in the pair's homophobic posturing is McGraw's homophilic plea when the manager realizes the irrevocability of the umpire's ruling. "Don't take it out on the kid, O'Day. Sweet Jesus, don't take it out on the kid" (140). The whole melancholy of McGraw's desire for the younger Merkle is compressed into these two sentences.

Merkle, at age nineteen, becomes the most shamed of baseball blunderers. McGraw, however, to whom most mental errors are anathema, absolves Merkle and hovers over him protectively during the evening that follows. When Jack meets them later, summoned by McGraw to discuss team rings, "McGraw took hold of Merkle's wrist. 'Better make Fred's extra large. Look at those hands! Look at that body! Give me a body like that and I'd have been twice the player I was'" (149). For *The Celebrant*'s McGraw, the appeal of managing is the ever-renewed access to the body of the neophyte, a role that remains as constant as his own of mentor. As the dying Mathewson explains, "We had to endure those dreadful harangues while Mac, as young as his youngest player, repurchased his youth by renewing his roster" (262).

The final panel in McGraw's triptych of young beauties is Ross Youngs, exhibited in a scene that revolts Jack. It is 1919, the final year of the novel, the year of the Black Sox and baseball's betrayal of the contract the sport has seemed to offer the Kapps. Youngs is twenty-two, and his manager is now forty-six. McGraw shows Youngs to a roomful of admirers:

> "Take off your trousers, Ross. The skivvies, too. Now get up here on the table."
>
> Naked, the boy sprang onto the table and made it his pedestal, standing in repose, his body white, his face still as a statue's. The men at the table leaned back in their chairs, studying him as if he were a slave at auction.
>
> "Look at that body," said McGraw in a low voice. "If I'd had a body like that I'd have been twice the ballplayer I was." (238)

The exhibition of Youngs focuses the consciousness Jack has developed of McGraw's vampirish evil. He faints, but not before receiving a prophetic vision of Youngs dying. Youngs *did* die in 1927, prematurely burned out, the novel's analysis suggests, by the older man's desire.

The Celebrant's use of Mathewson, Merkle, and Youngs as foils for its homophobic image of John McGraw is, I underscore again, histrionic rather than historical. What is most striking about this representation for my purposes is its dehumanizing of the homosexual, its denial of full actualization to the man who desires men. In the doublings of paranoid Gothic, the homosexual is the nonhuman half of the male self, the side that must be suppressed, cast out, or killed so that the human side can grow. The heterosexual is valorized through being made more fully real than the homosexual. In these formulations the homosexual appears monstrous, vampirish, or ghostly.

Such homophobia can be seen even within the bounds of novels that try to expand the boundaries of social inclusiveness. Marilyn Levinson's *And Don't Bring Jeremy* (1985) is first and foremost a text that teaches toleration for the retarded. Jeremy is the mildly retarded elder brother of narrator Adam Krasner. The Krasners have moved to a new neighborhood where Adam pitches for a youth league team in an attempt to make new friends. His attempts are frustrated by the embarrassment of being Jeremy's brother. Adam tries to get into the homosocial networks of his new neighborhood through a triangle that includes two of his teammates: Eddie Gordon, the coach's son, and Danny Martin, who is an artist and a set designer for the local theater, as well as a ballplayer. The Krasners' Jewishness is factored out of the novel's dynamics, although the familiar pattern of Jews assimilating to a neighborhood of Gordons and Martins anchors the text in its genre.

The triangle comprising Adam, Eddie, and Danny quickly turns Gothic. Eddie can be a cad or a loyal friend; Danny is far more consistent, but his interests are a bit queer. Danny is introspective and supportive, the one of the three most sensitive to their mutual triangle (33–36). Eddie turns ugly on losing a starting pitching assignment to Adam and punches him (39). When Danny and Adam have a jealous misunderstanding, Danny behaves furtively and secretly (54–55). Eddie oscillates between offering Adam his entire baseball card collection and flying into a rage when his father (the coach) prefers Adam on the field. "Being jealous of me was just plain dumb" (67), remarks Adam, signaling the real problem by means of his semantic imprecision. Eddie is jealous *of* Adam in the sense that he wants no one (and most threateningly, not his own father) to enjoy Adam's company or spend time with him.

Eddie is specifically jealous of Jeremy's existence as Adam's brother. Jeremy himself befriends a younger boy, third-grader Tommy Stein, acting out fantasies with Tommy like the following: "I will throw you into my dungeon and tear you apart, limb from limb, if you do not tell me where the jewels are hidden" (48). His parents are alarmed more by the inappropriateness of Jeremy's playing with a third-grader than by any incipient tendencies Jeremy shows toward the bondage scene. Throughout the novel the mother, Helen Krasner, plays a kind of hysteria into a heightening of the general paranoia, refusing to believe that Eddie has it in for Jeremy and losing her temper when Jeremy shows signs of wanting to play with Tommy (90–93). Eddie spends his time doing mischief like destroying the sets that Adam and Danny have built and framing Jeremy for the vandalism. Ultimately Eddie's machinations are uncovered, and a new primary bond between Jeremy and Adam becomes the novel's final tableau (120–22).

The novel's overt theme is that a family can regroup around a "special" member and support that member (Jeremy) in the face of divisive external pressures. As the foregoing summary suggests, however, *And Don't Bring Jeremy* is obsessed with the proper direction of homosocial ties among boys. Eddie Gordon *loves* Adam Krasner, to put it as simply as possible; his wild swings from flamboyant generosity to searing envy to calculating hatred are "not only hate but also love," as Patricia Moors might put it. Eddie's father is his problem and his ultimate salvation. Unlike the Krasners, who are indulgent, hysterical, self-surveillant yuppie parents, "Mr. Gordon was the sergeant type, always serious and tough" (89). He continually threatens Eddie with violence, and the implication at the novel's end is that Mr. Gordon will make good on these threats when Eddie's crime of set destruction is uncovered. Like any good coach, Mr. Gordon wants to meld Eddie and Adam into teammates rather than rivals, but his strict meritocracy in choosing Adam as an all-star alongside Eddie (the team's best player) causes Eddie to doubt his paternal affections.

The world of *And Don't Bring Jeremy* is relentlessly homosocial and relentlessly stricken with paranoid panic. In the face of the structures his father represents, Eddie becomes the book's most normal heterosexual. When Laura Lee Swanson, the only woman in his life, plays the strict meritocrat with him by refusing to help him cheat on a test, Eddie pumps her locker full of shaving cream (59). We can see the kind of life Laura Lee can expect. Eddie's spermatic self-assertions are again subject to the novel's punitive economies, for he is doubly punished, by his father for failing and by the school for creaming.

At least Eddie seems to be headed in the straight direction, however. I am not so certain about Adam and Danny. Although excluded from the final family tableau, Danny is the novel's main object of desire, and his relationship with Adam seems to prefigure a long life of closet circumspection. The few girls in the book are present mainly to cover the development of this love. At a class picnic Adam relates, "Somehow or other, Danny and I got to sharing a blanket with Patty and Michelle" (76). Safe in the presence of their dates, the two boys commence a badinage. "I punched him in the arm and we ended up wrestling, the girls laughing the whole time" (77). One wonders whether they know why they are laughing; perhaps they are reading *Women in Love* in their English class. As the Birkin and Gerald of the tee-ball set knock off their wrestling match, Adam tells us, "I made a mental note to ask Danny if he knew how to dance, so he could teach me just in case I felt like asking Patty" (77). One can imagine this as the first in a long series of mental notes made to a character's self regarding the dimensions of his personal closet.

But it would be absurd to say that this text is "about" the closet. It is "about" incorporation of ill-tolerated people—retarded children and perhaps, silently, Jews—into a mainstream that takes patriarchal homosocial bonds, patriarchal violence, and the imperatives of the closet strictly for granted. The Gothic triangles of *And Don't Bring Jeremy* are not the novel's subject but its setting, a setting that this children's baseball story ultimately derives from the atmosphere of its precursors in the genre—as so often, ultimately from John R. Tunis.

In Tunis's *Highpockets* (1948) the oft-immolated Roy Tucker runs into a concrete wall making a circus catch (60-61) and is carted proximately off the field and ultimately to Johns Hopkins, where he lies in a coma. In his absence the brash young slugger Highpockets lacks a role model and becomes increasingly selfish and preoccupied on the field. The Dodgers suffer as a result. As luck would have it, however, Highpockets drives as carelessly as he plays ball, and he runs over, mangles, and crushes a young boy named Dean Kennedy.

It is an accident, but an accident of destiny for both the runner-over and the run-down.

With responsibility for Dean's injuries hanging on his conscience, Highpockets befriends the boy. Dean needs befriending; his own male role models are none too good, and his father in particular is a pusillanimous sort who behaves "as if it was an honor to have his son run over by Highpockets" (99). While Roy Tucker languishes in Baltimore, Highpockets frequents Dean's hospital room in Brooklyn, transferring his affections to the injured boy. Emphatically Highpockets is "thankful also that it was a boy who had been injured rather than a girl. Boys understand baseball" (86-87). In the pre-Fiedler world of *Highpockets* the slugger's secret assignations with the boy are suspected never as homosexual but as heterosexual. The presumptions of the novel serve as an almost perfect closeting device for the relationship: "Must be a girl," suggests a teammate (133); another asks, "Whatcha got, some dame back there in Brooklyn?" (144)

Nor can Highpockets really explain his moonstruck behavior, because his relationship with Dean can amount only to love. When Highpockets returns after a road trip, "The face was rounder and fuller now, and there was a smile and a warming look of welcome on it that made the ballplayer warm also. He shuffled over and ran his long fingers through the kid's hair, the hair which had grown and was again falling over his forehead. . . . Boys never comb their hair; why on earth should they?" (147) In any context other than the blissful innocence of the young adult novel, these musings would be grounds for opening a police file on Highpockets. That he does not open a mental one on himself is due to three special factors. For one thing, it is unclear whether Highpockets will play the role of mentor/lover or mentor/father to the boy. The elder Kennedy will cede his role: "I aim to be a good father and all, yet one way or another, I don't understand, he wants you here tonight" (129). For another, the player's relationship with Dean is a chance to move the boy in a normative direction, a goal at which Highpockets aims with a sort of paranoid desperation. His initial assumption that he will be able to bond with the boy over baseball is untrue, for Dean appears to be the only child in Brooklyn who has never heard of the Dodgers, and his hobby is collecting stamps. Highpockets works assiduously at mastering the lore of philately, but always toward the end of establishing trust with the boy *over* the stamps to draw him *out* of stamps. He succeeds; by novel's end (173) Dean is collecting baseball cards and coming out to Ebbets Field to cheer him on.

The third dynamic that prevents Highpockets from suspecting queerness in his own affections for Dean is the usefulness of the mentoring relationship in catalyzing his own bonds with the other Dodgers—or in constituting them, for Dean becomes an entire education in homosocial etiquette. The catalyst is Roy, revived in time for the pennant drive and reclaiming his place in the Brooklyn clubhouse. When Roy returns Highpockets muses, "Why can't I be like him? . . . He loves folks and folks love him" (156). When Highpockets reaches out to touch Roy, he touches the rest of the corporate Dodgers body through the older man. Later that day, after Highpockets hits a home run, they welcome him at the plate: "He felt their bodies jostling his, the friendly contact of hips and thighs when he came across the plate, their hot paws extended to him, someone grasping his right hand, someone else his left. . . . Now he was one of them, now he was part of the team" (158-59). The ability to negotiate loving contact properly, which Highpockets has learned from Dean Kennedy during long hours of negotiation over the stamp album, reincorporates him into the homosocial group. The role of mentor seized in one relationship enables him to enact the role of peer in others. The final sealing of the newly established homosocial bonds is an all-but-sexual locker-room ritual:

> Suddenly someone slapped him with the wet end of a towel. In six long months with the Dodgers it had never happened to him before.
>
> He turned quickly, but the player had escaped to the other end of the room. Just then someone else slapped him with another wet towel. The blow stung his thigh. It also warmed his heart. (162)

Anonymous contact on the butt enfolds Highpockets into the sensual world of the team. It is a moment that establishes a certain space for the mechanics of the closet within the baseball novel, a space still useful for young adult texts, where the assumption of straightness coincides with genital innocence. Were Highpockets's primary relationship with an injured adult—or with a female—the sexual presumptions might disable the mechanics of making the team. He is in the sacred space of man-boy relations, however, sacred for this text, this genre. It is the one space where the closet can be open without paranoia.

When adults desire adults, or think they do, the closet space becomes one of claustrophobic as well as homophobic panic. The locker room is full of gossip; players who can let their bats talk on the field are never allowed to shut up and let their dicks do the talking off it. "Everybody in baseball likes to talk about women, even the queers, but not John Barr," worries Ricky Falls about his idol in *Sometimes You See It Coming* (K. Baker 55). In the same novel the fear of a queer locker-room dynamic excludes the sportswriter Dickhead Barry Busby, who longs to be a novelist rather than embrace the quasi-teammate status of beat writer (139–40). Teammates' chatter can be directed outward, homophobically taunting perceived queer threats (as Coker Roguski's mocking of a "swishy" TV producer in Mark Harris's *Southpaw* [192]). Just as common, and far more effective for the control that homophobia has over straight men's identity, the chatter becomes a running interior monologue.

The pitcher Apples in David Carkeet's *Greatest Slump of All Time* (1985) internalizes the homophobic panic that his status as a virgin male on a team of heterosexual men provokes. His lack of *any* sexual experience in a world where sexual experience is assumed to be naturally straight leads him to conclude that he must be gay. He begins to accommodate himself to this disturbing possibility. Apples's failures to feel heterosexual desire (or to be the recipient of it from women) send him into a panic about his orientation. For instance:

> Apples sits in his dentist's waiting room . . . trying not to think about the well-muscled young man sitting across from him. Their eyes met and locked briefly as Apples came in, then again after Apples gave his name to the receptionist, picked a magazine from the stand, and sat down. Apples is not sexually aroused, though. He is merely uncomfortable because he suspects the young man is a homosexual who desires him. But Apples has managed to mistake his discomfort for repressed arousal. (Also, the man isn't a homosexual at all. He's just a fan who has recognized Apples and is tremendously excited about it.) (79)

The tricky rhetoric of Apples's interior monologue as routed through the narrating voice of *The Greatest Slump* makes apparent a system of defenses and subterfuges in the everyday work of self-surveillance. The text presents Apples as a kind of pathological case, as a deviant consciousness. He is the heterosexual (his heterosexuality is about to be confirmed by the dental assistant behind the office door, a woman who becomes his lover), but he is falsely conscious of homosexuality. Even his sense of who is homosexual is false, as it is here. He becomes doubly unsure of identity, and his identity in fact becomes determined by a cycle of misunderstandings. The real subterfuge here is in the way the text passes off Apples's dilemma as exceptional. I argue that it is the classic modern heterosexual dilemma. Apples is *normal* precisely because he cannot be sure, because no man can be sure. The man who does not doubt his heterosexuality is the deviant, possibly more dangerous than the man who realizes his homosexuality.

Apples is a magical realist highlighting of a kind of homophobic self-surveillance that is the background noise for many of the characters in baseball fiction. In a world where panic and paranoia are endemic, strategies are developed for the proper therapeutic treatment of incipient homosexuals. Here the cultural work of baseball fiction is done on the ground of sexuality. The overriding imperative is not so much to establish the conditions of terror as to suggest ways of coping with that terror by establishing a stable heterosexual identity. Establishing such an identity is hardly easy. Interest in men, specifically interest in men's bodies, must be redirected, remanaged in directions that recall the primal workings of an incest taboo. It is a homosexual incest taboo: an all-male family must expel its brothers who desire one another and make them find mates among the women in the world at large. Central to these rites is turning the desired body into a scapegoat in a violent ritual that destroys that body's desirability as it controls its animal potential.

Given the pastoral calm of baseball mythology, a remarkable violence inhabits the baseball *novel*. Part of the motive for this ubiquitous violence is sheer machismo, as in the Western: "The physical punishment heroes take is not incidental to their role; it is constitutive of it. Prolonged and deliberate laceration of the flesh, endured without complaint, is a sine qua non of masculine achievement" (Tompkins 105). There seems to be far too much violent death in sports fiction, however. As Tompkins points out, death is the whole context of the Western, but why is there so much death in a genre where the context is child's play?

"When they talk about violence in professional sports . . . they almost never talk about the game of baseball, and they almost never talk about murder" (42), reflects Mickey Slavin in R. D. Rosen's *Strike Three You're Dead* (1984), a novel about the murder of a ballplayer, as are dozens of other baseball mysteries. Bump Bailey hurtles through a wall, enabling Roy Hobbs to replace him on the Knights in *The Natural*. Roy himself has been shot to open that novel. The virtual Damon Rutherford is killed by a pitch in *The Universal Baseball Association*, and his virtual killer, Jock Casey, is killed in turn by a line drive. Ron Carlson's Zanduce kills *fans*—lots of them—with line drives.[2] Bruce Pearson dies of cancer. Eddie commits suicide in *The Greatest Slump*. Stillwater Norman is slaughtered in a bar fight near the beginning of *Sometimes You See It Coming*, and John Barr dies in a plane crash at the end. Mathewson dies, racked with tuberculosis, at the end of *The Celebrant*, and Eli Kapp is a suicide. Gabby Gus Spencer buys it in a car crash in *The Kid from Tomkinsville*; Charlie Snow bleeds to death (he is a hemophiliac) in *Brittle Innings*, where later on the novel dissolves into unspeakable violence; and Ray Zajak spends *Chin Music* dying horribly of a brain lesion. For lesser injuries, consider Roy Tucker throughout Tunis's novels. We first see Bob Russell naked and mangled in *Keystone Kids*. Nor are the slapstick novels exempt; a turning point in the plot of Paul Molloy's *Pennant for the Kremlin* is a line drive to the kneecap of White Sox pitcher Jim Reeves.

It is not that these deaths and injuries are completely unrealistic; baseball history, from Ray Chapman to Lou Gehrig to Herb Score and beyond, is filled with the potential for sudden death or dismemberment. The disasters of baseball become connected, however, to the melancholy of displaced homosexual desire. The athlete dies young, as we know from Housman. Over and over again in the completely fictional situations of these stories, the athlete dies young *because* he is desired (and conversely is the more desired because he is fated to die young). In a dynamic that resembles nothing as much as that of *Jane Eyre*, interest can be shown in a dead, dying, or mutilated man when it can never be shown in that man at the peak of his potency.

Nowhere is the direction of such deadly desire in the baseball novel so clearly seen as in the archetypal pitcher-batter encounters that end in the death or dismemberment of one party or the other (it would be difficult to kill both on the same pitch, although sooner or later some baseball novel is bound to try it). Such encounters are often potentially Oedipal. Damon Rutherford and Jock Casey are killed on different pitches in different games, and their confrontation becomes the basis of the religion of the Universal Baseball Association. "A boy name of Muddy Rivers" (270) ends the career of the ancient Henry Wiggen in *It Looked Like For Ever* by hitting him in the head with a line drive. The archetype of archetypes is again from Tunis. Long before the days of the Griffeys, *Young Razzle* contrives to have a father and son playing major-league baseball at the same time—not only playing, but playing against each other, and not only against each other, but in the World Series. Old Razzle is a pitcher, Young Razzle is a batter, and they meet at a crucial point in the series. "Razzle let go with everything he had. The boy was waiting. He met it with the fat of his bat, and the ball came back like a bullet at Raz, who was way over in his stride and completely off balance. Unable to duck, unable even to throw up his hand in protection, Raz caught the ball squarely on the left side of his forehead" (184). Razzle is unhurt by this moment of Oedipal violence; it rather endears his son to him, much after the manner of John Wayne and Montgomery Clift at the end of *Red River*. Perhaps most remarkable in this primal scene is the reaction of Razzle's manager, Spike Russell: "That's luck for you. Your star pitcher knocked out at a critical point in the game by a lucky shot" (185). "No," one wants to tell Spike Russell, "he has been knocked out by one of the more overdetermined shots in the whole series of novels you've been in." But perhaps Spike's attribution of the drive to luck is how the text of *Young Razzle* rather transparently covers up its obsession with the sexual violence between fathers and sons.

As readers of *The Universal Baseball Association* know, pitchers are not hit on the head by line drives on account of luck. Men are fused together through violent atonement. Once one male has proved himself through inflicting sudden and hideous violence on another, an equation of sexual disinterest has replaced one of potentially unhealthy interest, and the father and son (who underlie all such encounters but are revealed as such only in *Young Razzle*) can be united in a loving final tableau. The anger that Young Razzle has borne toward his father on account of Razzle's treatment of his mother is dissolved in their relation of mutual reverence as on-field antagonists. The female in the equation has been solved for and erased.

Coover's characters have it even easier in one respect—they do not exist, and there are no dice rolls for women. Women exist troublingly on the periphery of the UBA, but they are well removed from the game within the game. Women threaten every other male baseball team in fiction, however, and they were posing insoluble problems for fictional ballplayers long before Harriet Bird shot Roy Hobbs. The problem that the men face is how properly to negotiate women as individuals and as counters in male homosocial relations. Razzle must thus convince his son that it was his mother's malice that prevented a crucial male-bond-cementing gift of a bat and glove from reaching him at an impressionable moment in his adolescence (Tunis, *Young Razzle* 148–49). So too we have the violence that is directed toward women in such scenes as Long Lew's rape of Fanny in *The Universal Baseball Association* or the disarmingly unself-conscious episode of Eileen the Bullpen Queen in *Sometimes You See It Coming*, where Eileen gives blow jobs to Mets bench players, who become erect and ejaculate in each other's sight, staring at each other's cocks. Nobody, apparently, checks to see whether Eileen is a queen indeed.

Therapeutic routes to straightness in the baseball novel are subtler, however, and involve exchanging women to construct a heterosocial order. This order replicates patriarchy; it also controls anarchy by restraining desires in the homosocial milieu. The earliest example from baseball fiction is already a parody—to an extent that makes later texts in the genre seem like solemn parodies of a satire. When Jack Keefe in *You Know Me Al* (1914) marries Florrie, the sister-in-law of his roommate, Allen, he not only bonds with his teammate over the bodies of the sisters they have married but exposes the flaws in such patriarchal arrangements. Florrie agrees to marry Jack because she is pregnant with another man's child but able to convince Jack that the baby is his; Jack, so ignorant that the mistaken paternity of his son never openly registers in his letters to Al back home, is pressured into appearing masculine and heterosexual in front of his team (and proud to acknowledge his heterosexual activities). By succeeding at being a man among men, Jack loses at the larger game of establishing a legitimate patrimony.

It is just like Ring Lardner to deconstruct the entire genre of baseball fiction in advance, so that it is built in literary historical terms on a foundation of sand. Nevertheless the fun poked at patriarchal exchange of women in *You Know Me Al* has never prevented the baseball novel from going in wholesale for the exchange of women, because homophobia and the homosexual incest taboo of the team continually drive such exchanges. When women appear on the scene, they are always tokens in a complex sexual-economic arrangement among male teammates. Ellie Jay in *Sometimes You*

See It Coming is a touchpoint of possible sexual competition between John Barr and Ricky Falls, till her evident mission to bring out Barr as a straight man becomes more functionally useful to Falls than is his own desire for her. Harvey Blissberg is briefly a murder suspect in *Strike Three You're Dead* because he and the murdered Rudy Furth maintain their relationship as roommates and teammates by engaging in rivalry over the woman sportscaster Mickey Slavin. Such rivalries are always more productive of male bonding than of male fallings out, because they guarantee that both males are traveling the straight and narrow.

When such rivalries are generational, they transform the Oedipal rivalries of the team into a way to sustain patriarchy. In *Schoolboy Johnson* (1958) Tunis's main plot concerns the bickering mentor/disciple relationship between washed-up veteran pitcher Speedy Mason and the hotheaded rookie pitcher of the title. Schoolboy will not listen to Speedy, and Speedy feels he cannot teach Schoolie anything. The proper relationship between the two men cannot be established until Schoolie reroutes his desires and his ambitions through the body of a woman. In Highpockets fashion Schoolboy Johnson finds his true love through hitting it with his car (the way to a man's heart in these novels is through his fender). The car he hits is Roy Tucker's, and the driver is Tucker's daughter, Maxine.[3]

As at almost every point in the long series of Dodgers novels, Roy Tucker becomes a surrogate for every desire and every dynamic; here, as a washed-up veteran in the last novel of the series, he offers his own daughter to a rookie teammate to integrate him into the team. Roy routes his own incestuous desires for Maxine through Schoolie—or for Schoolie through Maxine?—in a locker-room scene where he gazes longingly at "the tall boy tenderly stroking his thick hair" (103) and wishes he could be Schoolie's age, have Schoolie's body. As the relationship between Schoolie and Maxine progresses, Schoolie drops his obsessive antagonism with Speedy and becomes the model pupil. The Dodgers drive for the pennant behind the pitching of the rookie and the veteran alike.

Speedy throws a no-hitter to get the Dodgers to the deciding game, and Schoolie starts that game, with Maxine watching from the stands. At the crucial moment, with everything riding on the next pitch, Schoolie thinks, "I wish I was at Jones Beach" (177). However naive the thought, it is weirdly appropriate. Schoolie has won his niche on the team by dating Maxine, but having to play in her presence is a different matter. The pressure of performing feats of pure male innocence under the desiring female gaze sends Schoolie to fantasies of utopian retreats from the feminine—and it is always only a short ride, in these stories, from Ebbets Field to Jones Beach.

Schoolboy Johnson ultimately cannot be as hip, or as camp, as it seems. Nor can other juvenile fictions. If the children's baseball novel provides a space for the desires of men for men, it is no less concerned with providing spaces for the heterosexual couple. In Patricia Reilly Giff's *Left-Handed Shortstop* (1980), the young protagonist, Walter Moles, is brought the full distance toward normative heterosexual orientation, as well as the full distance toward integration with teammates. Walter, a fourth-grader, is a prospective scientist, and his friend Casey Valentine (a girl) is an aspiring writer —as are many female characters in baseball fiction (like Ellie Jay in *Sometimes You See It Coming* or O. A. Drummond in *Brittle Innings*). These characters either type the entire activity of writing about sport as feminine or simply get women close to the masculine world of the game by making them interpreters of it. Casey has fourth-grade come-hither mannerisms ("Casey ran her tongue over her braces and looked back at Walter" [3]), and her protosexuality is accented by Leslie Morrill's drawings for the book, the first of which (11) shows Casey's rear end but not her face.

Walter's favorite activity is to do experiments with Casey. The book opens with them filling a bucket with water to see whether anything will grow in it: "Maybe we should throw in some gunk. Help it along a little" (14), says Casey. While the couple is thus trying to spontaneously generate a nuclear family, Walter is pressured by the other fourth-grade boys to play shortstop on their team so that they can compete in the school league. Now Walter, a right fielder at best, is no ballplayer, and his awkward play as he helps to eke out the lineup aggravates tensions between him and the other boys. In particular Walter's friend J.R. turns into a potential enemy when the two compete in the science fair (for prizes and for access to time with Casey) as well as for positions on the baseball team. The novel's resolution depends on Walter and J.R. reaching an accommodation that will sort their respective skills into an efficient division of labor. As each defers to the other in the other's sphere of expertise, the novel moves toward the closure of the Big Game by shifting Walter's energies toward the science project and J.R.'s toward baseball. Walter and Casey win the science fair prize, Walter hits into a rally-killing double play, and J.R. comes back to win the championship with a home run.

What has really been won and lost in this shifting of roles? It is ultimately Walter's story, not J.R.'s—and certainly not Casey's. By accepting a subaltern role on the ball club, Walter maximizes his potential to enter the technocracy—and mate with a high-IQ female. In this sense *The Left-Handed Shortstop* is a fantasy of meritocracy as much as it is a fantasy of sexuality. Men are stratified into class and occupational groupings, with the meritocracy of sport reinforcing the social boundaries that grade-school activities begin to sketch out.

The female in this tableau, Casey, ultimately carries (for all her brains) nothing but the promise of ever-ready sexual access for the male. It is a tableau more Darwinian than Darwin, who so chivalrously placed female choices at the center of his theories of sexual selection. In the ideologies of *The Left-Handed Shortstop*, the males arrange the assortative mating, working out on the ballfield their own pecking orders, which they will then recognize and impose on a receptive female population. The most vivid visual image of this situation is in one of Leslie Morrill's illustrations (55). Walter faces us, his legs spread and an inflated balloon between them, while Casey, her face not visible, is on all fours facing away from us, her butt in the air with a heart-shaped patch showing on the seat of her pants and her back arched in delight. Walter, to go by the text, is getting water from a hose to mix with flour for papier-mâché: "You're getting paste all over the place," Casey says (54).

The Left-Handed Shortstop shows that the way to the world of the upper middle class is not necessarily through success in sports but through a swearing of allegiance to the values—meritocratic and heterosexual/homosocial—that sports inculcate in young males. Walter Moles is the typical upper-middle-class male who will "grow out of" sports but internalize their lessons. These lessons will reinforce his power as a scientist or engineer. The world beyond this children's game is the "real" world, but the real world is structured like a children's game. It is an irony in the genre of baseball fiction itself that the texts must outgrow their interest in sport and in "making the team" to become literary. At the same time characters must outgrow their childish preoccupations and move beyond the generic roles of athlete or teammate. The overwhelming bitterness of many baseball novels can be read as a kind of compressed melancholy for the loss of an innocent homosexual desire, a desire for one's teammates often presented as a desire for the paraphernalia of the sport.

Mike Kutner in *Man on Spikes*, the cynosure of Durkin Fain's gaze, appears for the first time in that text "working in the pocket of his glove, fondling the leather like it was a dame" (Asinof 2). The whole process of Fain's signing Mike is the courtship of a young man by an older one, of innocence by knowledge. Mike's innocent copulation with his glove is attractive to Fain precisely because Mike would *rather* fondle his glove than a dame, would rather exist in a world of preadolescent sexuality directed toward cowhide and neat's-foot oil. The Kutner family is not sentimental about Mike's first love. As his father Joe relaxes one evening in a scene of domestic intimacy, he asks about his son's whereabouts. "Where was Mike? Even as he asked, the answer was heard pounding through the house, the fist smacking into the still-virgin pocket, heard easily through the thin layers of walls that separated them" (20). Joe and Edna (Mike's mother) take pillows and slippers and begin to mimic Mike's pounding (apparently unconcerned about the cost of the psychotherapy this is bound to lead to over the next few decades). But who is the original pounder here, and who the mocker? Who is overhearing whose primal scene? Mike comes out and confronts his parents: "He saw Mike stare at the position of Joe's fist in the slipper, then back to his own, similarly buried in the pocket of his glove. Their eyes met for a moment, and Joe shrugged his shoulders. Well, that's it, Son. That's what's funny. It's nothing really . . . but somehow, it's funny" (21; ellipsis in the original). This is a joke only in the sense of its relation to the unconscious, of course; for Mike, the scene is nothing less than the Law of the Father asserting itself in the purest form. Mike throws his glove into the furnace and burns it, sacrificing the virgin to the wrath of the father. This is the primal moment of embitterment in *Man on Spikes*; it is also (uncoincidentally) the primal moment of goading Mike Kutner toward the heterosexual. The father is always by definition straight. By begetting the son he has placed himself in the only unblackmailable homosocial relation to that son. The best that the son can hope to accomplish is to emulate the father, to beget on another woman the son that he can humiliate in turn. For the father to empathize with the son would be to invite a transitive relation; it is the transitivity, the potential reversibility, of homosexual roles that makes them so feared by heterosexuals.

Mike learns his lesson well. He marries young, and when he is drafted during World War II, he takes an opportunity doubly to reject the childish: "Mike had wrapped his glove, cradled it in a box, and mailed it home. . . . 'I guess my wife'll get more use out of it than me,' he had said. With the glove gone Mike never mentioned baseball" (127). It is a new glove, of course, but it stands always for Mike's sexuality and for the direction of that sexuality. As Mike enters war, the most unquestionably masculine milieu, he detaches his sexuality and mails it home to his wife—the wife to whom he has first made love in the center field of a minor-league ballpark (214-15).

Mike's failure is that he cannot outgrow his primary homosocial joy in the game. He cannot leave behind the nostalgia for his unselfconscious youthful desirability, the first thing that had attracted Durkin Fain. His wife taunts him: "I want to be a real wife, Mike. I want to have a home of our own, with kids, lots of them. You know what that means to a girl? Just about everything, that's all" (221). Joe Kutner has in effect done his work too well, however. Mike is determined to emulate his father domestically and to repudiate his father professionally. He fails in both milieus—and finally misses his father's funeral because he is trying, and failing, to win a minor-league batting title (249-50).

The fully successful hero, in the terms laid out by the cultural work of baseball novels adult and juvenile, is the man who can beget a child in wedlock, form an unsuspicious yet intimate personal bond with a male teammate, and lead his team to victory in the Big Game. The fully successful hero of baseball fiction is, in short, Henry Wiggen in *Bang the Drum Slowly*. Henry grows up in *The Southpaw*, his break with the clichés of children's literature to create a serious literary voice of his own. He ends *The Southpaw* a man, but as Marianne Moore (quoting Robert of Sorbonne) might say, "no truth can be fully known / until it has been tried / by the tooth of disputation" (66). *Bang the Drum Slowly* tests Henry's masculine identity, pushing the limits of his interest in another man to their extreme. In the process Henry is suspected of loving Bruce Pearson and then exonerated of loving him. This is Henry's triumph, for *Bang the Drum Slowly* is not centrally an elegiac novel. The tragedy of an athlete dying young invokes Housman and (therefore) the suspicion of perverse erotic desire. The comedy within that tragedy is that a man is suspected incorrectly of indulgence in perverse desires and then cleared of that suspicion. It all turns out all right: in the end Henry is less interested in Bruce than in establishing his own heterosexuality. In turn his teammates, having discovered that Henry's desire for Bruce is not sexual, can celebrate this central relationship and justify their own straight identities and the corporate masculine identity of the team.

Bang the Drum Slowly begins with Henry in bed with his pregnant wife, Holly, the living proof of his straightness—and with the collect call from Rochester, Minnesota, that will send him off in pursuit of Bruce Pearson. The opening tableau both validates and excuses Henry's primary interest in his teammate, an interest strongly seconded by Holly herself. Henry leaves Holly, avoids a desirable stewardess, and flies directly to his friend's bed to find that Bruce has been diagnosed with Hodgkin's disease and is dying. Henry's first impulse is to tell manager Dutch Schnell about Bruce's illness, but when he calls Dutch, he loses his nerve and keeps the secret. In fact his call to Dutch becomes a reflection on Dutch's own character and his desiring relation to younger players; Henry remembers Dutch saying "When I die . . . the paper will write in their headline THE SON OF A BITCHES OF THE WORLD HAVE LOST THEIR LEADER, yet many a boy might shed a tear or 2 that I brung to fame and greatness" (20). Dutch's deliberate sentimentalizing of his own death in prospect, set against his self-denigrating assertion of toughness, becomes the context for Henry's elaborate subterfuge in keeping Bruce's secret from Dutch. Dutch's combination of maudlin clichés and tough-guy clichés is the established way for asserting one's own future mortality. Henry's fear, perhaps, is not so much that Dutch will cut Bruce from the team as that he will impose his own constructions of mortality and desire on the special relationship developed by Henry and Bruce as roommates and as partners in the secret of Bruce's disease.

Dutch more than anyone else becomes fascinated by that secret. He is suspicious when Henry's winter phone call turns out to be void of content: "I can not imagine you running up a big phone bill gassing over nothing" (20). (As I will show, the secret itself turns out to be void of content when finally revealed.) When Henry demands that Bruce stay with him, causing the flash of homophobic suspicion that gives this chapter its title, Dutch becomes obsessed with prying into the primal scene of his young batterymates. Henry's insistence on Bruce as his teammate, catcher, and roommate defies baseball's prime directive of meritocracy and seems like special pleading on behalf of a loved one. Dutch is the focal point and magnifier of the suspicions. Naked in bed, he interrogates Henry, probing for a sexual secret (99–103); the secret he gets is a false name for the stewardess with whom Henry has not been involved, a deception within a deception. Henry half-dismantles the scenario, claiming that he and Bruce have been half-telling the truth and half-pulling a gag—in a move that recalls one by Sam Spade in another American genre masterpiece of homophobic paranoia, *The Maltese Falcon* (Hammett 77–81). But the suggestion that he has been taken in by a confidence trick enrages Dutch still further. "He always knew it was a phony story, but he never knew just where" (103). Dutch even tries to change the venue of the story over to that of the detective novel, hiring a sleuth named "Mr. Rogers" to get the goods on Henry and Bruce (144–47), but the secret remains opaque to normal detective techniques, because it is not a secret on the same level as those that detectives usually investigate. The secret Henry and Bruce share is ultimately analogous to that of the open closet; mortality, like morality, is something that often dares not speak its name.

"Author, what is the secret locked in your head?" Dutch asks (83) when Henry goes out of his way to protect Bruce from Dutch's wrath over a missed sign. Missed and mixed signals build an open closet around the friendship of Henry and Bruce. A vital element in the mortar that connects Henry to his teammates, for instance, is Tegwar ("The Exciting Game Without Any Rules"), a poststructuralist's dream of free-floating signifiers that entraps linguistically realistic suckers on Mammoth road trips. That mortar begins to disintegrate when Henry insists that Bruce be let into the secrets of Tegwar. Bruce, unskilled in the linguistic play that the confidence game involves, does not merit inclusion in its rituals. Henry's prime Tegwar partner is the coach, Joe Jaros, a master at the art of signifying in the Henry Louis Gates sense. His Tegwar spiel begins "There ain't been a rule changed since the Black Sox scandal" (116) and proceeds to build into a pastoral rhapsody over the virtues of Tegwar as a bond among ballplayers and a part of American folk culture. Tegwar of course *has* no rules and is only a factitious game; it exists only to transfer money from sucker to grifter—just like the Black Sox series. As Henry and Joe are about to strip a young Washington outfielder of his money, Henry spots Bruce among the onlookers and insists that he play, spoiling the scam. "'No!' said Joe. 'No! No! What are you 2 anyway? Are you Romeo and Juliet?'" (116). Joe's jealousy is erotic, homophobic and homophilic at once; he plays for Henry's attention by casting Henry's attentions to Bruce as suspiciously homosexual.

Henry loves Bruce, but the love is not "fairy love" or some perverse twisting of romance tradition, some masculinized "Romeo and Juliet." If anything it is far more intimate. When the pregnant Holly quips, "I am thinking for 2," Henry answers, "I personally been doing the same for some months now. . . . It is keeping me hopping. It is a strain" (129). Henry fetalizes Bruce, who is now more to him than teammate or roommate; their bodies take on an umbilical connection. The revelation of Bruce's mortality has fused their relationship into this pre-Oedipal state before and beyond all social structures. Their central, privileged moment is when Henry holds the stricken Bruce in his arms: "I took his shoulder and held it, and he reached up and took my hand, and I left him have it, though it felt crazy holding another man's hand. Yet after a while it did not feel too crazy any more" (140).

This intensely private moment, free from even internalized suspicion, is enabled by Henry's having made the open secret truly open. Henry can hold Bruce because he has told their teammate Goose Williams about Bruce's condition just before this scene. Goose has been a leader in taunting the couple, a taunting spread by Joe's jealousy (121). He is a jaded, burned-out old ballplayer about to "die" in the baseball sense of being cut from the team. Catching sight of Holly at a ball game, Goose begins to talk to Henry about his own estranged wife. This gives Henry an opening to ask Goose to stop taunting Pearson—and to legitimize the request, Henry reveals the secret. They shake hands to signal their complicity, "which must of looked peculiar out there, 2 fellows shaking hands" (133). Once exposed, however, even to one person, the open secret becomes the empty secret. Bruce is dying, but so are all the Mammoths. He is only dying more quickly. "Everybody knows everybody is dying. . . . That is why people are nice. You all die soon enough, so why not be nice to each other?" says Henry to Bruce before holding him (140).

Bruce's mortality is the empty secret that Henry could not bring himself to reveal to Dutch Schnell, because of his fear that Dutch would load the secret with maudlin content, the content of an older, gazing, desiring male mourning the death of his beloved. Revealed to peers, the secret becomes totally banal. When first baseman Sid Goldman finally hears the secret, Henry "asked around, but everybody said they already heard it from so many different boys there was really no way of tracking it down even if you wanted to, and anyhow what difference would it make, for it was out and you could not call it back" (231).

The outing of Bruce Pearson as a dying man is what brings the Mammoths together as a team; scorned before as a dumb ballplayer and as Wiggen's too-close companion, Bruce now becomes the center of attention that gives the players a common cause. They win the pennant and the World Series, the latter after Bruce has already broken down and is headed for a quick death. In this respect *Bang the Drum Slowly* resembles dozens of other baseball novels where the solution to an interpersonal problem catalyzes team success. The catalyst here is anything but arbitrary. When Bruce is discovered to be dying, he is cleared of the suspicion of being gay—or more important, when the Mammoths find out that Bruce is dying, they stop insulting Henry Wiggen as gay and celebrate his disinterested love for his teammate. When the secret opens and becomes no secret at all, the novel stops being Bruce's tragedy and becomes Henry's comedy.

Bang the Drum Slowly is not a crudely homophobic text by any means. The openly abusive homophobes in the novel are its least redeemable moral characters: Dutch, Goose, Horse. Its central image is after all Henry holding Bruce and *not* thinking it queer. By clearing a space for that central physical contact, however, the text makes the space of homosocial desire sacred again, reattaining the innocence of *Highpockets*. The logic of *Bang the Drum Slowly* works something like this: while Bruce is suspected of being gay, no one thinks he is dying; when he is revealed to be dying, everyone assumes that he cannot be gay. The inference can be completed by concluding that gay men do not die—or rather, that they are not mortal and thus not fully human. Instead, images of the homosexual here are present only in Dutch Schnell's memory or Joe Jaros's jealous maunderings. To die is to be mortal, is to be a man—is to be, one supposes, like Socrates in the famous example, with the proviso that a distinctly straighter exemplar is required. As so often is the case, the imaginary gay man is the vampire, the ghoul, the Undead.

By becoming fully straight and mortal, Bruce and Henry avoid the fate common to series heroes in genre fiction, that of being reimagined by the reader as a gay couple. There are potentially gay reimaginings of Holmes and Watson (see the film *The Private Life of Sherlock Holmes*), and there is a long tradition of such imaginings about *Star Trek*'s Kirk and Spock.[4] Bruce dies (as Holmes, Kirk, and Spock try to and never seem to manage), however, and he thereby escapes revisionist reading. Hence come both the novel's self-protection against Fiedlerian interpretation and its insight into the need of the series to kill its hero, to assert the hero's mortality in the face of the mutual connotations of homosexuality and the eternally unchangeable.

Bang the Drum Slowly is a literary novel, distinctly and aggressively employing devices such as self-conscious narrative point of view, semiotic play, and intertextuality. The role played by homophobia, the closeting and uncloseting of secrets, marks this novel as participating in a genrewide project of constructing the heterosexual. I have shown some of the themes of homosexual panic and the construction of heterosexuality at work in many other baseball fictions, both adult and juvenile; it remains to show the pure form of paranoid Gothic at work in the children's novel, however, and for this I turn to Julian De Vries's *Strike-Out King*.

It is only serendipity that enables me to turn to this book. I am not quite sure that *The Strike-Out King* exists; the only evidence I have for its existence is a single copy in my possession, "A Falcon Book" from the World Publishing Company dated 1948. I have never seen it listed in a bibliography or in a library catalog. For the purposes of scholarship, it might as well be the Exeter Book or the Gawain manuscript. The cover shows a generic illustration of a pitcher in what is clearly a major-league ballpark (although there is no such scene in the book, which is solely about college baseball). The front matter vouches for the novel as "an action-packed story of the diamond that will appeal to the sports-loving instinct of every American boy" and suggests other Falcon titles such as *On the Forty-Yard Line*, *The Winning Basket*, and *Over the Hurdles*.

Every American boy may have a sports-loving instinct, but it is to be hoped that most American boys know baseball better than *The Strike-Out King* does. The text presents strategies of positively infernal subtlety, as when a coach calls for his pitcher to bunt when the team is two runs down in the bottom of the ninth (196). *The Strike-Out King* believes that grounding into a force-out constitutes a hit (79, 84) and describes a double play turned 1-3-2 on a squeeze bunt (85)—think carefully about that: with the runner breaking from third on the pitch, the batter bunts to the pitcher, who throws to the first baseman, who has enough time to throw home so that the catcher can tag out the runner coming from third. The text presents these weird simulacra of baseball in a prose style that should simply be presented without comment:

> Val Richardson, the Pennfield pitcher, seemed to consider the situation for a moment and then, suddenly, without a windup, cut loose with a low, fast ball that seemed to be aimed at Paul Winters' knees. Guardian of the keystone sack for Carson, Winters was speedy on the bases and a fast fielder, but his batting was something that Doc Meade, in his calmer moments, spoke of as erratic. No sane ball player would have made a try at Richardson's offering, but Winters had the reputation of passing up the good ones to swing at the poor ones and Richardson's present pitch was no exception. With a wide, roundhouse swing, the second baseman took a terrific cut at the ball and a moment later it was sailing through the warm, spring air toward the bleachers. A lusty roar from the Carson side of the field greeted the first home run of the season. (80)

Yet the subliterary quality of *The Strike-Out King* is what most makes this text available for the study of the cultural work of its genre. Without any other purpose than the express one of being "an action-packed story of the diamond," the text is free of constraints that force more self-consciously literary novels to manage their ideologies for the reader. *The Strike-Out King* is an uninhibited reflection on the nature of intrasquad competition and on the erotic obsessions that spring from such competition and drive it in turn.

Larry Murdock, the protagonist, is bound to win a place as a starting pitcher on the Carson College nine. Coach "Doc" Meade is sure that Larry is his best pitcher, and Dick Fletcher, big-league ace (who somehow has lots of free time during the baseball season to hang around Carson College cheering on its team) and cousin of Larry's sweetheart, Mildred Warren, raves about Larry's work. There is a complication, however. George Brayton has lost out in the battle for the pitching job, so Doc has moved him to third base. George begins to stalk Larry, making numerous but ineffectual attempts to deprive Larry either of his life or of the use of his pitching arm. Finally George puts out a contract on Mildred and some gangsters kidnap her. He breaks down, Mildred is recovered, and after a bit of decompression, George takes his place as a constructive member of the Carson College team and as Larry's sworn friend.

The event that incites the plot is George's move to third base instead of the pitcher's mound. "What if he is playing third base instead of pitching?" wonders Larry. "He's still on the team. The guy must be nuts. I don't get it" (29). Now that is the point of the thing, not to get it; George Brayton's jealousy lacks what critics might call an objective correlative. George himself masks the origins of his feelings as indignation at a corruption of the merit system: "Trust Murdock to put in a good word for himself, especially when Murdock, senior was in a position to make a handsome gift to the Carson athletic fund. Sure! That was it! Let little Larry pitch and Papa'll come across with a nice, fat check! The more he thought of it, the angrier he got and the angrier he became" (14). This interior monologue ends chapter 1. The central event of chapter 2, titled "Mixed Signals," is Larry's fall down a flight of stairs, caused by a "charging figure bearing down directly upon him" (20). When he stops seeing stars, Larry is helped to his feet by an obliging George Brayton. The mixed signals are apparently those that Larry's own common sense should be interpreting correctly, as time and again he is hurt, surprised, tricked, or endangered while Brayton is either suspiciously present or suspiciously absent. George decoys Larry so that he can take Mildred to the depot to collect Dick Fletcher (40); George crashes into Larry in the on-deck circle after overrunning home plate (49).

Larry puts team cohesion ahead of trying to figure out what is wrong with George Brayton. "If I were to try to settle things now," he tells his roommate, catcher Bill Taylor, "the team would take sides, you know that. And I'm not going to be responsible for disrupting the harmony and playing effectiveness of the team just for that" (56). Larry believes that Brayton is merely "the victim of his own imagination" (56). Meanwhile Brayton's attempts on Larry's well-being become ever more fiendish, not to say moronic. He throws a baseball right at Larry's nose on the practice field (61). Then he steals a copy of trainer Duke Williams's secret liniment formula from Doc Meade's desk and replaces it with one calling for "pentachromic ordanol," which, as we all know, "when absorbed in small amounts through the skin, would, in time, cause a form of paralysis" (104).

Larry starts to think about George Brayton all the time. George is stalking him, has some unknown and inexplicable interest in him. Mildred's honor is vaguely threatened by Brayton's presence. Larry is actually driven to hit George only when George confronts Dick Fletcher and says: "Naturally you'd stick up for him! You're his sweetie's cousin and everyone knows that Mildred War—" (70). George gets hit at this point and never finishes his somewhat incoherent insinuation. Whether he is about to say that Mildred is fucking Larry, and Larry hits him because it is true (or a lie), or that Mildred is fucking Dick, and ditto, or perhaps that Dick is fucking Larry and Mildred is their screen, his train of thought is permanently interrupted. But not before he lays out an important axis of the novel. "The Strike-Out King" could be Dick actually or Larry potentially; George is the outsider who cannot find a place for himself in this increasingly cozy male bond. Moreover, although Larry's ostensible interest in Mildred is as a heterosexual companion, it is clear that she functions mainly as a conduit for Larry's attentions to Dick, his mentor and publicist. Larry's homosocial bonds, either disastrous (in the case of Brayton) or invaluable (as with Fletcher) are the novel's foremost concern.

The Strike-Out King is a novel of the fraternity world at a purely fantastic all-American college, where "boys" spout a pseudo-educated argot that verges on bitchiness. When Larry flames a particularly prissy fraternity house steward over his finicky money management, another housemate and teammate calls out, "If you girls are finished swapping recipes out there in the kitchen . . ." (143). It is a world where the real mystery is not what drives George Brayton to his stalking doppelgänger behavior but why there is not a lot more of that kind of behavior going around. At Carson College a young man even of Larry's unquestioned athletic credentials must prepare an elaborate brief in defense of his own masculinity.

Many of the potential plot directions out of the first half of *The Strike-Out King* could lead to slapstick, to festive comedy, or to a general détente in the Larry-George relationship that would produce the usual team bonding for championship play. That none of these potential paths is followed marks the text even more strongly as a paranoid Gothic, deeply anxious about the direction of its young male characters' sexualities. In the second half of the novel George Brayton disappears. There is no plot necessity for his disappearance, for he has been able to move at will between the roles of ruthless stalker and disingenuously helpful teammate. By consigning him to invisibility the text makes vivid his function as Larry's own homophobic, hyperaware self-consciousness.

Invisible, Brayton becomes ubiquitous. Larry becomes paranoid. He is convinced that someone is hiding in the cellar of the fraternity house. (Someone *is* hiding in the cellar of the fraternity house; just because Larry thinks that there is someone out to get him doesn't mean there isn't.) Larry takes to prowling around the cellar himself, looking for the other prowler (174–76), but the intruder has always just disappeared around the next corner, just left his last footprint in the dust that was intact when Larry passed it a moment ago. Larry spends a whole chapter (chapter 16, "The Enemy Strikes") thinking feverishly about George, and in the middle "Larry sighed as he gave up trying to understand Brayton. He tried instead to figure out who was making his home in the fraternity house basement and raiding the icebox for his meals" (179). Well, who could *that* be? Larry's terminal slowness on the uptake, his inability to make his only possible persecutor cohere into a stable image, shows how deeply, at the key plot juncture where he is about to prove his manhood by pitching the Big Game, his entire identity is assaulted by homophobic self-suspicion. He is the object of George Brayton's desire, yet to let this desire show itself is to accede to the worst suspicions he could have of his own masculinity.

While Larry is working on the problem of the identities (the identity) of Brayton and the icebox thief, he crosses a desolate part of the Carson campus.

> The campus was utterly deserted, and Larry felt as though he were all alone in the world. Suddenly he looked up as the crunching sound of wheels on gravel reached his ears. The first of the busses bearing the two teams and their rooters was arriving. And the next instant Larry gasped in sudden pain as something struck him between the shoulders.
>
> Whirling around, he saw no one, but he dashed toward the grandstand which was immediately in back of him. A quick but careful search through the supporting posts under the tiers of seats revealed nothing. (180–81)

The invisible enemy has indeed struck, clamoring for recognition as himself, as the lover and the beloved, as (perhaps) the Enemy Within.

Ultimately the plot course of *The Strike-Out King* lies in a therapeutic direction. To set his life straight (in all senses) Larry must acknowledge who has a secret crush on him. After the game the brain trust of the Carson club assembles and tries to solve the invisible rock-thrower mystery. With Doc Meade as his confessor/analyst, Larry works through the event:

> "The only person who could possibly make a throw like that is a trained baseball player; an outfielder, perhaps, or a catcher or third baseman."
>
> No sooner had Larry mentioned the possibility of a ball player being able to make such a throw then [*sic*] both coach and player looked at each other with the same thought in mind, a thought that neither liked to put into words. Doc Meade finally broke the silence.
>
> "George Brayton?" he asked.
>
> "I've been thinking so all along," Larry confessed. (201)

This confession, more than any of the baseball action in the novel, is its climax. The real drama is not whether Larry will win the Big Game by striking out a record number of batters (we know he will, and he does) but whether he will acknowledge that George Brayton's persecution is serious, methodical, and of a piece—whether, by extension, he will choose to come out as a heterosexual rather than to keep the secret of Brayton in the open closet by refusing to admit the erotic sources of that obsession.

As if responding by a sort of telepathic connection to the progress of Larry's therapy, George goes completely over the top, instigating the kidnapping of Mildred and fleeing across country. As the final championship series is playing out, Larry turns detective, descending into the underworld (which is any world off campus) and trying to track down George, who, as he now knows for sure, will lead him to Mildred. The novel plummets to Dostoyevskyan depths:

> That night, he took a room in a cheap hotel in Webster City. The walls were thin and loud voices were issuing from the next room. Larry put his ear to a place in the wall where the plaster was cracked.
>
> He listened intently, but the conversation was about something that held no interest for him and he turned away in disappointment. He tried the opposite wall but with the same lack of success and, with a heavy heart, he went to bed. The next morning he began his search all over again, visiting all the cheap disreputable places the city afforded, in the single hope of finding the one person he would have given anything to find—George Brayton. (210)

The stalked has become the stalker; it is emphatically *George* whom Larry is out to find, not Mildred. The psychosexual content and even the outward form of a straight man's policing of a gay stalker are identical to those of the gay man's stalking of a straight crush, but the method is purified by the motive.

"Brayton's trail was soon picked up, and while Larry was searching the pool halls and other low resorts of Webster City," presumably having a fabulous time, "the local police there, at the request of the Federal men who located him, arrested him at one of the city's best hotels where he had been living on his guardian's credit" (211). His guardian's credit? Just who is this guardian? We have never known that Brayton is an orphan of sorts, if he is; the mystery of his parentage is unexplained. Is he a bastard, the natural son of somebody? Is he maybe Larry's evil twin? Is he Frankenstein's monster? Whatever he is, he is illegitimate, possibly immortal, and certainly queer.

Mildred is recovered, and she reinvigorates Larry. When he sees her in the stands at the final game, he strikes out twenty-one consecutive batters (214) (oh, the realism). The novel's resolution does not concern her, however, and never has. The denouement occurs at the opening of the next school year. Larry spots George, at first does not recognize him, and then turns to confront him. He shakes George's hand, "tears welled in the other's eyes," and "as Larry threw his arm around his shoulders, he was afraid to say more for fear the lump in his throat would choke him" (216). These are the final words of the novel. George is reintegrated into the Carson campus and ceases forever to be a threat to its heterosexual community. Alternatively, George is free to live with Larry again in his all-male milieu, even (who knows?) to become Larry's life-long inseparable friend, in later years playing pinochle with Larry and Mildred Murdock and laughing over that hilarious little contretemps when he fell off the sanity wagon and had Mildred kidnapped. The world is all before them, where to choose.

The baseball novel, even at its most obsessive, has rarely cast its homophobia in terms of negative images of gay people. Even George Brayton, its most rapacious of desiring men, is heterosexual and strives to prove his overt straightness through his crush on Mildred. In many dozens of baseball stories there are no homosexual characters with which to contend. Gay sex itself has entered the genre only lately and in exceptional texts. In Michael Bishop's *Brittle Innings* (1994) narrator Danny Boles loses his voice after being raped by a GI who claims to have known his serviceman father. Boles regains it only after Franklin D. Roosevelt shows up to tell him personally that his father is dead, and he is kissed by a boyish girl named Phoebe Pharram, who farts during the kiss, driving her tongue into his mouth. (Between these two incidents Danny establishes a crucial homosocial bond with his roommate, Henry Clerval, who turns out in literal fact to be Frankenstein's monster, but that is another story.) The sexual reasons for the loss and redemption of the narrating voice itself in *Brittle Innings* establish the homophobic bound of the continuum of sexuality in recent baseball fiction; the homophilic bound is marked by Peter Lefcourt's *Dreyfus Affair* (1993), where a shortstop and second baseman on a pennant contender fall in blissful and innocently romanticized love (and are caught necking in a Neiman-Marcus fitting room).[5]

But these are late entries in a genre that has till the 1990s been concerned, when it thinks of sex, with the establishment of mandatory heterosexual identities and the policing of those identities through self-surveillance, panic, and blackmailability. There are no really gay men in the baseball novel; there are only distant, monitory presentiments of the gay man, a category beyond life and reality, an Other against whom the straightness, and the realness, of the heterosexual male is defined. For the sports-loving American boy, such fictions have provided a model for the construction of adult sexuality.

Notes

1. I must stress that there is *absolutely no evidence* that the historical John McGraw was homosexual. Nothing in the definitive biography by Charles C. Alexander suggests that McGraw was gay, and I know of no anecdotal tradition that suggests so. Nor does *The Celebrant* specifically portray McGraw as engaging in genital homosexual acts.

2. As if to invoke this particular primal fear, the naughty little monkey Curious George becomes the hero of his own foray into the genre by *saving* fans from murderous foul drives. See Rey and Shalleck, *Curious George Plays Baseball.*

3. Where exactly Roy Tucker *gets* a grown daughter is another matter. He appears to stay unmarried through the entire series of novels, and the only woman in his life is his grandmother.

4. See "A New Enterprise" by Donna Minkowitz.

5. Lesbian baseball stories are literally a footnote to this chapter, but two recent titles of note are Celia Cohen's novel *Smokey O* and Lucy Jane Bledsoe's story "State of Grace." Both texts enthusiastically use erotic attraction between same-sex teammates as a theme, although Bledsoe's story, more realistic, represents and critiques homophobia as well.

3

"I Was in America and My Job Was to Speak English"

In baseball fiction the problems of becoming an American and becoming a man are worked out across the rules and strategies of the game. They are worked out also across the rules and strategies of language. The game itself is stable in fiction because its rules are immutable. It is therefore also transparent, in the sense that characters just play the game and do not take ideological sides over how it *should* be played. Natural language, by contrast, has shifting sets of rules. Fictional characters and entire novels argue over the proper rules for language. Language becomes a matter of contention. Finding a common language to speak is as much a problem as finding a level field on which to play.

When Al Lopez became manager of the Cleveland Indians in 1951, the Cuban star Minnie Minoso recalls, "Lopez spoke some Spanish, which made things a little easier and a bit more comfortable for me. Yet I did not speak to Lopez in Spanish. I was in America and my job was to speak English. I never wanted any special favors, no matter what the problem might be" (47). Minoso presents his negative attitude toward his native language as entirely admirable, and in many arguments about the proper role of immigrants in American society, it is admirable; learning English is the cornerstone of the archetypal immigrant achievement. Minoso's theorizing deserves a closer look, however. Why does learning English, for one thing, mean that Spanish has to be a "problem"? What does either language have to do with baseball? "My job was to speak English," Minoso insists, not to hit home runs or steal bases or catch fly balls. If he does not join the English-speaking community, his athletic accomplishments will somehow remain forever suspect.

The construction of a language community can even in real life seem more important as a goal in baseball than does the construction of a winning ball club. The linguistic imperative becomes all the stronger in fictional texts, which are constructed entirely of language. The sociolinguistic cultural work of baseball fiction falls broadly into two categories. First, English is constructed as the only natural language; next, the English language is purified so that it can convey masculine and meritocratic imperatives. The first dynamic involves race, and the second involves class. The educational, transformative power of language, however—the potential of language learning to effect cultural transformations impossible in the seemingly inelastic categories of race or class—tends to obscure the issues of race and class. Above all, language in baseball fiction is an instrument that works changes in human material. Its users can, should, and must learn the appropriate linguistic skills to make the team.

Shirley Temple Wong, the protagonist of Bette Bao Lord's *In the Year of the Boar and Jackie Robinson* (1986), faces the same problem in her fictional 1947 as Minnie Minoso did in his real 1951. She has come to the United States, an immigrant from China, and her job is to learn English. In the novel's symbolic space—an immigrant's first year in Brooklyn, corresponding with Jackie Robinson's first season in Brooklyn—Shirley becomes a model American. In a pattern that we have already seen, Shirley's transformation is not from an inchoate identity to a fixed identity but rather the other way around. Her "rawness" is a matter not of lack of form but of too much form; her allegiance to America becomes one of always renewing her unformed potential.

Shirley is not Shirley when the novel begins. She is Bandit, an inhabitant of the elaborate family structures of her Chinese home. The novel opens in China. Its Chinese dialogue is represented by standard literary English, offering American readers a strange description of Chinese customs and relationships that foreshadows the bewildering social landscape Bandit will enter when she comes, as Shirley, to America. Nevertheless this alien culture displays pleasing analogies to American culture, analogies that reach out of the text to assure the reader of the existence of universal human nature (a universalism that peculiarly tends to imply that the universal human condition is American). In the opening scene Bandit and Fourth Cousin, her relative, play a game of "pick-up beans" (3). Its rules are only dimly outlined, but it is enough like jacks to provide a bridge for the American reader to Chinese girlhood.

Bandit is renamed Shirley Temple Wong before she ever reaches America (18-19). She is preassimilated through the power of an American cultural institution (the movies) to make converts abroad. An American name is only the start of an American identity, however. Shirley's initial feelings when she arrives in Brooklyn resemble the feelings of Roy Tucker or the Russell brothers when they arrive in that city. This similarity points perhaps more to what the Tunis novels draw from American bildungsroman tradition generally than to what *In the Year of the Boar* draws from juvenile baseball novels. In any event, we see a commonplace construct of America as a place that is centrally metropolitan, leveling, and disorienting.

Shirley lacks everyday knowledge when she lands—or rather, she lacks Sunday knowledge. She "could not know that it was Sunday, a day when everyone stayed put, except to go to Church" (28). (One might note that this is an oddly Gentile default value for an American "everyone.") Shirley arrives with her mother to meet her father, who has preceded them to Brooklyn. The first accommodation the women must make is to the terms of the American nuclear family. In Shirley's extended Chinese family (presented virtually without consciousness that it is an upper-class family) there were servants to manage a large and intricate household; in Shirley's Brooklyn there are only three immediate family members and a few inscrutable machines: a stove, an icebox, and a washing machine (which Shirley assumes is for bathing [32]). "In America . . . the wife cooks" (30), and she washes and shops as well. There are no rivals with whom to contend, however; "with no servants there would be no Awaiting Marriage to spoil Shirley's fun either" (33), thinks Shirley as she recalls the dour virginal servant who has been her bête noire back home.

The emotional appeal of assimilation here is complex. Shirley's family has come down in the world. They are retreating to comparative poverty in Brooklyn so that they can advance in the future. Nonetheless there is an overriding implicit faith that earned success in democratic America is preferable to unearned privilege in China. In realistic terms there is no possible life of privilege ahead in China; as emigrants in 1947 Shirley's family are obviously escaping civil war and the breakdown of a bourgeois system. But political and socioeconomic contexts are elided. There are vague references to a war and to dangers in China, but the overall ideological map of the novel is drawn from stock images: abroad is a worse place materially, spiritually, and socially.

In America the wife cooks, and Shirley quickly adapts to this convenient system, as does her father. The novel is curiously unsympathetic to this privileged mother turned domestic worker, whether because Shirley foresees 1960s feminism and suspects that her mother's will be the only generation so domestically subject or because the novel simply underscores the "natural" gender roles of the American nuclear family, leaving Shirley's own gender unmarked for the time being. Whatever its take on maternal work, *In the Year of the Boar* presents Shirley as grateful for the absence of servants. America clears away the intrusion of class into domestic space. The private nuclear family can imagine a classless commonwealth of identical nuclear families outside; with its domestic work made either purely private or purely external and commercial, it no longer presents the contradictions of class in tandem with everyday work such as cooking food or washing clothes.

Shirley's assimilation is a process of riddles, beginning with the domestic machines that underpin the gender and class transformations of her passage to America. "Father struck a match and put it to the top of the second white box. *Poof!* Out came blue fire. Off went mother to hug the wall" (31). Answer: a gas range. "Pictures of men swinging a stick or wearing one huge glove" (46). Answer: baseball cards. Shirley at first fears her teacher, Mrs. Rappaport, because she sports a huge stick that Shirley supposes is used to beat children (45); when the stick is revealed as a window pole (47), Shirley is relieved and learns that in America teachers do not rely on the threat of corporal punishment. (The implication is that in China they did; abroad is a worse place.) Cultural power is transacted across these riddles, because they function as riddles only for an audience of American readers. An American reader—and only an American reader—knows what is being described in each case long before Shirley does. The genre "riddle" works only at a specific boundary between the foreigner's bewilderment and the native's blasé familiarity, and each instance is guessable only from the perspective of the native. To put the matter in literary terms, the object is defamiliarized, yielding delight (and difficulty). To put it in cultural terms, the experiences of immigration and assimilation are presented to American readers as no harder than a set of easy riddles. Once one knows the answers, one has arrived.

Shirley, as a brand-new American, lacks a vocabulary and must present her initial perceptions as visual riddles. She enters school innocent of English. As it poses its assimilative riddles, *In the Year of the Boar* represents English, *in* English, back to English readers from a Chinese perspective. The English language is characterized as "a string of nonsensical sounds" (36), "like gurgling water" (45). The effects achieved are so good that the reader tends to forget, in fact, that *there is nothing but English in the novel*; it has only the barest minimum of transliterated Chinese phrases. As Shirley thinks about the strangeness of the English language, her thoughts are couched completely in English. One perceives her hard-won journey toward English fluency less as the acquisition of a second language than as the dreamlike recovery of a native language she has known all along.

The immigrant novel in English, of course, has to be written this way, but "the immigrant novel in English" is itself a tendentious thing, not a natural one. A polyglot immigrant novel is an entirely possible genre—even (perhaps especially) a polyglot juvenile immigrant novel. *In the Year of the Boar and Jackie Robinson* is written in English, a fact that may be determined more by market forces and the conditions of print technology than by the ideologies of assimilation. The book's language is not factored out of its cultural work, however; rather, it is central to it. In common with other texts of its genre both juvenile and adult, *In the Year of the Boar* presents a world where the reader imagines what it would be like to learn English from the comfortable position of already knowing English— of existing, blissfully, in the target language.

In the course of this pedagogical drama, we forget there was ever a language other than English. As in *The Celebrant* and many other novels, foreign languages appear only in English translation. At first Shirley "could only speak a few words at a time" (51), as if she were a true Caliban. The text focuses to such an extent on her linguistic incapacity that it is almost a shock when she shifts to (Englished) Chinese and we find her there very fluent indeed. Shirley's incapacity is seen not only as linguistic but also as lingual, of the tongue; her physically realized mouth has trouble getting around the material of America, as when "tiptoe on the toilet seat, she peered into the mirror, trying to blow bubbles with her Juicy Fruit gum. Even the first graders blew bubbles as big as a full moon. Hers were no bigger than a button. Jaws aching, she tried again and again. She had to do something right. Had to" (56). It is the most poignant moment in the novel, because the fault is not in Shirley but in the stuff with which she has to work. It is impossible to blow bubbles with Juicy Fruit, but instead of mistrusting the chicle, she mistrusts herself.

Moving upward from this nadir of Shirley's lingual achievement, *In the Year of the Boar* offers a lovingly detailed analysis of an immigrant's progress toward linguistic competence and full assimilation. Shirley memorizes a Disney song and is derided by her classmates for her mimicry and by her mother for her lack of dignity (56-58). Shirley mistakes an assimilated Chinese girl for a Chinese speaker and is embarrassed when the other girl responds, "I come from Chattanooga" (65). Significantly Shirley's efforts to become fully American never stop at the purely linguistic; increasingly her entire body must become American. Roller skating (66-67) is her first physical success, but it is an individually won success, a mastery of a skill that, however inherently American, lacks a full social context.

The full exercise of physical Americanism is possible only in a team sport such as baseball. The cultural barrier to Shirley's participation in baseball is formidable, however. The game does not make sense to her: "All that effort just to hit and catch a silly little ball. All that hurrying just to step on a bookbag" (70). The description of the game, filtered through the text's defamiliarizing riddles, shows how unself-evident its conventions are to the immigrant and consequently how violent is the act of will needed to transform the immigrant into a baseball player or fan. Shirley's initiation into the sport is literally violent; heedlessly crossing the field of play, she walks into a big fifth-grader named Mabel, who punches her in the eye (72).

Up till this point in the story, Shirley has been on a streak of social failure: misinterpreting compliments, accepting them inappropriately, failing to understand the rules of games, unable to return insults correctly. In every case the text has made it clear that the social conventions involved in these cultural misunderstandings are arbitrary and relative. Her crucial response to Mabel's violence, however, is presented as a universal moral imperative: do not squeal. Shirley's response comes neither from a Chinese code of ethics nor from a learning of an American code but from what the novel presents as an instinctive sense of honor. Fortunately for Shirley, her instinctive sense of honor corresponds with the one that is valued in all American children's sports fiction. When Mabel realizes that Shirley has not told on her, the two girls become fast friends.

Mabel is African American, although this fact is not clear in the text until thirteen pages after her friendship with Shirley begins (76–89). (Marc Simont's illustration of a black girl pitching [69] is not initially connected to Mabel, and his picture of her sharing an umbrella with Shirley [77] shows the girls only in silhouette from behind.) In the novel's rhetoric Shirley is unconscious of race in the American sense, for her distinctions of racial identity extend no further than Chinese and not-Chinese. Crucially, she is not prejudiced against Mabel. It does not even occur to her to include Mabel's color in her first description of her (71). Mabel returns Shirley's lack of prejudice by insisting on Shirley's inclusion in the playground stickball club.

Only Mabel possesses the moral, physical, and rhetorical authority to guarantee Shirley's inclusion. When the team members sling anti-Chinese invective at Shirley ("Send her back to the laundry" [78]), Mabel proceeds to dissolve the apparent homogeneity of the team. She ticks off the insulters by ethnic origin, calling them "Spaghetti Snot," "Kosher Creep," "Brown Blubber," and "Puerto Rican Coconut" (79)—also "Damp Drawers" and "Dog Breath," obscurely running shortcomings in personal hygiene together with ethnic origins. Remarginalized by Mabel's interpellations (and the threat of Mabel's fists behind them), the team members acquiesce in Shirley's presence. Implicitly Mabel's own African-American identity lets her see the identities behind the American surfaces of her teammates— the kind of vision expressly denied to Spike Russell when he tries to include Jocko Klein in the Dodgers in *Keystone Kids.*

The team wins the first game Shirley plays. Shirley scores the winning run by overcoming a moment of linguistic uncertainty— specifically, a moment of idiomatic uncertainty, when she mistakes her teammates' cry "go home!" for a literal command to go back to her house (81). By realizing that "home" is a base in the game's dialect, Shirley finds herself for the first time "at home" in the American language and social order. Sport teaches Shirley her first English idiom. It is at this moment that Jackie Robinson is first invoked, as Shirley's pigeon-toed baserunning wins her team the game and they serenade her, chanting *"Jackie Robinson's on our team"* (82).

Shirley Temple Wong's connection to Jackie Robinson resembles Jack Kapp's connection to Christy Mathewson in *The Celebrant*; in each case an assimilant learns a culture by imitating a baseball hero. Whereas Kapp learns his otherness by contrast to Mathewson's centrality, however, Shirley meets Robinson on the grounds of their mutual otherness, an otherness that becomes interchangeable between the black man and the Chinese girl in the face of the American core to which both are to be assimilated. In this way stories of assimilation become universalized. The text combines a sanguine attitude toward otherness—nearly all the characters who are somehow Other are good—while insisting on the benignity of the America that they enter. Strikingly in *In the Year of the Boar* America has no ethnic center; it is comprised entirely of Others. It is the emergent national identity in its purest form, an identity from which the Anglo-American component has been completely (and ahistorically) extracted.

Even after she wins her first game of stickball, though, Shirley has taken only the first steps toward an American identity. Her neophyte status is brought home when her class recites the Pledge of Allegiance. The polyglot already-Americans approach this ritual with a brisk mastery: "Popping a last bubble, Maria Gonzales tucked her gum safely behind an ear" (86), as if to show that even a Hispanic girl can chew gum and speak English too.

> Shirley's voice was lost in the chorus.
> "I pledge a lesson to the frog of the United States of America, and to the wee puppet for witches' hands, One Asian, in the vestibule, with little tea and just rice for all." (86)

Losing one's voice in the chorus can stand for the blending of the individual into the American community, but here the blending does not result in a full participation in the unison of the pledge. Shirley constructs her own unconsciously macaronic parody of the pledge under cover of the general noise. She is not yet fully American; in the dreamwork of her mimicry, she is distinctly still "One Asian, in the vestibule." Yet America was first constructed when one of its culture heroes stuck a feather in his cap and called it macaroni; Shirley's appropriation at a distance of the Yankee Doodle gesture, with its fairy tale elements of frogs and witches, surrounds the distinct and unalterable "United States of America" with a series of provisional verbal gestures that ends on the egalitarian note of "just rice for all."

Shirley's macaronic pledge to an America conceived of more as mantra than as a historical nation, however it is presented here as a comic linguistic failure, may turn out to be the keynote of the text, particularly as the text uses baseball to center its conception of America. When Shirley, still at a loss, asks Mrs. Rappaport who Jackie Robinson is, the teacher launches into a civics lesson on the theme "what is it about baseball that is ideally suited to Americans?" (91). Mabel's initial commonsense answer—"it's a great game" (90)—does not satisfy the teacher, who demands a location for the answer not in what is intrinsic to the game but in what is intrinsic to the nation.

No one in the class can answer Mrs. Rappaport's question; the silence is so deafening that the official portraits of "President Washington and President Lincoln . . . exchanged a look of shared displeasure" (91). Finally she has to answer it herself. In a speech that Shirley finds unforgettable, Mrs. Rappaport constructs baseball as the ideal American sport. She moves from exceptionalism ("Baseball is not just another sport. America is not just another country" [92]) through individualism and meritocracy, ending with what Shirley hears as an argument for the human rights of emigrants. "In our national pastime, each player is a member of a team, but when he comes to bat, he stands alone. One man. Many opportunities. For no matter how far behind, how late in the game, he, by himself, can make a difference. He can change what has been. He can make it a new ball game" (92). The fusion of a team out of individuals, the *e pluribus unum* theme, is familiar. Mrs. Rappaport adds an illogical insistence that in both baseball and in America *history can be erased.* Her insistence applies to the game only in the narrow sense in which a tie score means a "whole new ball game"; if a player contributes to tying a game his team has been losing, he changes an imbalance back to an original balance, although he hardly rewrites the box score. To make the allegorical leap to American history, as Mrs. Rappaport does, means believing that history can always begin afresh.

This is in effect what Jackie Robinson has done (in her analysis).

"Despite hostility and injustice, Jackie Robinson went to college, excelled in all sports, served his country in war. And now, Jackie Robinson is at bat in the big leagues. Jackie Robinson is making a difference. Jackie Robinson has changed what has been. And Jackie Robinson is making a better America.

"And so can you! And so must you!" (93)

The spin that Mrs. Rappaport puts on Robinson's achievement is startling—or perhaps more startling is the way its illogic can pass as commonplace. Robinson changed not a jot or a tittle of the past, yet it has been a commonplace of much American thought that the facts of de jure desegregation, civil rights law, and antidiscrimination policies *have* erased the past. Equally odd is Mrs. Rappaport's insistence that Robinson made a difference *by himself.* It is perhaps preferable to the idolatry of Branch Rickey that one finds in, for example, Ken Burns's film *Baseball,* but it curiously blames, by implication, all Robinson's black predecessors who somehow, through some fault of their own, failed to make the difference that Robinson made.

Most important for Shirley Temple Wong, Mrs. Rappaport's rhetoric blames *her* for any future failure to make a difference. Mrs. Rappaport blames Shirley prospectively for future inabilities to change what has been, to erase the past and as a consequence to erase her particular original identity. "Suddenly Shirley understood why her father had brought her ten thousand miles to live among strangers. Here, she did not have to wait for gray hairs to be considered wise" (93). The accumulated weight of historical tradition, and the concomitant need for an individual to grow old within that tradition to speak with its full weight behind her, is suddenly lifted from Shirley. She is granted freedom from her traditions at the cost of vigilance against falling back into those traditions. This is the fulcrum of the novel's plot. The weight of Shirley's identity shifts from the Chinese half of her hyphenated identity to the American half, the half she shares with all her equally hyphenated classmates and teammates.

"She must never forget China or lose her Chinese. But then . . . there would be baseball games on the radio, games to listen to all summer long" (97). Baseball Americanizes Shirley not just physically but aurally, as it enters her consciousness through pure language in the person of Red Barber. The insidious presence of the radio and the instant access it gives to the American culture of baseball transform Shirley's interior speech.

> She still spoke Chinese with her parents, but even then foreign words were substituted for those that did not come easily. Mother corrected her. "Make an effort, Shirley. You must not forget you are still Chinese."

"Yes, Mother." But then out would pop another English expression, one for which there was no Chinese equivalent—Gee whiz! Baloney! Just for kicks! Party pooper! Fat chance! What's up? (119)

Everything but "the catbird seat." Shirley worries that if she begins to think in English, her hair will turn blonde (119); language may have direct physical consequences. Shirley has a literal nightmare of becoming an alien to Chinese culture (120-22). The erasure of identity and history in assimilation can inflict disastrous psychic pressures on the assimilant.

These pressures are eased finally by a meeting of identities across the game of baseball, as Shirley, her new friend Emily Levy, and Jackie Robinson are brought together to form an American polity across the centerless functionalism of sport. As African Americans, Robinson and his avatar Mabel are both native and minority. They validate Shirley's progress from exclusion to full participation but fail to provide adequate models for a specifically immigrant experience. Emily Levy is important as a test case for Shirley's mastery of the American identity, because Shirley meets her in September 1947, as she begins the sixth grade. Emily is the new girl, Shirley now the old hand fully accepted by her fellow Dodgers-fan classmates ("Maria offered them a fistful of Double Bubble" [123]). If Shirley can mentor Emily through her assimilation, she can validate both her own new identity and the American condition at the same time.

Emily reminds Shirley vaguely of Fourth Cousin, the best friend she has left behind in China, which provides a universalizing reassurance. Shirley offers Emily basic school-survival skills. Emily offers Shirley class—the literal and literary promise of a route to class improvement through education. The Levys are indiscriminate readers—except on the basis of gender, for Emily reads Nancy Drew, whereas her brothers read Zane Grey—and for once Shirley's mother heartily approves of Shirley's use of English, since she uses it to read the texts that Emily lends her. Emily and Shirley reach their strongest bond over a text, Emily's psychiatrist father's copy of *Gray's Anatomy*, over which the girls huddle in secret silence: "Even an unborn baby. Yuck!" (129).

Gender in *In the Year of the Boar* fuses with national identity and the theme of secrecy when Emily and Shirley stare at the female reproductive system together. The shared text is graphic, fusing the body with its visual and textual representations. The girls reject their own gendered bodies ("Yuck!") at the moment they master the English language through texts. They do so without ever acknowledging that Emily Levy has (or has shed) an ethnic identity; Emily's Jewishness (like that of the Krasners in *And Don't Bring Jeremy*) remains entirely presumptive throughout.

The ideologies of *In the Year of the Boar and Jackie Robinson* are based on the principle that categories cease to exist in America. There is no Jewishness, no Chinese identity; there is no gender; there is no Babel of languages. All the marked categories sink into the default categories: universal maleness (typed as a lack of gender), universal American ethnicity (typed as a lack of group identity), universal language (as it has always already been, English). The moment of maximum erasure comes when a couple of assimilated Italian Americans converge in one of the great plays in World Series history. When Al Gionfriddo catches Joe DiMaggio's line drive, "forgetting thirty-nine generations of Confucian breeding, Shirley hugged everyone in reach" (146). The novel ends with a multicultural love-fest, as Emily insists that Shirley be the one to present an award to Jackie Robinson himself at a school Christmas pageant (169).

In the Year of the Boar and Jackie Robinson nevertheless tempers its annihilation of identities in the American melting pot with a sense of the maintenance that assimilants must perform on their new identities. Shirley's assimilation is performed over the resistance of her mother, whom she comes to see more and more as hysterical. Terrified by everything in a Brooklyn she will not try to understand, Shirley's mother faints dead away at the sight of a pet parrot (100) and screams when there is a power outage (112). Her mother can be integrated into the American system only by conceiving a native child, and when she does (164), Shirley dreams of how thoroughly American her new brother will be (she is sure that it must be a brother), how she will initiate him into American mysteries. For her mother, there is no initiation possible; there is only the honorary status conferred on her as the mother of an American. Trapped in immigrant hysteria, she must become literally hysterical, all-womb, to reconcile herself to her place.

For Shirley as an immigrant girl, her mother's unassimilable nature is a warning that she must maintain a double (or triple) consciousness of her own Chinese-American female condition (by contrast her father's unassimilable foreign nature rarely appears, as problematic or otherwise). The ideal is an ability to traverse the compartments of a divided personality at will. The process of crossing and recrossing the boundaries within a multiple consciousness is made dramatic for Shirley by a favorite story of her grandfather's. The story of "the filial daughter and the loving bride" (152) is actually the story of just one woman, destined by her father to marry his best friend's son. When she runs away with a fisherman instead, the lovers suffer from guilt; when the fisherman returns to beg her parents' forgiveness, he is told that their daughter has never married and never left. The filial daughter *and* the loving bride appear and merge into the same person. The moral of this story, for Shirley, is that you can both leave home and stay, that the feminine consciousness of identity is so multiple that a woman can perfectly fulfill both the duties of tradition and the duties of self-actualization.

Most telling of all the circumstances in which Shirley tells her story is its linguistic situation. She tells the story "as Grandfather would, slowly" (152), and to her mother; the language she speaks in the scene must therefore be Chinese. Of course the story appears in the text in a perfect idiomatic English. The novel signals that the story is "translated" without explicitly saying that the story *is* a translation. The representation of language at this moment in the novel, so apparently uncomplicated, is actually more complicated than ever. Shirley manages linguistic double consciousness perfectly and simultaneously, in two exclusive registers: the story of the filial daughter told, for her mother, in perfect Chinese and the story of the loving bride (for she is as much the bride of Jackie Robinson as any nun is the bride of Christ) told in perfect English—for the *reader,* here imagined as the ideal interpreter of Shirley's divided allegiances. As interpreter the reader, situated in the target language, can have the best of both worlds, open access to Chinese traditions along with a sense that Shirley's linguistic identity is oriented firmly toward English. The reader him- or herself is the ravishing fisherman bridegroom of the story.

The beautiful transparency of the transition from Chinese to English in *In the Year of the Boar and Jackie Robinson* and the way that this transition comes across as a heroically won passage from a marked, confined (even hysterical) identity to the freedoms of the liberal subject mark this text as one of the most positive constructions of the English-language community in baseball fiction. That it can be so is perhaps due to the exotic nature of Chinese languages for the implied Anglophone American reader. Further to enlist the sympathies of the Anglophone reader for its Chinese protagonist, *In the Year of the Boar* employs a move so common to the baseball novel as to be almost one of its defining generic features: it makes scapegoats of Spanish speakers. In a drama of assimilation where the native speaker of Chinese is presented as the exemplary learner of English, a counterweight is provided by the image of the Hispanophone, unable to learn English idioms, unable to become a fully linguistic human being.

Shirley (who will say, well into her lessons, "I hate the piano" [124]) is taught piano by Señora Rodriguez, a grotesque, Falstaffian woman who has been a "sinister shadow" behind curtains as the landlady of Shirley's building (59).[1] Shirley, traumatized, can barely introduce herself to the señora when they first meet; stammering hello, "she eked out the words as if squeezing dregs from a squashed tube of stale toothpaste" (59). Señora Rodriguez brings Shirley's oral insecurities to the surface. They are quieted somewhat when the señora reveals herself as even less lingually competent than Shirley is. "Without a word, the Señora grimaced and out came a set of upper and lower teeth, which she then casually set on the music stand. Stuck between the molars, something green. String beans or broccoli? Shirley tried not to look, but the teeth were exactly at eye level" (60). Toothless, an inept eater, the señora communicates in the most broken Spanglish.

> "I weel teach these hands to make mewsic. Mewsic, the language of angels. Angels who geeve happiness to all living tings. Tings like leetle girls. Si?"
> "I see."
> "*Bueno.* We begin." (60)

The señora's primary teaching device is a parrot named Toscanini, who screams the names of the notes at her pupils until they play correctly (61-62). Unable to get far herself in communicating musical instruction via the English language, she is supplemented by a talking animal.

Señora Rodriguez is at best a talking animal herself and at worst an animal that cannot even talk. Being subjected to the señora's discipline is one of the low points of Shirley's career; freeing herself from it is one of her linguistic triumphs. Likened to animals and constructed as grotesque, Señora Rodriguez exerts a tutelage over

Shirley that lowers her beneath animals, demoralizing her, deforming her fingers. The señora's incapacity for English-language learning presents a point of leverage for Shirley, however. Shirley expels the señora from her life when she herself is completely humanized as a speaker of the only natural language: English. The señora becomes the child in their relation and Shirley the adult; power flows down from the more competent English speaker in the relationship.

Señora Rodriguez is made into an infant because she cannot perform the act of will that would make her an American. Like a child or an animal she lacks a fully voluntary consciousness. She wallows in nostalgia for an unspecified "old country." "I weesh to be with my Nonnie," says the old woman of her "leetle girl" back home. "I weesh every hour," but "Who care for house? No rent, my people no eat" (101). Her Gordian "probleema" is cut through by the Alexandrine intelligence of the immigrant sixth-grader. Shirley explains that her father will act as surrogate landlord while the señora is abroad. In the end the señora simply departs the American polity altogether, taking her fractured language and her mossy false teeth with her.

> The idea pleased the old woman, for her lips parted until her pink gums showed in a huge smile. Then she giggled like a maiden. "Si! Si!"
> "I knew you would see." (102)

Shirley, to the end of her relationship with Señora Rodriguez, refuses to comprehend the simplest word of Spanish, taking *sí* as "see," interpreting the words of the señora's native language as childishly mispronounced or misapplied versions of true English words.

In terms of the baseball novel as a whole, Shirley's responses are typical. In this genre Spanish is not a human language. In Tunis's *Keystone Kids* (1943) pitcher Razzle Nugent says, "A guy I know who lived in Havana told me the Spanish have no word for shortstop. Whadd'ya think of that?" The reply is "Neither have the Phillies" (95), but the linguistic imperialism of the comment cannot be joked away. *The Spanish have no word for shortstop*, and that deficit, in the rhetoric of baseball fiction, is more than a semantic blind spot. Baseball novels are unrelentingly realistic, in the linguistic/philosophical sense, and to say that there is no word in Spanish for shortstop implies that Hispanics have no concept for shortstop and indeed cannot understand the logic, self-evident to English speakers, of needing a fourth infielder when there are only three bases.

Of course there is a word in Spanish for shortstop, *paracorte;* its obvious status as a literal translation from the English word, however, somehow gives it less authority. The devaluation of words because of their borrowed or translated status has political significance. Once, when he was the U.S. ambassador to the United Nations, Vernon Walters asserted on *Firing Line* that Hispanics have no word for "leadership" and therefore cannot comprehend one of the essentials of American democracy. When William F. Buckley countered as unctuously as possible, "what about *liderismo?*" Walters simply said that his point was proven; Spanish speakers had the word only because English-speaking Americans had given it to them.

The long and porous history of contact between English speakers and Spanish speakers in the Americas can serve to exacerbate the formers' assumption that not to speak English is not to possess human language. Since American Spanish is filled with American English words (and vice versa), and since the languages are cousins from Western Europe and share a cultural legacy from Latin, Hispanics are sometimes accorded less linguistic credit than Chinese speakers (like Shirley) who speak a historically more alien language. Like those English people who are convinced that the French really speak English at home, Anglo-Americans can easily be convinced that Hispanics have no true language of their own—that the words they speak are part of a complex and hostile refusal to communicate. It was by no means personal idiosyncrasy or private fear that led Minnie Minoso to feel that his main job in the American League was to speak English.

David Carkeet's *Greatest Slump of All Time* (1985) crystallizes the image of the Hispanic whose lack of English becomes a lack of human language and at times a lack of consciousness altogether. Jaime van der Pijpers is the right fielder for Carkeet's depressed ball club, depressed because he is impotent, impotent because he cannot speak any language, languageless because he cannot think, and ultimately cured of his impotence by a brutish insistence on expression—an insistence that does not register on anyone around him. Jaime brings together race, sex, gender, and economics in Carkeet's novel. "He grew up speaking an Iberian-based creole quite different from the Spanish of Caracas, his home after his tenth birthday. His attempt to learn conventional New World Spanish was foiled by the heavy nasality and useless Dutch vocabulary of his native tongue, which also began to deteriorate through disuse and the family-wide deaf ear he was given, making him a wretch inarticulate in three languages" (50). Jaime is the literary extrapolation of the Garrett Morris character from *Saturday Night Live* ("beisbol been very good to me"), and his English consists entirely of interview clichés: "We no pay masha goo behine eem" (50). Since his linguistic competence consists solely of conditioned responses to stimuli, Jaime's psychological existence is subhuman. He moves through the novel in a twilight world between consciousness and pure animal instinct. Of course, sport clichés demand that he be a good ballplayer; in the stretch when the entire team is about to collapse from overwhelming clinical depression, Jaime plays like a maddened beast, single-handedly winning games with aggressive hitting and baserunning. He fits the stereotype of all minority ballplayers, the player whose natural talent is unleavened by reflectiveness. The ball club is populated by "normal Spanish speakers" (51), but they are bench players, undepressed and uninteresting; Jaime is the only Hispanic player given a name and a role in the novel. His status is all the more interesting because, in a pattern that will appear again, Carkeet's novel is black affirmative. Its black characters span a range of complex emotional types, and Bubba, the black second baseman, is carefully established as being its smartest player.

"Jaime's thinking, which unfortunately is no more successful than his speech" (76), can even interfere with the semiconscious activity of chewing tobacco, an important rite of belonging on any ball club. Here is a sample of Jaime's mental process delivered as free indirect style: "He knows about food. You chew it and swallow it. Gum: you chew it and swallow your sweetened saliva. Tobacco: ? He hasn't mastered the intermittent spit. He chews and chews, his mouth becoming a liquid toxic-waste dumpsite, and then he finally erupts like a Caribbean volcano, clearing the bench on both sides of him" (76). One can imagine readings of the novel in which that passage is hysterically funny, but for me its humor depends too much on the debasement of the character's lingual abilities that has started with language. When they can stay out of the way of his tobacco spit, Jaime's teammates converse with him as one might with an intelligent ape. In the middle of a group discussion, Jaime breaks in with "You combersá me nada. . . . Me no surdu. Me no muda. . . . Me no gagu. Scuchámi" (141). The English speakers get a Hispanic player to translate (despite the transparency of what he is saying); the interpreter translates, "A burro is not a beautiful animal, but neither is it an ugly one" (141). "Let's just forget him and keep talking," someone suggests, but someone else answers, "That's it. . . . He's saying we don't talk to him. We converse with him nothing nothing" (141). Jaime's expression is buried under a double linguistic barrier, because translation makes him harder to understand. His meaning is clear to one clever English-speaker, but the Spanish speaker who "translates" for him, on account of deficits or treacheries of his own—or more likely because of a deep Anglophone distrust of all Hispanophones—obscures communication still further.

We last see Jaime on the ballfield "at third, pounding his chest with pride" (186) after a triple, transformed for the novel's purposes into the ultimate baseball Tarzan. An earlier throwaway line marks his connection to one of the genre's paradigmatic novels, however. When Bubba pulls off one of his spectacular trick plays, the uncomprehending Jaime asks "Qui?" [sic] and is answered "Forgit it" (11). The response echoes a scene from *Bang the Drum Slowly* where Diego Roberto (or Roberto Diego; Henry is not sure), whose only role on the club is that of interpreter, is translating for star third baseman George Gonzalez. Diego's "translation" of Dutch Schnell's labored metaphor of the Washington club buzzing around the Mammoths consists of acting out Dutch's pantomime a second time for George's benefit. When Dutch, irritated, tells Diego to "forget it," Diego

> whipped out his dictionary. "Mister, forget is not remember, but is too quick to not remember. She just now happen."
> "Forget it means fuck it," said Dutch.
> Roberto threw his dictionary away. (124)

Diego Roberto's inadequacy as a translator is almost total, beginning with his conception that nonverbal gestures require rendering into the target language. His final comeuppance is one most of us share when we are translating: an incomprehension of idiom. It is the same idiom that Manuel cannot comprehend in *Fawlty Towers*: "You're going to forget everything you know about [it]." . . . "*Sí, sí sí,* eventually. . . . at the end." "No, no, no, forget it *now!*" (Cleese and Booth 172). If misapprehension of idiom means helplessness in a foreign language, the mastery of idiom is the mark of a linguistic insider and the site for scathing disparagement of the foreigner who cannot understand the most self-evident expressions. (The underlying suspicion, in the case of both Diego and Manuel, is that their native language has no idioms and indeed may consist only of directly indicative terms; the foreigner is always inhumanly literal-minded.) Recall Basil Fawlty's contemptuous despair with Manuel: "Please try to understand before one of us *dies*" (172). Basil's ultimate recourse is to poke Manuel in the eye or hit him over the head with a frying pan, but Dutch Schnell, more adept at his culture's construction of the Spanish speaker, communicates with Diego Roberto by rendering his phrase into idiomatic obscenity. "Forget it" may be impenetrable to the Hispanic, but "Fuck it," arguably at the end of a far more mediate chain of signifiers, renders the dictionary unnecessary in its immediacy. The various Hispanic interpreters in baseball fiction may be able to manage neither the English language nor their own, but they speak fluent four-letter-word.

One might ask whether I am being too sensitive to offhand stereotypes in a novel published in 1956. One cannot locate the stereotypes of baseball fiction in some politically incorrect past, however. Bobby Roddy in Kevin Baker's *Sometimes You See It Coming* (1993) is a direct literary descendant of the Hispanics in *Bang the Drum Slowly*. "Bobby acted crazy, like a lot of the Latins I know in the majors. All he would ever say was 'Fuck you.' Didn't matter if he booted a ground ball or hit a triple into the corner. He'd still come back into the dugout an' look at everybody an' say, 'Fuck you'" (56–57). The speaker here is Ricky Falls, "The Old Swizzlehead," the most prominent narrator in Baker's novel. Falls is a black ballplayer who speaks what the novel thinks is African-American vernacular (mainly because he drops the g's at the ends of participles and gerunds) as he tells the story of its white protagonist John Barr. Bobby's catch phrase is simply an unexpurgated version of George Gonzalez's only bit of English, "Up yours"; the only change in the stereotype is to unite black *and* white Anglophone characters in their stereotyping of the Hispanic.

Another recent novel goes a step further by uniting black and white gay protagonists in stereotyping Hispanics. The Hispanic player in Peter Lefcourt's *Dreyfus Affair* (1993) is "Angel 'Spic' Mendoza," who "had been in the bigs for five years and still barely spoke a word of nonobscene English" (75). His typical utterance is something like "Bastard prick shitass mother" (168), and he stalks about the novel for all world like a baseballing La Tourette sufferer, but without the quiet dignity of Jim Eisenreich. (One might pause to consider Mendoza's nickname, which is not cute even in a Rabelaisian way.

In a novel that is openly pleased with its command of baseball idiom, the Hispanic player is given a nickname that assuredly no ballplayer has ever sported even in jest.)

The Hispanic stereotype in Lefcourt's novel is compounded by gardener Manuel Rodriguez. Even Rodriguez's thoughts are marked by the most inane of xenophobic figures of speech: "as thin as tortillas," "the whole enchilada" (113). His direct speech consists of phrases like "Quien sabe?" and "Jesus Maria!" Rodriguez's role in the novel is to skulk around the shrubbery lusting after protagonist Randy Dreyfus's wife. His one contribution to the plot, despite the narrator's assertion that "Mexicans were very fond of animals" (113), is to try to poison the Dreyfus family dog.

It is no news that Anglophone xenophobia is alive and well in 1990s California. What makes the anti-Hispanic thread in *The Drey-fus Affair* so difficult to understand or accept is that as baseball fiction the book breaks ground in the extent to which it is black affirmative and gay affirmative in an unself-consciously explicit way. The novel's central plot has Dreyfus, the white and presumptively straight star shortstop, falling desperately in love with D. J. Pickett, the black and unashamedly gay star second baseman. One could argue that there is a latent racism firmly closeted within the novel's explicit and romanticized gay friendliness. All it takes is a look from the white man for the man of color to fall desperately in love with him, so that Randy and D.J. resemble nothing so much as a twenti-eth-century queer rendition of Disney's John Smith and Pocahontas. Nevertheless the book's overt rhetoric is clearly affirmative about its interracial homosexual love affair. As in one baseball novel after another, a progressive stance (here an antihomophobic stance) is pur-chased at the expense of Hispanic scapegoats.

Scapegoating Hispanics is only the most common form of a per-vasive othering in baseball fiction, an othering that constructs En-glish as the only language. In this process English in the United States becomes both naturally and logically inevitable. The various historical and political forces, deliberate and accidental, that led to the dominance of English in America are obscured. The persistence of such ideas about English in present-day fictional representations reveals how xenophobic cultural work continues in the face of con-tact with other languages. The English language skirmishes at these linguistic front lines with other tongues, taking them prisoner by reducing them to mangled versions of true language. Receptiveness to bilingual or multilingual communities is unthinkable in these fictions; America must be an English-only monologue, or it will cease to exist.

In *The Celebrant* Jack Kapp's younger brother Arthur, the most fully assimilated of the family, scorns his uncle Sid Pincus's Yiddish accent. Arthur's agenda throughout the novel is to remove all trace of perceived un-American elements from the family business, including foreign-sounding English. For Arthur, Uncle Sid is a comic figure, barely competent linguistically. When Uncle Sid speaks Yiddish, however, he sounds like anything but a buffoon. *The Celebrant* renders Uncle Sid's English as "Siddish," a stock character comic argot; it renders his Yiddish as idiomatic literary English, ironically indistinguishable from Arthur's own masterful English. On the grounds of Yiddish Sid becomes master, telling Jack "Talk English, your accent is awful" (157). The grounds of Yiddish, however, are not the grounds of the United States, which demands from immigrants an allegiance to a single common English as loyal as their allegiance to any political tenet.

Presumably Sid's mental essence does not change as he shifts languages; his thoughts are as cogent in the deep structure of his English as they are in the deep structure of his Yiddish (or alternatively, in the surface structure of the Yiddish that he haltingly renders into English/Siddish). *The Celebrant* shows a problem that is everywhere in literary renderings of baseball. Jack and Arthur Kapp speak and write standard literary English—although Jack's, in one of the novel's great beauties, is always a distanced, formally attained literary register; we are aware of Jack as the immigrant *not* speaking his native language. When one writes literature, one writes *always* in literary English, by definition. To render spoken English, with its heteroglot variety of regions and registers, into Standard English involves problems akin to those of translation, however. Standard English becomes that into which one translates everyday speech. Baseball fiction is a large-scale exercise in the rendering into Standard English of vernacular—and in meeting the challenge that the vernacular poses to Standard English.

Standard English, after all, is ultimately just that—the literary language of a nation by definition not the United States. English too is a foreign language in America, and its use in American literature is often suspect. At the same time, however, the long associations of Standard English with literature make for the countervailing suspicion, that American vernaculars may never be truly literary. This is the problem that bewilders slugger Tiny Tyler when he reads *Huckleberry Finn* in Heywood Broun's *Sun Field* (1923):

> He seemed to enjoy it a good deal but not without misgivings. At least half a dozen times he asked Judith, "Are you sure this is a good book?" Judith replied dogmatically that it was a great book and each time Tiny returned to the story eagerly enough. The thing which bothered him was that "Huckleberry Finn" was simple, understandable and enjoyable throughout. He had a deeply engrained feeling that the thing which people called "literature" was intensely painful and could only be endured and mastered by sacrifice and terrific concentration of the will. (147)

Easy does it not, as I discuss in chapter 5; literature must be difficult. Tiny's reading experience of *Huckleberry Finn* foregrounds the problem of an American literary dialect. If *Huckleberry Finn* is indeed the Great American Novel—a critical opinion taking shape in academic circles during the 1920s—then the center of American literary language must shift from standard to vernacular. The language of the narrator of *The Sun Field*, George Wallace, is decidedly not the vernacular, however, but rather the received dialect of George's Ivy League, New York club, and literary circles. The drama of *The Sun Field*, in which George's upper-class friend Judith rejects him for the uncouth ballplayer Tiny Tyler, is not really erotic but linguistic. Standard-speaking Judith, who idolizes Huck Finn, meets Huck's linguistic equivalent in Tiny. She recenters her social universe on Tiny (and in turn turns Tiny into a reader, a rhetorician, and a candidate for Congress). George can only watch helplessly as the Darwinian advantage in mating passes to the better master of true American speech.

The characters of *The Sun Field* enact an American cultural drama in miniature; in many ways their story is the eternal one of the redskin outwrestling the paleface (Rahv). The language of this drama presents an acute problem to the baseball writer and the baseball novelist. Should one translate vernacular into standard, carrying across its meanings without its specific vocabulary and syntax? Should one leave the vernacular "in the original" to be realistic (or to go slumming)—or perhaps to advocate a more vital redskin vocabulary for the paleface standard itself? How can one be sure that one is reporting vernacular without distorting it? "Grow bigger ears," suggests Mark Harris in "Easy Does It Not," but that is hardly a comprehensive theory.

The larger issue governing these technical inquiries is the relation of language to social class in America. The literary text, a package for elite culture, reaches out to include lower-class voices and to appropriate those voices in the service of democracy. This cultural work is specious, though, because whatever becomes literary becomes in turn elite and exclusive. For *American* literature particularly this cultural work is fraught with the dangers of denying, ignoring, or misrepresenting class dynamics. Nor do linguistic registers reduce simply to class strata. The culturally central text in American literature is frequently one that can balance argot and universal intelligibility, region and nation, elitist and illiterate, black and white. The "English" that seems so limpid in immigrant narratives, or when opposed to Spanish, is itself fragmented and full of tension. The central narrating voices in baseball novels can work as lenses to focus the problem of language in American fiction as a whole.

Striking a balance in the language of literary baseball fiction may therefore be seen as a microcosm of similar projects in general literary fiction in America. The struggle of *The Southpaw* against *The Kid from Tomkinsville* is a continuation of the struggle of *Huckleberry Finn* against *The Last of the Mohicans* or that of *Leaves of Grass* against elevated Victorian poems generally. In these struggles the literary text establishes itself as more authentically of the people than its elitist forerunners were. The literary's move toward the vernacular is exactly what Tiny Tyler mistrusts; the move is counterintuitive. Texts aim for the vernacular center to create a common ground accessible to all classes, but claiming that accessible common ground masks other forces that maintain the exclusiveness of literature. Tiny may be right; George Wallace's arch description of Tiny's reading experience may be the archetypal "literary" representation of the vernacular reader. The same cultural forces that put *Huckleberry Finn* in the canon surround it at the same time with the critical apparatus—even if that apparatus frequently amounts to no more than highfalutin *praise*—that mystifies the untutored reader. The content of the literary ultimately matters far less than its scholarly encrustations.

Arguments for the literary status of the texts such encrustations accompany reveal the role of the democratic common language and its connections to the kind of relation between the literary and the nonliterary that I study in chapter 5. The dust jacket of the first edition of *The Southpaw* invokes *Huckleberry Finn* directly:

> [Henry Wiggen] talks like Huck Finn, pitches like Lefty Grove, and thinks like a cantankerous Yankee liberal. . . . Obviously Henry has nothing in common with Frank Merriwell or Baseball Joe, just as *The Southpaw* has nothing in common with the sentimental, saccharine and completely improbable sagas which keep popping up under the general category of "baseball books." *The Southpaw* is a novel about baseball, true, but it is the most authentic and adult treatment of the sport ever attempted. . . . [The ballplayers'] talk is salty and their jokes are bawdy. . . . What Mark Harris has achieved in *The Southpaw* has been to combine a searching commentary on life with the most realistic descriptions of the game itself ever written, all of this tempered by a rich strain of native humor that stems directly from Twain and Lardner.

The cluster of adjectives here—*native, authentic,* and *realistic* opposed to *sentimental* and *saccharine*—shows where the claim to literary status is located. Another cluster of linguistic categories—particularly the linking of *adult* and *salty*—shows the literary status of the novel not so much as one-half of a pair but as the point of a triangle. To be both salty and adult distances the text not only from the insipid and the childish but equally from the distilled and the transcendent. The dust jacket claims for its novel a certain adult childishness, locating a truly literary voice at a point where the usual claims of literature to have put away the child are returned against it and the elevated is shown to be child's play after all.

This continual thinking of the literary as the adult, of the precursor as the child, is a complex form of one-upmanship. (It is very different from the precursor-as-father models of Harold Bloom.) Vernacular adult texts disparage previous literary texts for trying to sound too adult, which is the surest sign of childishness. Around we go. Within the text of *The Southpaw* Henry Wiggen constructs his own ironic canon of baseball stories directly against the claims of his slipcover: "There was also some books of baseball stories, such as those by Sherman and Heyliger and Tunis and Lardner, although Lardner did not seem to me to amount to much, half his stories containing women in them and the other half less about baseball than what was going on in the hotels and trains. . . . Heyliger and Sherman and some of the others give you a good baseball story that you couldn't lay it down" (34). As Henry constructs his reading taste, he aggressively distances himself from Ring Lardner, the author that his own surreal misspellings and his distinct focus on women and on "what was going on in the hotels and trains" establish as his literary model.

Henry creates his character through the appropriate relation of his own language to literary and vernacular languages. Like Jack Kapp or Shirley Wong, he physically imitates star ballplayers: "I pitched about 5,000 games of baseball against the back of the house with a rubber ball. . . . Out behind the house was Moors Stadium in New York City, thousands of people and a good deal of cheering. Sometimes the ball would hit the clothesline, and there was no way to explain that, and I did not try" (24). His more decisive models come from baseball texts, in particular the memoir of Sad Sam Yale, who will later become his teammate and negative role model as a drunken, embittered veteran. Henry's career path is as much to the role of Author, the self-conscious literary ballplayer, as it is to star pitcher.

Henry begins his literary trajectory ironically, disparaging the style of Lardner and admiring the series novels of William Heyliger (*Bartley, Freshman Pitcher* [1911] and its followers) and Harold M. Sherman (the "Home Run" series, starting with *Bases Full* in 1928). As a boy Henry rejects anything literary, such as *Moby-Dick:* "we begun to read it together, Holly and me, and we never come to the whale so I give it up" (25). The book that becomes the ideal in his young readerly life is *Sam Yale—Mammoth.* Its hypercorrect prose and banal sentiments lead him to steal it from the library and stow it "in a secret place in the closet" (34)—about where we might expect to find Henry's love affair with an older man. The text of *Sam Yale—Mammoth* calls to Henry personally, like a Whitman poem, as in the following passage: "This book is written in the hope that every American boy now playing the great game of baseball in his home town, wherever that may be, will take inspiration from my straightforward story. Some of my readers, in the not-too-distant future, will be wearing the uniform of one of the big-league clubs. His success or failure in reaching that goal, and in remaining there once he has reached it, depends on him and him alone" (32). The crushingly mechanical, world-weary quality of this language seeps into Henry's youthful enthusiasm even before he meets the jaded Sam Yale in person. The language is crucial for Henry, however, because it sets a model against which he will oppose a more authentic literary voice.

Henry's status as "Author" is ostensibly, and humorously, filtered through the role of someone called "Mark Harris," the eternal "told to." "Punctutation freely inserted and spelling greatly improved by Mark Harris," reads the title page of *The Southpaw*; "certain of his enthusiasms [are] restrained by Mark Harris" in *Bang the Drum Slowly*; and *A Ticket for a Seamstitch* is "polished for the printer by Mark Harris." The role of "Mark Harris" in these texts, however, is more to preserve Henry's authentic voice than to polish it the direction of *Sam Yale—Mammoth*. If "Harris" is really charged with editing Henry's text, he is incompetent. If Henry believes that his text ought to aspire to Standard English, he has been betrayed by his "editor."

Henry ends up sounding like Huckleberry Finn, albeit a thousand miles to the east and a century further on. Henry resists the identification, saying of *Huckleberry Finn* only that it "was a dirty trick to start a book that you no more opened then the writer was telling you to read still another as well" (25). Henry resists how literary books relate to each other. He resists, possibly more than any other feature, the literariness of literature. His story will not be literature; it will be something different, better, uncharted. In a word, finally, it will be literature.

The Henry Wiggen novels parallel Lardner's *You Know Me Al* (1914) and *Lose with a Smile* (1933) in the way they represent a vernacular that tries to run out of the basepaths of literary language and establish itself as more literary than Standard English. The spellings that "Mark Harris" fails to improve are never random ones, as in the following from *Bang the Drum Slowly:* "libel" for "liable" (111), "isle" for "aisle" (175), and "General McCarthy" for "General MacArthur" (175). Henry's verbal tics—the expanded contractions ("do not," "will not"), the self-conscious reflections on the craft of language ("When in doubt I punctuate" [*Southpaw* 29]), and the run-on sentences—are a mix of things that a copyeditor would change to make the narration more natural or the text more intelligible. They are thrown together in exactly the *wrong* order for literary English, and therefore, of course, they are in exactly the *right* order for American literary English.

The playing field is that of class. The text reaches down into a vernacular, seizes a narrator who cannot understand the rules of the literary dialect and at best can only mock them, and displaces the literary dialect by recentering literature on that narrator. As Kerry

Ahearn observes, "Ring Lardner's 'Alibi Ike' and James Thurber's 'You Could Look It Up' succeed very well in advertising the distance between whom the fiction is *about* and whom it is *for*, but they also suggest that a condescending sort of comedy is as necessary for the formula as are the dialect-burdened narrators" (3). At the extreme limit of this project and in an excellent demonstration of Ahearn's point, Lardner's *Lose with a Smile* is so difficult, its grammar and spelling so idiosyncratic and its plot line so headlong and filled with inside jokes, that it marks itself as unreadable by the very people it represents. *Lose with a Smile* has more in common with James Joyce's *Work in Progress* that was to become *Finnegans Wake*, more in common with Faulkner's *As I Lay Dying* or *The Sound and the Fury*, than it does with sportswriting or sports memoir (such as *Babe Ruth's Own Book of Baseball* [1928], as ghostwritten by Ford Frick).

That is precisely my point—not that we should feel specially uneasy about the class representations and co-optations of the Lardner novels but that we should feel equally uneasy about the way that Joyce's texts represent Ireland and Faulkner's represent Mississippi. It is the nature of literary language to canonize (and colonize) "lower" strata of a language community. Each colonizing leaves the educated—or the coming-to-be-educated, the newly empowered readers—as bewildered as ever and preserves literature as a detached pure category.

The Lardnerian mode in fact becomes Lacanian. When Jack Keefe spells "colic" as "collect" (Lardner, *You Know Me Al* 197) and "apologize" as "apollojize" (195) and talks of touring "San Dago" (216), one sees a far more psychoanalytic understanding of language than that displayed in the work of Susan Glaspell or even Joyce, because the linguistic play of *You Know Me Al* is all on the surface. Keefe's narration adheres exactly to what Jacques Lacan calls "the insistence of the letter in the unconscious," because its "dream-work follows the laws of the signifier" (93). One kind of baseball fiction, naturally, follows a more conscious deployment of metaphoric symbolism, as in the sexually turgid symbols of *The Natural*. More commonly, however, baseball fiction rejects the metaphor for the pun. Most baseball novels, and most baseball stories fictional or nonfictional, play with words rather than with symbols. Words, as a quicker route to the unconscious and to the political, offer a chance to play for higher stakes.

The literary effect of such texts as *You Know Me Al* and *The Southpaw* therefore depends not so much on a belabored joke about class as on the same thing on which *Huckleberry Finn* depends: the texture of a new literary standard created in opposition to the old. Its methods are linguistic, unconscious, and playful rather than realistic, meaningful, and serious. Jack Keefe calls the World Series the "World Serious" so often that the language rearranges itself around free play with its own pretensions.

One might then call the language of the "serious" baseball novel a kind of higher-order slumming. In the young adult novel the ability to move between linguistic registers is presented less ambivalently. It becomes more or less another element in the protagonist's tool kit of American skills. In *The Strike-Out King* the college men speak their curiously cultured argot while the maids, mechanics, and trainers use quaint dialect words such as "floppola" (De Vries 25) or speak broad stage Negro: "Nawsuh, she ain't" (38). At home in both worlds is our idol Dick Fletcher, who can summon up a "Texas drawl" ("Mildred's ben a-tellin' me 'bout yo'" [41]) for "the newspapermen" and move flexibly back into Standard English when he wants to. Roy Tucker, too, slips into his most vernacular when talking to reporters—"Nosuh . . . mebbe. . . . No'm. . . . Yessir" (Tunis, *The Kid from Tomkinsville* 197)—but his thoughts are rendered completely in Standard English (unlike Spike Russell's). These texts seem to tell us that anyone we would be interested in really speaks Standard English at home and that all down-home dialects are a populist sham.

In recent baseball fiction the appropriation of "lower" speech works with race as well as with class. In several novels with white protagonists, a black voice is central to the concerns of the novel: *The Greatest Slump of All Time, The Dreyfus Affair,* and especially *Sometimes You See It Coming* (1993) by Kevin Baker. I want to touch briefly on the last of these three and to speculate on the reasons that underlie the text's need to focus its portrait of a white hero through the lens of a black character's voice.

Ricky Falls, called "The Old Swizzlehead" after his own favorite expression for anyone who gets on his nerves, is the main narrator in *Sometimes You See It Coming.* He is black and speaks a fluent black vernacular—or what the text tries to represent as fluent black vernacular. Like Eddie's in *The Greatest Slump of All Time,* Ricky Falls's speech is represented in eye dialect, where the inflections and endings of his words are lopped off to give the impression of nonstandard pronunciation.[2] For instance, here is his description of protagonist John Barr's hitting style: "The only movement was when he would roll that bat around a little bit in his hands, like a big lazy cat swishin' its tail. Then the pitch would come in, an' it was like somebody pushed a lever. His whole body would turn on it. Legs an' knees an' arms an' head, all moving together" (5). The passage is pure eye dialect, because if the terminal *g*'s and *d*'s were added back onto the words, the text would be almost standard diction. The elisions mark the speaker as black in a facile way. It is not especially the skill or lack of skill in representing a black man's speech that concerns me directly here, however. Eliding final consonants from Ricky Falls's words establishes a contract with the reader that is other than something crudely racial; it continues the way language is represented, however feebly, from Jack Keefe and Henry Wiggen.

The vernacular narrator, however stylized, is an attempt to seize linguistic authority in American texts. By contrast to Ricky Falls, the other narrative voices in this novel seem, well, *white:* Dickhead Barry Busby, the sportswriter; Ellsworth Pippin, the Great White Father; "The Color Commentary," which comes in now and then as a more detached, "authorial" voice. These white voices are stilted, humorless, in a higher or less real register.

If *Sometimes You See it Coming* posited the "black" eye dialect of its main narrator merely as a contrast to white voices, or even as a vehicle for the story of an African-American protagonist, one could critique the execution of the dialect on its own terms. A subtler cultural work is going on, however. The previously quoted passage is typical of the entire novel, for Ricky Falls spends most of it describing John Barr in one way or another. His first words about Barr, his white teammate, are "He was the best" (3). That is the heart of the narrative; the rest is merely an elaboration. Barr, the cold, mechanical, "drowned man" perfect ballplayer, is by turns a mystery, a friend, an annoyance, and a source of joy for Falls. His status as the greatest ballplayer of his time is never questioned, and the worship that should be accorded the greatest ballplayer is never denied him.

Barr is the focus of Falls's gaze, the object of his desire. Falls says far more about Barr in *Sometimes You See it Coming* than Henry does about Bruce in *Bang the Drum Slowly*. Himself energetically heterosexual, located in a plot that drives John Barr inexorably into the arms of veteran sportswriter Ellie Jay, safeguarded perhaps by discourses of homosexuality more widely public in the 1990s than in the 1950s, Ricky can sidestep the issue of gay desire. We are now well and truly past the Fiedler moment. But another of Fiedler's dynamics, that of race, is reversed. The man of color is now voluble; the white man is his strong, silent (and deadly) companion. The white man has gained in this transfer the natural power of the colored companion, and he has gained something that the colored companion never had in the Fiedler pairs: the linguistic work of the speaker in his behalf.

In a dynamic where the black man cannot "win," the white man is typed either as the producer of language or as the receiver of verbal praise. John Barr becomes a figure of glamour and seriousness, whose death (in a Clemente-like plane crash) is ultimately tragic. By having Falls tell Barr's story, *Sometimes You See It Coming* gives his story the added authority of multicultural assent; a black man too finds the essence of the white man to be the most fascinating human issue in his life. In an sardonic twist John Barr's story is wrapped around a kernel secret modeled on the life of Ty Cobb, one of the most extreme real-life racists in the history of the game. Barr's mother has shot his father dead. By having Falls serve as the narrator of how Barr unpacks his nightmarish past, the text argues that white people's stories are central—all the more so for borrowing a black voice to tell those stories.

Ricky Falls is no naive narrator. It is all the more interesting that he should stand for a cliché that characterizes the literary baseball novel as a whole, even when that novel is most eager to present its plot and themes as a departure from cliché. We work around and around again in these texts to the image of the straight white hero, his concerns and struggles but above all his determination to be represented as *representative* of America as a whole. In *Sometimes You See It Coming* the black man is granted an imitation of language, but he is granted it only the better to show how the white man's family romance, athletic skill, and personal moral integrity are greater than his own.

The straight white male is the default value American, the condition to which immigrants continue to aspire in these cultural representations. His language, English, is the only language. Even foreign languages exist only as they can be represented, or misrepresented, in English. The closer other voices come to rivaling his linguistic authority (an authority so vital to culture), as in the case of Spanish in the United States, the more desperate and unremitting is the cultural work performed against those voices. Above all the white man's language must take a central (and therefore a literary) place as unmarked natural dialect. Wherever he chooses to speak, he speaks with original authority, and the other voices of the culture align themselves around him. He clears a space for the literary, which becomes the natural criterion by which other literary voices are measured.

Of all the controversial seizings of the middle ground by white male rhetoric in these texts, the ground of meritocracy is both the most pernicious and the least examined. It is also the one where making the default value of white male is the hardest to overcome. The rhetoric of meritocracy arises not only from ideas about the liberal subject (uncomplicatedly white and male in so many founding theories) but also from racism and sexism, which propose meritocracy as a way to rationalize the perpetuation of inequities. Meritocracy is connected to class in a complex reaction to old constructions of class as a matter of birth and inheritance. This connection tends to obscure and leave beyond the possibility of challenge constructions of class that are based on inequities in wealth and in control of means of production.

Meritocracy is neither natural nor positive. It is created through language, and it seeps into readings of immigrant, assimilant, and even sexual discourses. The next chapter of this book reads the baseball novel in an entirely new way—as a defense, and a mythology, of meritocracy.

Notes

1. Señora Rodriguez reminds the reader of Walter Moles's *grand-mère* in Giff's *Left-Handed Shortstop* (29–31), as well as of Shirley's own mother; all three older immigrant women are hysterical, nonsensical, and exist on the edge of emotional trauma.

2. D. J. Pickett in *The Dreyfus Affair* and Henry Adams in Barry Beckham's *Runner Mack* (1972), by contrast, speak not in eye dialect but in Standard English.

4

Hitting the Bell Curve

. . . .

After Castro's revolution George Gonzalez of the Mammoths leaves the America that has never understood him for his native Cuba. Asked about his baseball career, he tells an interviewer: "In U.S.A. baseball I was a third baseman but in Cuba as a patriotic player I play every thing but pitch" (Harris, *It Looked Like For Ever* 200). This is more than just another of George's failed encounters with the English language. The revolution has given him an opportunity to roll back the whole capitalist history of the division of labor. George seems to imply that in some precapitalist past, in some noncapitalist place, all players play all positions; no one's labor on the ballfield is constrained within a tiny, alienated part of the team's entire objective.

The visceral, almost religious resistance some fans and commentators still have to the designated-hitter rule (by which the pitcher's role is divided into offense and defense, one player taking the field while the other—the designated hitter—bats in the pitcher's place in the lineup) is perhaps similar to George's holistic rhetoric. Surely those who want to abolish the designated hitter do not want to do it because they have fond childhood memories of watching Sandy Koufax trying to hit.[1] I think that what they object to, almost unconsciously at times, is any further fragmentation of the athlete as productive worker. Teams with designated hitters score more runs than teams without, but are they better for the soul?

Moreover, one might ask, are they better for baseball's use as a cultural fiction in America? Every division of labor subtly changes the rules whereby one's work will be judged and valued; the designated hitter still gets three strikes, as do the relief pitcher and the platoon batter, but when divisions of labor are introduced into the game, its rules change for the people who must prove their worth to earn a living at the sport. As these "rules" change for the players, the lessons of the sport change for the audience. Those who apply baseball to their own lives in search of moral or metaphoric guidance find their attitudes toward professionalism, the value of work, and merit changing as well.

Without nostalgia there would be no interest in baseball. Warren Goldstein shows that the sense that the game has become too professional, commercial, and mechanical dates at least from 1868 (1). It probably dates from five minutes after Abner Doubleday picked up the first horsehide in a Cooperstown meadow (an almost certainly apocryphal event). Considering the early decades of the sport as American public spectacle, the older fans of 1868 had a point. Baseball in the beginning was played by amateur clubs dedicated to social activity and individual recreation. Pictures, descriptions, and accounts of this game date from the mid-1840s. The earliest known newspaper game story (*New York Morning News*, October 22, 1845) refers to the sport already as "the time-honored game of Base" (Sullivan 11). The anonymous Ur beat writer who described the match between the New York Ball Club and an apparently less organized group of "Brooklyn Players" left intriguing traces of the spirit of the game by means of the things that he (probably *he*) left out. The game account is entirely about batting; not a single field position is mentioned, not even the pitcher. The primitive box score lists the number of runs each player scored and the number of outs he made, but not his position (12).

By 1858 a description of an all-star match between Brooklyn and New York teams lists each player's position and describes plays made in various defined parts of the field (Sullivan 28-29). Full statistics are given for the pitchers, each of whom threw a complete game. The box score is recognizably modern, although it does not list some things we would expect (such as RBIs) and includes others one can only infer from 1990s box scores (such as outs made).

I suspect this difference is a development in play and not merely an artifact of media coverage. The players in 1845 probably rotated around the field, each player pitching to a few batters in turn and then moving out to fluidly defined defensive positions. No one "was" a pitcher or a first baseman, because no one stayed in one place very long.[2] By 1858, ten years before the point at which, according to Goldstein, nostalgia for the good old days of baseball first emerged, the advantages of a rudimentary division of labor were making themselves felt. A player who specializes in a single position can train continuously for the situations that arise there and handle them better than a generalist can (Goldstein 22). By 1860 *Beadle's Dime Base Ball Player* was printing a list entitled "The Positions on the Field," with a full rundown of the strategies and talents needed at each position; significantly the list starts with the most specialized positions (catcher and pitcher) and becomes vaguer about the other positions as it proceeds, saying of the final position, right field, simply that "it is only occasionally, in comparison to other portions of the field, that balls are sent in this direction" (Sullivan 41).

Ever since this early division of labor became the necessary organization for the workplace of a winning ball club, baseball rhetoric has hankered after the Edenic condition of the complete ballplayer. The complete ballplayer, driven by love for and appreciation of the game as a whole, would also naturally be an amateur. Ominously this division of labor was asserting itself as the original amateur clubs were beginning to employ professionals. This is the moment of baseball's original fall from grace, a fall with obvious repercussions in the 1990s. Amateur clubs of the 1850s concentrated as much on charity fundraising, winter socializing, and commercial boosterism as on baseball (Goldstein 29). Prominent in the 1845 game story is a description of the dinner held afterward (Sullivan 12). Most matches were intraclub, and competition among members of the same club led to stratification of the clubs into "first nines" and others—much as present-day chess clubs maintain member rankings with a view to staffing the first five "boards" in an interclub match. But the practice of intraclub competition was drawn inexorably into the service of interclub competition. Instead of the playground model, where roughly equal sides can be drawn up by alternate choosing, by the 1860s "baseball commentators had a more sophisticated approach to training. . . . Clubs, they urged, should practice so as to concentrate on the skill of the first nine by playing the 'first nine against the field'—that is, the starting lineup against everybody else. That way the best players would get used to each other and to their set positions" (Goldstein 21-22). The best players were soon being offered exemptions from dues as an incentive to play ball for specific clubs (Goldstein 94-96). Such negative compensation turned into positive salaries; clubs began to hire professionals. The first club pros may have been analogous to modern golf club pros. Their job was to train, instruct, and generally schmooze with serious dues-paying amateur members

(Goldstein 70). As clubs tried to emulate the success other clubs won by using professionals in interclub matches, however, the logic of professionalism moved swiftly toward the all-professional first nine, a team now composed not of members but of employees of the parent ball club.

The first all-professional first nine was that of the 1869 Cincinnati Red Stockings, a nine (ten including one substitute) that completed a national tour without defeat and lost only six games in 1870. As the only club to hire a professional at each position, the Red Stockings were naturally better than anybody else. They easily defeated all-amateur nines or the nines of amateur clubs that were eked out with a few professionals. In 1871 the club nevertheless disbanded its professional team and returned to entirely amateur competition (Goldstein 112-19). The Cincinnati club's decision to disband its professionals is popularly seen as the result of discouragement after their long winning streak ended in 1870 (as it is in Ken Burns's *Baseball*), yet exactly the opposite is likely to be true. The Red Stockings collapsed not because they lost once in a while (not even Cincinnati fans are that fickle) but because they had cornered the talent market. They were too good for their own good; people stopped paying to see a team that routinely won all its games.

No team in professional sports (except the Harlem Globetrotters) can make money by winning all its games. Business models that point toward monopoly as the ultimate and desirable outcome of unfettered competition cannot work in sports. Time and again in the history of baseball, lack of competition or the fear of that lack has paralyzed the business. Most of the Red Stockings went to play for Boston after 1871, where these original Red Sox so dominated the new National Association that the entire league folded five years later. The subsequent history of organized baseball has been one of attempts to manage the level of competition, so that the competitive parity necessary for the illusion of struggle could be maintained in the face of the natural tendency of success on the field to translate into financial success and for financial success to translate into even stronger teams. As the best team in the nation's largest market, it was natural for the New York Yankees to win the World Series annually in the 1950s, but it was disastrous for the business of the sport; the Yankees' success drove both their local competitors (the Giants and the Dodgers) out of town and condemned distant competitors like the Athletics, Senators, and Browns to abject failure and similar transcontinental wandering. Fears of this dominance's repeating itself drove the passionate union-busting of "small-market" owners during the 1994-95 baseball strike.

Nonetheless the tribulations of major-league baseball are only the tip of a complicated iceberg of national competition and management of that competition. In prelapsarian baseball local clubs, largely composed of skilled artisans and other workers who could lay claim to some control over leisure time (Goldstein 26-27, 75), played matches with other local clubs; membership was determined along trade and guild lines, by neighborhood or city, or by school.[3] In twentieth-century "organized" baseball whole systems of ball clubs function in the sole interest of developing players for the major-league clubs, which are located in the largest metropolitan areas, at the centers of vast regional broadcast markets and merchandising agreements. Local clubs function as colonial outposts of the metropoles, so that Oklahoma City, Tulsa, Charleston (South Carolina), and Port Charlotte (Florida)—Texas Rangers' farm clubs of the mid-1990s—"belong" to Dallas-Fort Worth in the baseball sense. The minor-league franchises may be independently owned, but they depend on the major-league franchises for most of their players and for financial subsidies.

The farm system of organized baseball grew during the 1920s, 1930s, and 1940s, its growth the expression of the economic power of cities in a rapidly urbanizing America. The chief architect of this internal colonization of the country by the city was Branch Rickey, who figures in most mythologies of the game mainly as the integrator of the majors. The chief advocate for independent minor-league clubs was the segregationist Kenesaw Mountain Landis; after his death in 1944 (and after World War II pushed the national demographic balance decisively toward industrial cities), independent minor leagues ceased to exist (James, *Historical Abstract* 164-65).

Replacing these independent minor leagues was the organized baseball that we see today, a system finely tuned to sort men by their skill as ballplayers. This system of organized baseball is in turn the backdrop for modern baseball fiction, the rise of which as a young adult and then an adult genre, in the 1940s and 1950s, parallels the rise of the farm system. Each midsummer, in a draft instituted in the 1960s (although less dodged than other 1960s drafts), amateur baseball players—in effect, graduates of high schools, junior colleges, and colleges—are chosen by the major-league organizations. The drafted players, if they sign contracts, start out in rookie leagues that play short late-summer seasons. The best move up to full-year rookie ball, then to A leagues (most systems have two class-A teams), and then to AA, AAA, and the majors. At each successively higher rung the cities are bigger, the competition is better, and the pay is higher.

Professional sports—sports as business—run themselves into the ground if competition goes unmanaged, for the richest team will buy all the best players and make a mockery of competition. To manage that competition and keep the interest of spectators, organized baseball has developed a system that places an equal proportion of talent at the disposal of each franchise. The system manages and monitors the level of talent so as to keep each team's stockpile nearly even with the others: players must play in one minor-league system for only a few years before another major-league team can draft them, to prevent hoarding of young prospects, and players can be sent up and down from the minors only a few times before they are "out of options" and can move to another club's system.[4]

Organized baseball may be the most perfectly meritocratic social organization in modern America. Better players rise higher in the organization, become more famous, and make more money. "Excellence," that vaguest of qualities in American corporate life, is demonstrable on the ballfield—a team either wins the game or it does not. The individual qualities that contribute to a winning ball club are far more uncertain; they are the well-known "intangibles" that constitute the fatal flaw in any meritocratic system. At the surface level of basic statistics, however, the player with the higher batting average or lower earned-run average (for a pitcher) is on the face of it probably a better player.

The strict logic of the game provides for continuous comparison among players to ensure that a team fields its best lineup and that the best players in a league or age group are consistently recognized for their talents. Meritocracy is therefore on every page of baseball fiction. One looks through these representations of meritocracy directly to an underlying cultural value of merit that is never challenged. The better an individual's performance, the more that individual should be recognized and rewarded.

The value of merit in sport is identical with the value that Martin Luther King Jr. thought lay somewhere beyond the walls of American racism: "I have a dream that my four little children will one day live in a nation where they will be judged not by the color of their skin but by the content of their character" (2485). King rejects judgment by color. He does not reject the basic value of *judgment*, a judgment he specifically links to moral attributes. The ideal America is not one where judgment is suspended, an America of "to each according to his needs"; it is an America like that of Sam Yale and Mrs. Rappaport, where a child's "success or failure . . . depends on him and him alone" (Harris, *The Southpaw* 32). Nowhere in this rhetoric can we see a space where neither success *nor* failure might be the outcome of everyday work.

Nevertheless, one can appreciate the strong attraction that meritocratic ideologies held for King. An honest meritocracy is color-blind. If a black pitcher can win games and a white pitcher cannot, that black pitcher will get the call. The logic is compelling; segregationist businesspeople and ball club owners who refuse to hire talented people of color are simply harming the productivity of their own organizations. It is an argument that could sway even Richard Nixon; in 1956 he argued that "America, the people of the United States, cannot afford the cost of prejudice and hatred and discrimination. We can't afford it morally, we can't afford it economically, and we can't afford it internationally . . . at a time when we have to keep ahead of the Communist world" (quoted in Ambrose, *Nixon* 417). For the reactionary who sees the whole world as a playing field, integrationist meritocracy is the rational approach to the civil rights issue.

It is thus not surprising that Branch Rickey, organized baseball's first integrationist, was also its leading meritocrat. He realized that Jackie Robinson, Roy Campanella, Don Newcombe, and other African-American players could help the Dodgers win pennants, and they *did* help the Dodgers win pennants. Nevertheless, meritocratic rationalization of baseball destroyed free competition at lower levels of the sport, drove many minor leagues out of business (including the independent Negro leagues), and subordinated the interests of local communities to the interests of metropolitan regions. Most important of all, it placed entire ways of organizing the world at the service of a meritocratic ideology that could (being color-blind) as easily turn against people of color as work for them.

Meritocratic ideologies work in the closed system of sport; fielding better players makes a better team. They demand a terrible price, however: the allegiance of the entire being to the ideal of merit. In children's stories such allegiance is completely uncomplicated—and when children's stories leave no room to imagine a way out of a value, one does well to be wary of it. The young adult baseball story is about the team's progress toward victory in the Big Game. It is also geared toward aligning that victory with the proper composition of the team, so that the deserving players participate in proportion to their talents. As Michael Oriard says of early football stories, "Behind many of these narratives lies a basic question: who would succeed in America, and on what terms?" (*Reading Football* 188)—and, one might add, who will fail? If white people happen to succeed in a meritocracy, their success is doubly validated. If black people fail, it somehow is really their own fault.

In the ideal meritocracy of the young adult novel, the talented player makes the team by learning to fit his (or her) individual strengths into team goals. Stretch Evans in Home Run Stretch (1991), by S. S. Gorman, starts out as an individualist. When his coach, Miss Hyland, announces that "Defense is fifty percent of a winning team. . . . To win, you not only have to score runs but also keep your opponents from scoring," Stretch answers: "You guys stay with defense. I'll stick with hitting home runs" (15). This opposition of individual statistics to the total team effort is a point of tension throughout the novel, but Stretch is ultimately not hard to win over. His individual merit, Miss Hyland assures him, will finally be judged by the success of his team: "You're one of the most talented kids in the league. . . . But sometimes raw talent isn't enough. That's when technique comes into play. When talent and instinct let you down, you have to have hours of practice to back you up. . . . Besides, it's all part of being a team. You can't play baseball without a team" (104–5). *Home Run Stretch* exemplifies the most basic form of the meritocratic plot element, the balance of individual against corporate functional "merit" that must be struck to ensure success in team sports.

Nothing in these stories is easily limited to mere team sports. In Walter Dean Myers's *Me, Mop, and the Moondance Kid* (1988), Mop makes a multiethnic youth club as a catcher but suspects that an entirely different agenda is at stake in her tryout. She believes that coach Jim Kennedy and his wife, Marla, are going to adopt her: "He's still trying to make up his mind if he wants to adopt me or not. It's like the Yankees. When they want to see somebody, they send a scout to check them out" (25). It seems that even family membership must be based on merit; nothing is taken for granted. The constant judgment and scrutiny that one undergoes to prove membership in the social unit of the team are not easily distinguishable from basic "family values," given the abundance of family imagery for the team ensemble and the highly moralistic quality of meritocratic rhetoric. Nor is Mop simply letting her imagination run away with her; when her catching helps the team to win the Big Game, Marla and Jim *do* adopt her (148).

Primal scenes of merit abound in the baseball novel. The sport, with its clear demarcations of success and failure, is a natural setting for them. As a cluck's wife tells Henry Wiggen, "at least at the ball game you find out" (Harris, *A Ticket for a Seamstitch* 37). You find out who is better than who, who deserves to be in the lineup and who deserves to ride the pine. You find out as well that "better" is more a matter of corporate function than individual talent. In a circular way, however, one's adaptation to the corporate role comes from a moral merit far more intrinsic than athletic talent.

When Roy Tucker originally bursts on the major-league scene in Tunis's *Kid from Tomkinsville* (1940), veteran catcher Dave Leonard initiates him into the mysteries of the meritocracy. "Any youngster who's fast and can throw and can stand up to the plate should make the grade," says Leonard (61). Something additional is required, however. "If he has one thing. Y'know, I've seen lots of ballplayers, lots that had everything except courage. They just didn't have it. And they wouldn't work" (61). Merit is continually constructed in baseball fiction as a complex of physical talent and just one more thing, or physical talent plus mental talent and just one more thing, or physical plus mental talent plus toughness . . . and just one more thing. The leftover missing ingredient, which for Stretch Evans is technique won through practice and for Minnie Minoso is fluency in English, becomes such a commonplace element in sport fiction that it can be the focus of parody, as in George Abbott's song "You Gotta Have Heart!" from *Damn Yankees.*

The banality of this supplement does not make it meaningless. On the contrary, the construction of merit is a matter of mystifying the obvious. "You find out," but only to the initiate are the real processes of "finding out" made clear. This mystique can be used to make merit a pliable value, even when it seems to be as inflexible as humanly possible, as in a ball game. Ultimately it scarcely matters what the extra term in merit may be: heart, courage, team spirit, collegiality, good grammar, "It." Whenever the lines of meritocratic evaluation appear to be etched in steel, they can be shifted and pulled into the evaluator's sphere of interest. The ability to evaluate merit can take on the power of an esoteric knowledge.

> Look here, has a kid got it; that's all I wanna know. No scout can crack open a kid's head and find out, has he got guts. If he could, baseball would be a cinch. Every team would be the Yanks. . . . When I was a kid breaking in like you . . . I thought I was hot stuff, but they soon showed me I didn't have an idea what it was all about. Just when I got convinced I was a flop and waiting for that pink slip in the mail box, this old fellow took me aside in the lobby of the hotel one night. . . . "Courage," says this old-timer, "courage is all life. Courage is all baseball. And baseball is all life; that's why it gets under your skin." (Tunis, *The Kid from Tomkinsville* 65)

Courage, baseball, life: all are matters of making the grade, of making the team. Evaluation and credentialing are only half of the meritocratic equation, however; the other half, perhaps even harder to see, is that of reward. For the meritocracy to function, differential degrees of merit must be apportioned differential rewards.

Reward is the theme of Vernon Simpson's discussions with the regents of his college in Valentine Davies's *It Happens Every Spring* (1949). Vernon is a self-made academic success, someone who has used academic credentials to move from the country to the metropolis in America, "an eager, gangling youth from somewhere in the upper part of the state. His widowed mother was a small-town librarian or something of the sort. . . . He had worked his way through college from the start" (6). To pluck and work ethic Vernon adds technological know-how; he invents a "biophobic" compound that allows baseballs to avoid bats and surreptitiously uses it to become a star pitcher in the major leagues.[5] His on-field success makes him an academic star as well, and he shrewdly holds out for a merit increase to his base salary (so that he can marry the college president's daughter). "The sum of money which I received for teaching the science of chemistry to the youth of this state for an entire year was a little less than I could make in a single afternoon by tossing a five-ounce rawhide sphere past a young man holding a wooden club" (221).

The whole issue of merit pay is one that will no doubt provoke (at the mildest) a grimace from any academician reading this book.

In the university, and in almost any corporate setting where performance is linked to reward, the evaluation of merit is a notoriously suspect process. Baseball fiction works to place the determination of merit above suspicion.

The more magical elements of the baseball story participate in this exoneration of merit processes. Fictional representations of merit rewarded tend to reincorporate the divided labor of the team into a single player: Miss Hyland makes Stretch Evans a complete player by having him try out at every position; Roy Tucker, his pitching arm shattered, returns in *The Kid from Tomkinsville* to succeed as a star outfielder. In magical realist baseball stories the invariant plot device is that the magically assisted hero must win the Big Game on his own. Joe Hardy turns back into aging, balding Joe Boyd but makes the catch that ensures that the Yankees lose the pennant. In the film *Rookie of the Year*, the protagonist loses his miraculous arm speed at the end of the film but wins the Big Game by guile. The angels desert the ball club in both versions of *Angels in the Outfield*, but the team wins the Big Game through human effort alone. In the film version of *The Natural*, at least, Roy Hobbs hits the winning homer without benefit of Wonderboy. And in *It Happens Every Spring* Vernon Simpson, his biophobic potion lost because his roommate thought it was hair oil, pitches his team legitimately to a series victory.

More important than magical aid is how meritocracy turns into a spectacle. When a hero wins on his own, without the magical devices he thought he needed, he is in the realm of fairy tale; he is Dumbo flying without his magic feather. When merit wins out on the playing field, however, the representation repeats what really happens every fall, complete with moralizing color commentary. What happens on the field is not significant only to the men who do it; the players' own appreciation of the workings of the merit system pales by comparison to the object lesson offered to thousands in the stands and millions beyond. When Vernon Simpson's Cardinals play in the series, "mixed in with the typical crowd of baseball fans, who jammed the stadium, were a surprising number of staid professors who had not witnessed a baseball game since the turn of the century. And many an elderly dean was astonished to find himself rooting and shouting with the best of them in a most undignified manner" (183–84). Meritocratic baseball works by providing a rational foundation for the social order. Pure meritocracy is on permanent display.

The best man always wins, validating the status quo in the stands. The winners who watch—the deans who enjoy their tenure, pay, and perquisites—are by reflection the best men in their fields as well. It matters little if their status was achieved by nepotism, gerontocracy, or sheer inertia: the game cleanses and purges the achievement of its spectators, validating their achievement as fairly won.

Baseball as spectacle, however important to its cultural work, is the source of worrisome doubts about meritocratic ideals. Like the assimilative ideals of the baseball novel, its meritocratic ideals can be eroded by hypocrisy. In Tunis's *Highpockets* (1948) the title character is a loner, an individualist who has trouble fitting into the postwar corporate ethic of Spike Russell's Brooklyn club. Unable to get along with his teammates, Highpockets plays to the crowd, gets his positive reinforcement there, and is obsessed with his own status as spectacle. "The rookie was fascinated by city crowds, and was invariably to be found in the lobby of the hotel in which they were staying. . . . He was excited and interested by the throngs who poured past, by the bellboys paging visitors, the continual stream of men and women coming and going" (49–50). "He's gotta stop playing to the crowd" (48), Spike avers, but even the manager is taken aback by the bluntness of Highpockets's philosophy: "'They pay off on the long ball in the majors, Skip.' . . . The youngster's obstinacy annoyed Spike. Perhaps what also annoyed him was the fact that the kid had some truth in his remark" (51).

Spike takes Highpockets in hand, teaching him to do less spectacular things like bunt and hit to the opposite field (53–55), but Spike's instructions are not self-evidently functional ones. The relation between a player's home run total and his team's success is a gray one; clearly it is not *bad* to hit home runs. Therefore Spike's unspectacular, team-oriented approach to the game may not really help the Dodgers win more than Highpockets's all-or-nothing batting style. Is management paying Highpockets to help the Dodgers win or to impress the crowds? The relation between competitive success and corporate financial reward is also a gray one here.

"All-Star games don't put no groceries on the table," says Highpockets as he defends his demand that *Life* magazine pay him $250 for a photo opportunity (85). He cannot be sure that his allegiance to Spike Russell's interests (the manager will surely be fired if the team does not win) is in his *own* interest. As Casey the columnist dryly notes, "it is not likely that *Life Magazine* would offer him a job as executive editor if his eyes go and he loses that home-run punch" (85).

As I discuss in chapter 2, Highpockets is assumed into the Dodgers fold only when he falls in love with a young boy, and that is a slightly (if only slightly) different chapter of this book. In terms of the basic issues of team and individual under a meritocratic system of rewards, however, he remains a permanent dissenter from Spike's series-long set of team values. Unable to win him over with rhetorics, the text wins him over with erotics, but the problems he raises do not therefore disappear. In fact they return with a vengeance a few novels later in Tunis's series, in *Schoolboy Johnson* (1958).

This novel is about youth and age, as I discuss in chapter 3. It too is erotic, but its other themes include the victory of age and treachery over youth and skill. It opens with a meditation on the release of ballplayers who are no longer good enough, a category that now includes Roy Tucker. Plummeting into the minors, Roy befriends the similarly washed-up Speedy Mason. Although they play for different teams, their age and veteran status make them friendly enemies. When Roy gets his inevitable recall to the majors (because the Dodgers' third baseman has broken his leg, and Roy must assume yet another position for the club), Speedy asks a favor: "Gimme a build-up with Spike Russell" (34).

When both were stuck in the minors with no hope of advancement, Roy empathized with Speedy's sense that his merit was neglected. Now Speedy's protestations that he can still win in the majors seem merely pathetic, a play for Roy's emotions that may help Speedy to gain an unfair chance. If prejudice against Speedy's age has led to his demotion, then he deserves another shot; if he has been fairly demoted, however, should friendship be the reason for his repromotion? The question of merit in *Schoolboy Johnson* turns into a spiral of suspicions, as the characters cannot trust themselves to identify pure merit.

Speedy soon wins promotion to the Dodgers on the basis of Roy's recommendation. He wants to be a starting pitcher, and Spike wants him to relieve. Speedy's desires are based not on vainglory but on what he thinks is functionally efficient; he is sure that he can get batters out only if he starts regularly instead of relieving on an erratic basis. (Of course one should not ignore the fact that in the 1950s starting was more prestigious and more highly paid than relieving.) When Speedy threatens to retire rather than relieve, Spike muses on the balance sheet of the old pitcher's merit.

> Baseball is a business; sentiment is out—if you want to survive. You must be impersonal, bring 'em up and send 'em down. A player has to prove himself out there on the field and do it alone. But this veteran is different. No matter what he may claim, I think he keeps that slap-happy young pitcher from going out too much at night. . . . And there's another big-leaguer, that Tucker. They both get out before anyone else, they take batting practice, they throw batting practice. . . . Pros—that's what they are. (76-77)

It scarcely matters what Spike actually decides, because after the eternal manner of the Dodgers novels, one of his starting pitchers is careening into a car crash even as they speak, giving Speedy a slot in the rotation. Most significant in Spike's thoughts is how judging merit in a coldly objective way leads to the undercutting of merit by the intangible. Spike Russell, who knows a little about the melding of business and sentiment in the composition of a ball club, can distinguish the tangible from the intangible—and is led to value the intangible even over his best objective judgment of the needs of his club. Speedy and Roy have proved that they have the "it" of the moment; they are *pros*. They may be on their last legs, but from where Spike is sitting, it looks like forever.

Through the tortured manager of the Dodgers, we can see what problems arise in the evaluation of merit. The human factor in merit-based decisions is unavoidably biased. Sure, Spike wants to keep Speedy and Roy around; sure, he wanted to take the cocky Highpockets down a peg. But isn't that just because the old guys are his peers, his old teammates? Wasn't his desire to break Highpockets of the home run habit just an older man's natural envy for the power of youth? We can sense in Spike's dilemmas the uncertainties that feed a desire for a stricter objective system of evaluation, one that would remove the personal from the mix and displace responsibilities onto a machine or formula. The same gray areas that make meritocracy so powerful tend to undercut its authority as a system.

If meritocracy is unstable as a social system even in the children's texts that serve as primers to teach it, it is positively explosive in the adult novel. Disillusion with merit is most pervasive in Eliot Asinof's *Man on Spikes* (1955). Mike Kutner, the protagonist, is a minor-league ballplayer who never quite makes the majors. His story is one of merit denied and neglected, and he thus becomes a painful object lesson in the supplemental intangibles of merit.

Mike plays inside ball, complete ball, winning ball—but he can get no one to appreciate his talents, which are general and holistically expressed. The scout Durkin Fain, who discovers Mike, raises the ancient cry: "Baseball has changed since you played it. It's the goddamn long ball they want now. . . . Baseball had become less a matter of winning games than the way you won them" (4-5). Joe Kutner is reluctant to let his son sign a professional contract because the game does not seem like legitimate work to the old miner. Joe argues that Mike's chances of making the majors are like those of a girl waiting at a soda fountain for a Hollywood director to discover her. Fain replies, "But this is baseball. A game of skill" (33). His words are belied by his own analysis of the situation in the sport, however. He himself feels that baseball is becoming more like Hollywood all the time.

Mike's progress through the minor leagues is beset by the refusal of the empowered to recognize his true worth. A succession of stock characters comment on his progress. Herman Cruller, "The Old Ballplayer," knows that no business really rewards merit and that baseball is not distinct from other businesses: "Baseball is a game of personalities, like any other business, I suppose. Some cruddy skipper don't like the way you part your hair and you sit on your ass for a season. You never can tell" (60). Mike's roommate, Charlie Caulfield, is a master of the social niceties needed to get ahead in the game. He is college educated and his thoughts are given in learned language ("he wasn't going to back down for some tripe about propriety" [95]), but like that of Dick Fletcher or Roy Tucker, his direct speech descends to whatever register is needed: "Lemme interdooce ya" (95). Charlie criticizes Mike for thinking about and working at baseball all the time. When Mike thunders, "I've always thought you had to sweat for what you want, and if you're good enough, and you sweat hard enough, you get it!" Charlie simply replies: "Get the skipper patting your back and swapping a few gags and it goes a long way—longer than all your sweat" (109).

Charlie's rejoinder is a direct rebuff to Mike's meritocratic ideals. These very ideals are intertwined with Mike's particular tendentious evaluation of his own merit. He cannot summon a rhetorically convincing argument from authority: "he was not a 'record' ballplayer. His value lay in abilities not altogether apparent in record books" (209). Charlie is a "record" ballplayer *and* a showman and thus gets the major-league career that he does not need in order to earn a living; Mike, who lives on his baseball salary, has to sustain him only a faith that the mundane things he does on the field contribute to winning. Mike would "rather play ball than eat" (146), but his full justification will only come when he can play ball *to* eat.

In a children's novel Mike would get his big chance in the Big Game and hit the home run that would vindicate his own faith in himself. *Man on Spikes* is an adult novel, however, and the reader knows that this is never going to happen. The basic ideal is the same: somewhere, as hidden from mortal view as divine providence itself, there is a perfect order of merit, and the hero ranks high.

The visible state of affairs is considerably less perfect. Mike is sandbagged on a farm club, his upward progress blocked, in violation even of the basic restraint of trade that governs player movement in organized ball. When he brings his case before the commissioner, he delivers a scathing critique of the system: "You tie up ballplayers like they were real estate. The rules limit you to forty, but you buy up ball clubs that net you control over four or five hundred" (200). Both law and equity are on Mike's side. "The man belongs in the majors and the rules are written to see that he gets a chance," screams the commissioner (203). Nevertheless another factor only partially detachable from law and equity is against him: the nature of the sport's whole organization as a patriarchal family. The commissioner's role as grandfatherly arbiter requires him to hear the case of the rebellious son but ultimately to rule on the side of the owner-father.

> Baseball must remain a game and the baseball world a big family, whose house he would keep in order.
> It seemed, now, that Mike Kutner would have to become an obedient son. (206)

There is no room for sentiment in the business of baseball, as everyone from Spike Russell to Roy Hobbs knows very well. Nevertheless, when a baseball player tries to read the authorities their own unsentimental riot act, their final line of defense is to dissolve business entirely in sentiment. Baseball is suddenly a game again, where merit and meritocracy vanish in the freedom of child's play. When it suits the rulers of the game, the club is a family where love and mutual sacrifice, not the cold relations of merit and reward, determine interpersonal relations.

Faced with this maddeningly shifting context, Mike changes the way he plays. He starts to dive histrionically for batted balls. His wife "Laura watched him, knowing he had learned to dramatize these rolling catches. Years ago he would have rolled with the catch and jumped right up. Now she speculated whether he was prepared to admit this piece of crowd-teasing artifice for what it was, even to himself" (213). Laura's deconstruction of Mike's ambitions is his final disillusionment. Accepting her own role in the patriarchy as baseball wife, Laura has always implicitly supported Mike's career. As he reaches his midthirties, washed up as a big-league prospect, unable to provide a stable home life for her, she summarizes the results of his lifelong faith in meritocracy:

> "Lots of guys are good and don't make out. Not only in baseball, Mike . . . in everything. Show me where there are guarantees. I've never seen any. Don't you see? You have to be *more* than good. You have to be lucky; you have to be a bootlicker, or part your hair the way some dumb manager likes it. You're none of them, Mike. You're just good, and that's not enough!"
>
> "You're wrong, Laura." His voice was subdued. "You've got to be wrong." (222)

She is not wrong. Given his final chance to make the big leagues, he strikes out in his crucial at-bat.

Mike's failures are inevitable, because by trying to avoid kids' books' clichés, his story lands in adult books' clichés. By so relentlessly inverting every part of the children's story, *Man on Spikes* critiques the apologia for meritocracy that the children's baseball story so cheerfully undertakes. This is no children's matter, the novel keeps reminding us. Mike, whose conflicted relationship with his father has been a driving force behind his pursuit of athletic success, finds himself at the end of the story bargaining with Laura's body for the attention of Clark Mellon, a club executive: "Clark Mellon, the bedroom scout. Line up, ladies, one at a time. Get your husbands a big-league job. Only AA and AAA wives eligible. The best lay wins" (239). Mike's batting average, his class status, and the sheer attractiveness of his mate unite in a kind of social Darwinist profile of his evolutionary advantages.

Ballfield merit is ultimately only one of many things that adult baseball fiction speaks of in evolutionary and eugenic parables. Success at the game is not just a metaphor for success in life; it is directly connected to social, sexual, economic, and dynastic success. When George Wallace takes his friend Judith to the ball game in *The Sun Field*, her attraction to the game and to its star, Tiny Tyler, carries with it a strong odor of social Darwinism. Judith is an upper-class WASP, like George. She is keenly aware that in her social circle, antifeminist prejudice interferes with her intellectual career, yet her underlying "female" instincts run counter to her overt feminist rhetoric. Deep down, Judith wants to breed children for a supremely qualified male, because that is the eugenic route to ultimate success. She implicitly resents the weakness of men like George who allow her even partially to succeed in their effete world. Even though she knows that men unfairly hold her back at work, she believes in a meritocracy of brute sexual appeal. Competing with George in an idle smoking contest, she says: "If a woman succeeds at law they say she has a mind like a man; if she writes a good book they call it 'virile' and now I find I'm blowing rings like a man. It almost tempts me to have a baby and then there won't be any fool to say I did it almost as well as a man" (Broun 53). She then tells George, "The father of my child, the fathers of all my children, must be able to blow rings better than I can" (53). George cannot, so Judith loves George but will never mate with him; Darwinian sexual selection leads her to mate with Tiny.

In this contest of sexual selection, Judith is participant, judge, and prize. Her unique status both grants and denies her power: she lacks the penis that would let her into men's intragender competition, and she possesses skills and qualifications to judge that are forever denied men in intergender competition. Emotionally, affectively, the different roles and registers of the competition become confused in the participants' minds (not least in the weird fantasy of working-class reproductive potency that troubles George and troubles apologists for eugenics generally).

So it is with competition and social Darwinism in all spheres of American society. Basic definitions and basic distinctions become blurred by emotion, political interest, and even irruptions of common sense. The ideology of merit is so basic in America that one rarely examines or analyzes its claims. Only when discourse about meritocracy becomes starkly political does it become visible enough for debate. The baseball fiction studied here is one such highlighting of ideologies of merit; another stark political example is the mid-

1990s debate over race, genetics, and intelligence catalyzed by Richard J. Herrnstein and Charles Murray's book *The Bell Curve* (1994).

The connection between baseball writing and *The Bell Curve* goes beyond the Lacanian conjunction of language that allows Stephen Jay Gould to title his review of the book "Curveball." The social mechanisms that led to the development of intelligence testing in the early twentieth century led in the realm of baseball to elaborate statistical analyses. The need to fit large numbers of recruits into graded training levels, the need to defend white upper-class privilege against immigrants and racial minorities by means of "objective" techniques of measuring merit, and the need to improve organizational efficiency through time study and eugenics have all combined to drive pseudoscientific distortions of testing (Gould, *The Mismeasure of Man*). They also combine, rather more innocently, to drive the recordkeeping and interpretation of baseball achievements.

In fact, however, although the forces driving baseball's statistical analyses may be more innocent than are those behind the more general tests of human abilities, nothing is innocent here. The validation of the meritocracy has perhaps nowhere been better reinforced than in over a century of newspaper batting and pitching statistics, from the agate type in the Sunday paper to the 1990s Internet website. With the extreme incentives for employing the best ballplayers come meritocratic methods for identifying the best ballplayers. Baseball statistics are nearly as old as baseball rules; the 1858 New York–Brooklyn box score includes such arcana as the average number of pitches per inning and the number of balls caught on the fly or on the first bounce (both types counted as outs in those days [Sullivan, *Early Innings* 29]). The statistics grew up with the game and remain part of its pedantry and its poetry.

> It is not just baseball that these numbers, through a fractured mirror, describe. It is character. It is psychology, it is history, it is power, it is grace, glory, consistency, sacrifice, courage, it is success and failure, it is frustration and bad luck, it is ambition, it is overreaching, it is discipline. And it is victory and defeat, which is all that the idiot unconscious really understands. . . . How else can one explain the phenomenon of baseball cards, which is that a chart of numbers that would put an actuary to sleep can be made to dance if you put it on one side of a card and Bombo Rivera's picture on the other. (James, *Baseball Abstract* 25)

In baseball the numbers tell the real story, and the real story will never be told in the numbers.

The real story is hidden by the numbers because the numbers are only the tip of the iceberg. For every player with a record there are dozens without; their lack of a record, in fact, is the condition for the records themselves. Jack Kapp, bewildered by the success of his brother Arthur's time-study methods in transforming the family business, thinks about the concomitant rationalization of the baseball industry:

> Of the millions of boys who ever put bat to ball, how many had signed a professional contract in . . . fifty years . . . ? Twenty thousand? Of these, how many had advanced even a single stage, let alone to the big leagues, and of each year's rookie crop how many played a second year, or a third? . . . Fewer still found a place in the game when their playing days were done, fewer than two hundred; that was the survival rate out of millions. How long could their fragile celebrity support them once outside the game? . . . They ended as statistics in . . . neatly filed books, mere measurements against today and tomorrow, gravestones. (Greenberg, *The Celebrant* 234)

Yet the numbers then *do* tell the real story, of course, because the real story comes to be what is validated by the numbers, just as the village graveyard validates the beliefs of the living regarding the hereafter. The faith kept in the record book is the faith of the community in a providential meritocracy. If you do not have a batting average, you do not exist.

Baseball provides controlled experimental conditions for a test of social Darwinism. Its teams compete against one another like species in the wild or groups of people in society. Within those groups selection pressures operate on the individuals who compete for roles on the team. The team so constituted maintains its competitive existence in the environment of the league. If it does not meet the minimum requirement of stabilizing selection for the environment, it can become extinct (fold, leave town, or see its niche occupied by other sports or entertainments). Fictional baseball players forge their characters in the cauldron of intrasquad competition much as biological organisms do in the natural environment.[6] This is what the pitcher Castorious tries to teach young Chase Alloway in Zane Grey's *Short-Stop* (1909): "The players on your own team will get after you, abuse you, roast you, blame you for everything, make you miserable, and finally put you off the team. This may seem to you a mean thing. But it's a way of the game. . . . On the field ball-playing is a fight all the time. It's good-natured and it's bitter-earnest. Every man for himself! Survival of the fittest! Dog eat dog!" (109). "The best thing," Castorious adds in a sublime afterthought, "is that the game is square—absolutely square" (109). The naked, violent attrition in *The Short-Stop* can be justified if (and only if) it is absolutely square—utterly true to the impartiality that characterizes evolutionary outcomes in nature.

The problem with this analogy (and with most analogies between society and evolutionary processes in nature) is that evolution is impartial to a fault; not only are its outcomes "careless of the single life," as Tennyson put it, but they do not make sense, either as they happen or in retrospect. As Gould says, "We came this *close* (put your thumb about a millimeter away from your index finger), thousands and thousands of times, to erasure by the veering of history down another sensible channel. Replay the tape a million times . . . and I doubt that anything like *Homo sapiens* would ever evolve again" (*Wonderful Life* 289). Life, in evolutionary terms, resembles Laura Kutner's worldview far more than it does Castorious's: some guys are simply lucky. The agents caught up in natural evolutionary struggle cannot make sense of it as it happens, but human agents in culture *need to* make sense of the unequal distribution of societal rewards, and they clearly have it in their power to reorder the distribution.

A substantial amount of rhetoric is therefore directed by the cultural work of baseball fiction toward making meritocracy seem both natural and reasonable. In Martin Quigley's *Today's Game* (1965) an extremely unlikely convocation of egghead social scientists assembles in the office of manager Barney Mann. They are meeting to learn from the sport (and convey to a cold war audience) what special qualities make American baseball central to the free world. The Soviet delegate is of course gobsmacked at the idea of rewarding better performance more highly: "Winning, I think it is, winning depends your job?" he manages to ask (61). Barney explains that this is true in any business, but an American anthropologist from Chicago demurs: "In business, in government, and in education and research, success is often ambiguous. We do not often know ourselves whether we are succeeding or failing. . . . But in baseball there is no ambiguity. The score and the complete record of the game are recorded instantly and permanently. There is no way to conceal a flaw or to hide a mistake from the multitude of knowledgeable and observant critics, who discuss and debate every tactic and action" (61–62). "We charge admission," Barney admits, "so they've got a right to see what goes on and to complain if they don't like it" (62). The point then becomes lost in a spate of joking, which obscures the great force of what has passed. The Chicago anthropologist is arguing that baseball is artificial, a hothouse environment in the social jungle. Barney maintains that there is perfect correspondence between professional baseball and the larger socioeconomic environment. It is an argument Barney is bound to win, less by the force of logic than by the entire context. The researchers have come to him for answers, the book is about baseball, and his views have a prima facie coherence that is lacking in the rebuttal of "old Chicago U.," which begins to sound like special pleading for the exemption of academic life from the hard realities of meritocratic competition. The ivory tower may confess that its merit procedures are mysterious, but baseball proposes its clinical realities of competition as a model for every other endeavor.

The conversation wanders off onto the issue of platoon baseball. Barney patiently explains how a right-handed batter has an advantage against a left-handed pitcher, as does a left-handed batter against a right-handed pitcher. The explanation is technical, and Barney mixes environmental factors (right-handed batters become accustomed to rare left-handed pitching as they gain experience in the game) with natural arguments from design (it is simply easier for a right-handed batter to see a ball thrown by a left-hander). "Moscow" interrupts impatiently, "We do not come to talk techniques, but ideas" (68). The Russian proposes a question in the form of a statement: "In American professional sports, winning is everything." Barney's answer, inevitably, is "Winning is not everything. . . . It is the only thing" (68), but he immediately repents of this clichéd response. Stirred by his Soviet listener's incomprehension, Barney Mann rhetorically elaborates a definitive justification for the meritocratic spectacle of baseball. It is a gem of a speech, perhaps because it pushes its own banality to the limit:

> I will tell you about a talk I had with a sportswriter this morning. This man said that baseball is to Americans what the theater was to the Greeks in olden days. He said the Greeks came out to see their heroes and gods suffer and sweat in situations familiar to everybody. He said that Americans feel the same way about baseball. They know the players and they know the game, so they come out to see how the

players respond to the challenges of a particular game. But I think he was wrong about one thing. The difference between the Greek theater and American professional baseball is that they played with heroes, and we play with people. I know my players, but I am not sure what they will do, or can do in any game. Baseball is a game that boys play for fun and men play for keeps. Baseball is our living. Our living is a baseball game that we must try to win. There are no tie games in baseball, and there is only one winner. (69-70)

"The simple facts of life" (70) are these: life *is* a game, and someone must lose it.

Put aside for a moment the misstatement "There are no tie games in baseball."[7] Barney Mann replaces logic and common sense with sheer insistence in an astonishing way. Baseball is a spectacle; people come to see it because it is artificial, because it distills reality into a customary form. Yet the very fact that they come to see it makes it real. A culture *is* its carnivals, its stage plays, its sideshows and circuses, yet not all these are identical in cultural value. The spectacle around which *Today's Game* centers the midlife melodrama of its white male protagonist is a zero-sum game, where there must be a winner and a loser, where nothing is done by halves or shared equally.

Need it be said that Barney's team goes on to win its game, after possibly the dullest, most protracted game narrative in the history of fiction? The white, middle-aged middle manager, pulling the strings from the dugout, becomes the hero of this 1960s corporate romance, a Beowulf for the gray-flannel-suit set. Does the narrative even need a hero? "'With all the data available, it would seem to me that a manager could be replaced by a computer in the dugout,' said Dr. Southern California. 'You could give the computer all the data on the alternatives and let it work out your problem'" (65). Barney dismisses the notion, pointing to his noggin as "The only machine I've got." But why not use a computer? If the decisions to be made are so clear-cut, if the success or failure and the percentages and probabilities thereof are so starkly outlined, if, as one of the eggheads puts it, "There is probably no form of competitive human endeavor on which there are such complete data as baseball" (64-65), why not turn it over to a machine?

The fantasy of the machine that makes decisions is both seductive and feared. It is just such a machine that gives "The Great White Father" Ellsworth Pippin his limitless power in *Sometimes*

You See It Coming. To sign the best ballplayers for his Mets, Pippin has invented the Vacuum.

> This was a system carefully divided into districts balanced by computer analyses of ballplaying demographics per percentage of the population, complete with separate scouts to study every aspect of the game. . . . Which all made its way in the blink of an eye back to New York and the Vacuum, the apex of the whole pyramid, which carefully sifted and balanced it all and within seconds spit out a ranking of each and every prospect in the world, what his percentage chances were of making the major leagues, and how much money he should be offered under current market conditions. (K. Baker 12)

The Vacuum is in part a theatrical gesture; Pippin designs the machinery to look more like "a computer from an old science fiction movie" than is strictly necessary. In fact the idea of a computer that can run an entire human organization is so imposing in its audacity that Pippin signs all the best ballplayers anyway.

That is, he signs all the best players except John Barr; the greatest Met of all (in the story) is signed in a Roy Hobbsian, Shoeless Joe Hardy way out of, well, left field. The story seems to resist its overweening perfect computer. The archetype of the Vacuum can exist only in the fiction that most completely dispenses with the human element: the baseball fiction in which there are no ballplayers at all, Robert Coover's *Universal Baseball Association, Inc., J. Henry Waugh, Prop.* (1971).

Coover's book is one of the most critically admired baseball novels, one that occasionally works its way onto syllabuses of the contemporary novel in general. It is a reflexive novel, one in which the main character writes a book. It can therefore be read as a postmodern cousin of the novels by writers such as John Barth and William Gaddis. It has been read as being about perfectionism (Candelaria), history and metahistory (Messenger), pastoral and antipastoral (Mount), play (Berman), myth (Westbrook), and even the impossibility of determinate meaning (Wineapple), and it is about all those things, much as Coover's Nixon novel *The Public Burning* is about all those things. I read the novel as being about the political fantasies of meritocracy, and mine is a partial reading of a rich work. It is also a reading that seeks to draw the postmodern reflexive novel itself back into the sphere of responsible cultural work—to hold it, for all its technical twistiness, accountable for its ideals and its values.

There is nevertheless a great deal of truth to Brenda Wineapple's contention that *The Universal Baseball Association* avoids meaning by critiquing the notion of fiction. The text is notoriously hard to interpret; the whole text is an allegory of God the Father and the Messiah, but as Michael Oriard points out in *Dreaming of Heroes,* "it is . . . impossible to determine who is the Messiah" (238). J. Henry Waugh, the main character, who creates the Universal Baseball Association (UBA) out of dice and paper, is clearly the Hebrew God, but the text refuses to reveal much beyond that correspondence. Damon Rutherford, star pitcher in Henry's imaginary league, throws a perfect game—and is killed by a pitch in his next start. His killer, Jock Casey, is killed in turn, but not by an accident of the dice; Henry kills him deliberately. It seems simple enough on the face of it that Damon should be the devil (*daimon*) and Jock Casey should be Jesus Christ (note the initials), but Henry loves Damon, even tries to become Damon, and seems to have only an accidental relationship to Jock. In the novel's fantastic final chapter, moreover, Jock and Damon have become culture heroes in a weird ritual that may be Easter, something out of *The Wicker Man,* or both, their deaths ritually reenacted during every UBA season.

I focus here less on the text's mythological and theological resonances and more on the mechanisms by which J. Henry Waugh plays his game. Henry, a bookkeeper who hates his job with the firm of Dunkelmann, Zauber, and Zifferblatt,[8] has become addicted to games: specifically, dice-driven solitaire simulation games. The games are dice-driven because he wants to distance himself from the events of the game and to avoid predestinating their outcome; they are solitaire because he cannot find a partner or opponent who has the dedication to play the games with him. Henry's games simulate organized systems of human endeavor and are populated by realistic characters; most precious of them all to Henry is the Universal Baseball Association. "Not the actual game so much—to tell the truth, real baseball bored him—but rather the records, the statistics, the peculiar balances between individual and team, offense and defense, strategy and luck, accident and pattern, power and intelligence. And no other activity in the world had so precise and comprehensive a history, so specific an ethic, and at the same time, strange as it seemed, so much ultimate mystery" (45).

The game Henry plays is not much different from the kinds of dice baseball games that have been in print for decades (and for some reason seem so lifeless when translated to the computer). Players are represented by cards or charts, with outcomes of plays represented by dice rolls. The charts are designed so that random multiple dice rolls over the course of a "game" or "season" produce statistics much like those that players might compile in the same span of play. If you have a card that generates Lou Gehrig's lifetime statistics, then over ten thousand "at-bats" your Gehrig card will make about 3,400 "hits," to match the real Gehrig's lifetime batting average of .340. Over a limited trial of only a hundred at-bats, the card might get 50 hits or only 15; one's virtual Gehrig is in a streak or a slump. These random fluctuations make the game fun.

If the game includes injuries (in Henry's "these occurred with a dice roll of 3-3-3 on all nine of the basic charts" [54]), this virtual Lou Gehrig will never be injured, because in real life, he never was. Neither will he ever get Lou Gehrig's disease, however, and here is the subtle difference between the dice games on the market and Henry's imaginary game. Gehrig is not famous because he hit .340 or even because he played in seven World Series; he is famous because he played every day till he walked off the field a dying man, because he looked like Gary Cooper and was played by Cooper in a movie, and because his dignified maturity on the field so wonderfully offset the Rabelaisian extravagance of Babe Ruth, the garrulous self-satire of Lefty Gomez, and the callow beauty of the young Joe DiMaggio.

Henry's players are like that: they have personalities. Their personalities matter far more to him than their numbers do, yet their personalities as well as their numbers are generated by the fall of the dice. Henry's players are not fixed. They age; they learn skills that later fade; they have career trajectories, including sudden injuries and deaths; they participate in extraordinary occurrences; and they beget children who carry their names on in the game. The only push Henry gives the dice is his initial act of naming. He is as much Adam as God here; for him, the name is crucial:

> Now, it was funny about names. All right, you bring a player up from the minors, call him A. Player A, like his contemporaries, has, being a Rookie, certain specific advantages and disadvantages with the dice. But it's exactly the same for all Rookies. You roll, Player A gets a hit or he doesn't, gets his man out or he doesn't. Sounds simple. But call Player A "Sycamore Flynn" or "Melbourne Trench" and something starts to happen. He shrinks or grows, stretches out or puts on muscle.

Sprays singles to all fields or belts them over the wall. . . . Not easy to tell just how or why. (47)

But it is easy to tell why the game has not become a franchising spin-off from Coover's novel. It places too great an Adamic responsibility on its proprietor. Its "ballplayers" are real human characters, but they have no existence other than an actuarial one. It is as if human nature were finally solved, by sociobiology, behaviorism, or psychometrics, and found to be no more than a set of probabilities, more opaque than most, but explicable by nonlinear equations and the dimensions of complex systems.

If we could develop a science of it from the inside, the game would be like discovering the occult dimensions of God's hidden providence—or, to put it in 1990s terms, like mapping the human genome. The genome project, from the point of view of those eager to draw social conclusions from its data, is akin to a reconstruction of the hidden player card that determines our success in the UBA of life. For the players in the final chapter of the novel, such a science is as yet impossible; the only routes to truth are mystical and involve a spiritual rejection of analysis: "Casey, in his writings, has spoken of a 'rising above the rules,' an abandonment of all conceptualizations, including scorekeepers, umpires, Gods in any dress, in the heat of total mystic immersion in that essence that includes God and him equally" (240). To the reader, on the outside, the actions of these distant descendants of the original Damon and Casey are revealed as no more than the sum of a number of throws of dice. God *does* play dice with the universe.

And God/Henry writes it all down. Most intriguing of all the features of the game is the Book, Henry's permanent ledger of the history of the UBA.

> It consisted of some forty volumes, kept in shelves built into the kitchen wall, along with the permanent record books, league financial ledgers, and the loose-leaf notebooks of running life histories. He seemed to find more to write about, the more he played the game. . . . Into the Book went the whole UBA, everything from statistics to journalistic dispatches, from seasonal analyses to general baseball theory. Everything, in short, worth keeping. Style varied from the extreme economy of factual data to the overblown idiom of the sportswriter, from the scientific objectivity of the theoreticians to the literary speculations of essayists and anecdotalists. (55)

On one level Henry's Book is clearly the Bible; on another, it is any shelf of Great Books; on another, it is the core belief of meritocracy. Somewhere in black and white is the record of everything, the encyclopedia, the Hall of Fame, the library of Babel. *Everything* is in the Book, but the people whose lives are described there cannot read it for themselves. Their search to discover the Book's totality, its centrality, is like the search Casaubon makes in *Middlemarch* for the "Key to all Mythologies." For late twentieth-century America, the key to all mythologies would be the key to merit.

The Book conceals as much as it reveals, for it requires continuous interpretation to make its meanings available. Like the correlations between IQ and "achievement" so dear to the authors of *The Bell Curve*, the real statistical sources of human achievement in the UBA are not evident to the players themselves; it would not occur to anyone that they existed if no expert pointed them out. "Functional details of the game were never mentioned—team analyses, for example, never referred to Stars and Aces except metaphorically, and, intentionally, erred slightly" (56). The Book hides the "true" records. Henry, like any good dishonest accountant, keeps two sets of books.

The pliability of merit makes it duplicitous. In baseball the brain trust of coaches, managers, and scouts has the only immediate access to the priestly knowledge of merit. They can read the indicators of merit that never make it into the Book. Alternatively, as in the case of Mike Kutner, they can fail to, for their decisions are frequently inscrutable. In the larger society psychometric experts take it on themselves to interpret the huge mass of variables that constitutes any individual's statistical profile, a mass so complicated that its central meaning becomes clear only through the operations of factor analysis.

The Bell Curve: Intelligence and Class Structure in American Life (1994), by Richard J. Herrnstein and Charles Murray, is the Book of meritocratic theory. It reads for all the world like a fantastic elaboration of the Universal Baseball Association into society at large. Like Henry's books, *The Bell Curve* is duplicitous, even in a morally neutral sense, for it is divided into text and appendices and further divided into technical and nontechnical text, as the authors are at pains to acknowledge right away: "We have designed *The Bell Curve* to be read at several levels" (xix). These levels correspond to degrees of initiation into the arcane truths of the text; they also correspond, in a disturbing way, to their implied readers' own merit, as expressed in the IQ level needed to understand the technical sophistication of the given textual level.

The Bell Curve has also been accused by its harsher critics of duplicitousness at worst and disingenuousness at best. According to some reviewers its authors "seem unwilling to admit the consequences of their own words" (Gould, "Curveball" 14) and are "blind to both contradictory evidence and the human consequences of their own work" (Gardner 34–35). I suggest that *The Bell Curve* shares an even greater duplicity with cultural constructions of baseball in general and with much baseball fiction in particular. It provokes controversy about how merit should be identified in American culture, without ever opening for question the principles of meritocracy.

By deferring any debate about meritocracy in favor of a controversy about the hidden essence of merit, *The Bell Curve* makes meritocracy all the stronger as an ideology. Even its critics find themselves debating the correctness and precision of the methods or the scope of the claims made in the book rather than arguing the basic morality of assigning social and economic rewards to people on the basis of their perceived worth. Of the widely published reviews of *The Bell Curve,* only Alan Wolfe's seriously takes issue with its depiction of a meritocratic America. Moreover Wolfe does so only to assert that America is *not* a meritocracy (but should be) and that Herrnstein and Murray's book is ultimately not meritocratic but racist, bent on reviving a vision of America along the antimeritocratic lines of caste privilege.

Wolfe finds unrealistic Herrnstein and Murray's picture of America as increasingly divided into classes by cognitive ability. Although such a picture is clearly a fantasy, it is a fantasy to which many of *The Bell Curve*'s critics aspire as an ideal. They would simply draw different lines than Herrnstein and Murray do; they would draw them along less clichéd boundaries, they would draw them in a color-blind way, or they would use better tests and more holistic evaluations of individual desert.

In Herrnstein and Murray's view Americans who are poor deserve to be, for the United States has in the 1990s become a perfect engine of meritocratic reward. "As affluence spread, people who escaped from poverty were not a random sample of the population. When a group shrinks from over 50 percent of the population to the less than 15 percent that has prevailed since the late 1960s, the people who are left behind are likely to be disproportionately those who suffer not only bad luck but also a lack of energy, thrift, farsightedness, determination—and brains" (129). The text does not offer any particular evidence for this assertion. It simply proceeds from certain axiomatic assumptions. First, there is a quality called "g," first proposed by Charles Spearman in the early twentieth century, which is the underlying determinant of success on mental tests (including IQ tests). G cannot be measured directly (in this it resembles the Cat in the Hat's Little Cat Z: "Z is too small to see. So don't try. You can not" [Seuss 55]). It can be measured only as a statistical effect, the "loading" of many kinds of correlations from many tests on different equational axes in factor analysis. G is *so* hard to measure, in fact, that Spearman was forced to invent factor analysis just to do so.

In one sense factor analysis is just pure mathematics; in another, it is a system that makes the invisible visible and gives it the appearance of reality.[9] Statisticians name the axes of their factor analyses arbitrarily, like mathematical Adams, so that a mathematical fact several layers of abstraction deep can emerge into everyday discourse with a name like g, short for "general intelligence" (Herrnstein and Murray 3). Once posited, g is given extensive powers to explain and cause: "the predictive power of tests for job performance lies almost completely in their ability to measure the most general form of cognitive ability, g, and has little to do with their ability to measure aptitude or knowledge for a particular job" (75).

According to this line of thought, then, a test for performance in any job will reduce to a test for g, which is the secret ingredient of all success. G is the determinant of differential success within jobs and of differential sorting of people into different kinds of jobs; high-g jobs are highly rewarded, and so society can be sorted into cognitive losers and winners. The higher your g, the less chance you have of being poor (this "logical" implication turns 180 degrees around in *The Bell Curve,* so that the authors can present tables showing that black people are poor—e.g., pp. 331-39—with the unspoken conclusion that they must be dumb too).

Finally, g is heritable and genetic, and the average g of white people is higher than that of black people. Affirmative action, race norming, and any preferential treatment for historically disadvantaged minorities hence show a refusal to face the facts of intelligence and are disastrously inefficient and morally wrong as public policy. It is extraordinarily difficult to catch *The Bell Curve* actually saying any of that, but that is the inexorable drive of its argument: "White children of dull women will, on average, be closer to the mean for whites in *their* generation than their mothers were in *their* generation. A parallel statement applies to black children of dull black women. But this does not necessarily imply that the IQ scores of black and white children must be closer to each other than their mothers' IQ scores were" (357). Fair enough, mathematically, but the text resists stating the implication: that white people are on the average really smarter than black people, smarter inherently, eternally, and irredeemably. The success of the white races has finally been located by Herrnstein and Murray not in historical accident but in biological law.

This position is speciously reconcilable with a perfectly color-blind meritocracy. "We cannot think of a legitimate argument why any encounter between individual whites and blacks need be affected by the knowledge that an aggregate ethnic difference in measured intelligence is genetic instead of environmental" (313). Of course, the future that *The Bell Curve* proposes will be one where highly rewarded key positions just happen to be filled, and deservedly so, almost entirely by white people, so perfect will be sorting by *g*; a future where black people, happy in the realization of their own inadequacy, cheerfully give up all ambition for a better life and adopt the roles of neighborhood idiots.

Recognition of individual differences in merit has scarcely slowed racism, of course; it has merely created a different kind of racism in integrated milieus in America. Mike Kutner is well established as a minor leaguer when organized baseball integrates, but he then finds himself in a desperate, losing struggle to make the majors against his teammate Ben Franks, a black man. "Up in Chicago [general manager] Jim Mellon had his eyes on Brooklyn, shifting from the gate receipts to Robinson's ability and back to the gate receipts" (Asinof 161). Ben is a much better player than Mike and will help his club win, but Mike sees their competition as unfairly linked only to an opportunistic appeal to black fans. He tells Ben: "I was due to go up because I've fought for it and deserve it. Then you come along and I get shoved over" (169).

There in a nutshell, and not in any revelation of the nature of *g*, is the whole argument of the white worker against affirmative action. Shifting the terms of merit away from ability and toward general moral desert, he claims that he deserves to have his previous expectations fulfilled. The appearance of the black job candidate (who has clearly "fought for" the job every bit as much as the white one) is in itself a betrayal of the white man's "privilege" (for that seems to be the only way to describe it).

It is easy to see why even a societal consensus that g exists, can be measured, and is heritable would not allay but intensify such feelings of white privilege and white self-pity. What is perhaps harder to see is that the system and ideals of meritocracy itself, not just its betrayals, are the causes of such virulent suspicion and hatred. Alan Wolfe, in a searing critique of *The Bell Curve*, asks "What is so wrong with the idea that a society should distribute its scarce resources based on merit?" (120). He challenges the book for breaking faith with meritocratic ideals. These ideals might be expressed best in a statement like the following one, from the book that coined the word *meritocracy:*

> Why has society been so stable in spite of the widening gulf between the bottom and the top?
> The cardinal reason is that stratification has been in accord with a principle of merit, generally accepted at all levels of society. . . . Since bottom agrees with top that merit should reign, they can only cavil at the means by which the choice has been made, not at the standard which all alike espouse. (M. Young 123-24)

This straightforward condensation of the meritocratic ideal is the soul of irony; like everything else in Michael Young's 1958 dystopian fantasy, it means the reverse of what it says.

Young invented the term *meritocracy*—now part of the common language, so that his book is uncited in *The Bell Curve* and in most commentary on it—to critique antisocialist ideologies in postwar Britain, where the initial dedication of Labour governments and the consensus welfare state to an equal distribution of resources in British society was being eroded by ideologies of merit. Merit, in Young's analysis, is basically class privilege dressed up in different garb. Young's alternatives to meritocracy would appall any believer in g: "The trouble started when the left wing emphasized a different interpretation of equality, and, ignoring differences in human ability, urged that everyone, those with talent as well as those without, should attend the same schools and receive the same basic education" (41). Too horrific to contemplate. For some of Young's contemporaries (and for many of ours, of course), it *was* too horrific to contemplate. Young quotes Eric James, high master of Manchester Grammar School in 1951 (this quotation is a real one, from James's *Education for Leadership*): "The demand for such a common culture rests either on an altogether over-optimistic belief in the educability of the majority that is certainly not justified by experience or on a willingness to surrender the highest standards of taste and judgement to the incessant demands of mediocrity" (50). Meritocracy is here linked intimately with an aesthetic based on "taste and judgment." The link is familiar, of course—so familiar that one may not even notice that neither merit nor taste is an inevitable value.

And what *would* be wrong, finally, with distributing the good life according to merit—supposing that any basis for sorting people by merit could ever be found? Meritocracy is wrong because unequal distribution of resources produces envy. If I have more or better of something than you do, you will resent my having it. In addition I will want to hold onto it despite any merit on your part. In Michael Young's meritocracy the system collapses when the cognitive elite try by all means to transfer their privileges to their lower-IQ children. Equality (to use phrases dear to sound-biters) is finally never equality of opportunity alone; true equality is equality of *result*. Equality of result has been banished from American political discourse, however. To suggest it is to risk anathema (true anathema, not the sense of pique displayed in *The Bell Curve* when it claims that its investigations are stigmatized as politically incorrect).

Even Iris Marion Young's *Justice and the Politics of Difference* (1990), the most thoroughgoing recent critique of "the myth of merit," is reluctant to critique merit so directly. Her critique of meritocracy is based almost entirely on faulting the methods that are used to determine merit: "Use of a principle of merit to allocate scarce and desirable positions in a job hierarchy, and in the educational institutions that train people for those jobs, is just only if several conditions are met" (201). The conditions are culture-neutrality, a limit to technical competence, strict adherence to job-related criteria, and individual rather than group discrimination. Since meeting even these conditions is a meritocrat's pipe dream given the differences that historically and culturally divide our society, Young advocates instead a democratic apportioning of jobs and rewards and a participatory workplace.

Nonetheless, not even in Young's conditions or in her attractive notion of a democratic workplace is the basic equation challenged: that the reward of labor should be determined by market conditions. Certain jobs will apparently always be "scarce" and "desirable," a virtual tautology. Scarce jobs are in demand, they pay more, and people want them, and the cycle thus reinforces itself. (Except it should not work like that: if scarce jobs are in demand, people should want to do them for less or even for *free*. This is part of the reason that professions where jobs are truly scarce, like movie acting and professional baseball, now have the strongest remaining unions in America—one protects very strongly a job that others really would do "for free").[10] By Iris Young's reasoning it should be very difficult to recruit people to take tickets at the movie theater or stand behind a convenience store counter at 3 A.M., yet these jobs are rarely unionized, are pitifully rewarded, and are always filled. The reality is that people do not demand *jobs*; they demand the pay they need to live. Electing law school candidates or shopfloor foremen does not change the basic inequities of reward in the workplace or the fact that the winners live better than the losers.

The wonder is that people stand for inequities of reward. The unequal reward of effort and talent in our society is defended and justified only by the constant maintenance of cultural work. The availability of sports as an analogue to (or allegory for) the more general workplace in American society is a major underpinning of the meritocratic ideal. Business success is sold in terms of winning at sports. The ideologies of *The Bell Curve* depend on justifying testing as an indicator of merit. As Iris Young explains, such tests—IQ, "aptitude," and other psychological tests—tend, oddly enough, to impress people more the further the tests are from testing knowledge or skills directly related to a job or a school opening.

> Employers and school officials have put so much weight on tests because they seem to offer a means of satisfying two of the requirements of merit evaluation . . . a precise measure of the competence of each individual, and a comparison or ranking of all individuals. Tests appear to satisfy the merit principle's demand that persons be rewarded according to their own individual achievement. Because they are universalized and standardized, however, the individuality of test results is illusory. Through the process that Foucault calls normalization, tests produce the reconstituted individuality of a "case" or "score." (209)

The Verbal SAT of 800, the IQ of 125, the GPA of 3.96—what are all these "reconstituted individualities" but a fantastic sociological echo of techniques first applied to professional athletes? Those numbers resonate with the same kind of associations as .406, 61, or 190.

Through use of what one might call the sabermetric model—after the Society for American Baseball Research, or SABR, which has promoted much statistical research on baseball—one set of numbers, "raw," "biased," or "apparent" numbers, is transmuted into a single number that crystallizes individual achievement and potential. In book after book recent baseball writers have tried to compute the single statistic that would crystallize the total individual ballplayer and make possible a linear ranking of baseball greatness "depictable as a single number, capable of ranking people in a linear order," as Gould says of g ("Curveball" 12). Thorn and Palmer have their "Total Player Rating"; Robert E. Kelly has his PAB number; A.W. Laird has his single rating number; and Bill James lists others: "DX . . . total average . . . Linear Weights" (*Historical Abstract* 445). These single numbers, as elusive and unreliable as g itself, are hardly a trivial pursuit. They are a manifestation of faith in something unseen but fervently wished for and stubbornly cherished—the Final Average, the Number of Life.

When Henry Waugh wants to preserve the brilliance of Damon Rutherford's rookie year in the UBA, he thinks:

> The smart thing would be to baby Damon through the remaining fifteen or twenty innings he needed, pitching him against weaker teams, using him in one-inning relief stints in which, according to the rules, he would pitch as an Ace, so as to make sure he made that all-important leap next year, without which no great career was possible. . . . So why shouldn't [manager] Bancroft do it, why shouldn't he baby him? Because Barney Bancroft didn't know what Henry knew. He didn't know about the different charts. He didn't even know about Aces and why it was the good ones often stayed good over the years. Of course, he must have sensed it, they all did: that peculiar extra force that these great players seemed to radiate. (Coover 39)

Merit, value, the nature of art, literary quality, g, and the content of one's character all come together in the relation of Barney Bancroft to Henry Waugh. All of them are displacements of a responsibility to deal with people in person onto the theological belief that

Someone Somewhere knows what the real statistics are. In the name of that transcendent "peculiar extra force," we draw some of the most divisive lines across our society.

Notes

1. Koufax, the greatest pitcher of the 1960s, batted .097 over his entire career.

2. Cricket, where both the rules and the length of first-class matches dictate rotation of bowlers and fielders and where defensive positioning is more flexible, is probably a good analogue to this early labor situation in baseball. First-class cricketers do specialize, but some stars are still all-around players, able to bat, bowl, and field with skill.

3. Cordelia Candelaria says of early baseball: "Its emergence in the United States as a formal leisure activity for gentlemen provides historical precedent for the racial and gender exclusivity of the modern organized sport. Racism and sexism pervade society regardless of class, of course, but baseball's particular social biases correspond, at least symbolically, to its original overt classism" (13–14). Candelaria's point may be partially true, for early clubs did not include the true urban industrial proletariat. Neither were they exclusively for gentlemen, however. Research by Goldstein, Sullivan, and others (see especially Harold Seymour's *Baseball: The People's Game* 215–17) indicates that the early game flourished among skilled workers and tradesmen. The ideal of the amateur baseball player has more to do with workers' relations to their earned leisure than with gentlemen's exemptions from all work.

4. The whole institution, ensuring that the best players at each level are siphoned into the next higher level and that the worst fall or fail, resembles nothing so much as Thomas Jefferson's pyramidic system for education as proposed in his *Notes on the State of Virginia.* Jefferson proposed a system of lower schools that would feed their best students to grammar schools, which would in turn feed their best students to colleges. His was the original plan for a farm system.

5. It seems not to interfere with the plot of this novel that Vernon succeeds by throwing a spitball; however magical his methods, he is cheating by the plain rules of baseball.

6. The concern with teamwork in baseball rhetoric is parallel to socio-biological concerns with group selection. In each case the success of the individual is related uncertainly to the success of the team (or species). For a technical survey, see Donna Haraway, *Primate Visions*, especially 213; for a general overview, see Roger Lewin, "Evolution's New Heretics."

7. "Any regulation game called due to weather with the score tied . . . is a tie game" (*Official Baseball Rules* 4.12b). This situation comes about a few times every season and used to occur more frequently in the days before domed stadiums and modern drainage systems. The 1908 Merkle game was a tie.

8. Dark Man, Magic, and Clock Face; nearly every name in the novel means something outrageous.

9. There are many legitimate uses of factor analysis; its main use is "as an aid in conceptualization" (Gorsuch 2). Herrnstein and Murray misuse it by uncritically seeing factor loadings as actual biological properties.

10. The persistence of the tenure system in American education may be a weird form of unionization. (Sometimes tenure is linked to strong teachers' unions.) Many people would teach for free, especially in a university; some untenured and nonunionized adjuncts virtually *do* teach for free. In addition to protecting academic freedom, tenure makes the profession possible by safeguarding work against its own desirability.

5

But Is It Literature?

· ·

Some baseball fiction is obviously literary. Start with *The Natural*; if *The Natural* is not literature, it is nothing at all. Even if it is not *good* literature, it has generic qualities that prevent critics from placing it in any other category. It is symbolic, intertextual, archetypal, portentous, and ambitious. What it lacks in high seriousness, it more than makes up for in irony, and for a novel published in the 1950s, irony is the academic literary value par excellence. One can more easily make the case that *The Natural* is not about baseball (the sport in the novel bears little resemblance to the real thing, as Gerry O'Connor notes) than the case that it is not literary. In fact one senses that *The Natural* becomes literature precisely as it leaves baseball behind, that it can approach literature only by ceasing to be a sports story.

The lines that adjectives such as *symbolic* and *intertextual* draw around the category "literature" are not inevitable ones. There is no way of deducing where literature must begin and end, and the definition of the literary is always debated among authors, academic critics, publishers, reviewers, and general readers. To read the cultural work of genre fiction, one needs a map of how criticism in the broadest sense has defined literature and discriminated among genres and parts of genres, allowing some works into the category of the literary and excluding others.

An objection to this theoretical project might be that the distinction between the literary and the nonliterary is no longer useful or interesting for criticism—that it maintains a false distinction from the past that would be better off unexamined. A general agreement to abolish the distinction between the literary and nonliterary and not to consider the matter any further would quiet the canon debate and open up large fields of material for literary and cultural criticism. There are plenty of things for which the question "Is it literature?" is impertinent: Krazy Kat, L=A=N=G=U=A=G=E poetry, the drama of Ethyl Eichelberger, the TV of Ernie Kovacs, the books of Robert James Waller. When these artifacts are studied in English departments by professors and students of literature, they are given the status of having their status held in abeyance—which is one possible definition, as I will show, for the genre "literature" itself. Cultural custodians of many kinds voice profound and widespread objections to such holding in abeyance, but suspended-status status is the norm for the cultural object of late twentieth-century academic criticism.

In the case of genre fiction, however, the suspended sentence of literary or not literary is always being executed, and every new work does its own plea bargaining. Texts published as works of genre fiction are sometimes granted a quasi-literary status with the remote possibility of someday getting full literary status. The vast majority of genre novels never break out of their initial assignment. They are *novels*, but not *real* novels. There nevertheless is always the possibility that the next genre novel that one reads—or rediscovers—will make the jump and become a real, if minor, work of truly literary fiction.

Where do we see this assignment and reassignment? It resides somewhere in the complex interplay among readers, writers, reviewers, adopters for courses or libraries, bookstore managers, and others. This interplay cannot be reduced to a single decisive factor. Someone with or without "literary" ambitions writes a detective novel; reviewers for the "mystery pages" of major book reviews reject its consciously displayed literary ambitions or, perhaps, detect unflaunted ones; a bookstore stocks the novel with "New Fiction" rather than "New Mystery," possibly because of a publisher's marketing strategy; readers are influenced, sometimes crucially, by such things as where in the store they bought the book, on which rack in the library they found it, or the tone taken by the flap copy; a college professor adopts the book, with some apology, for a course in "contemporary fiction" or, with a special qualification as "literary," for a course in "detective fiction"; a publisher decides on a reprint in trade rather than mass-market paperback, perhaps as part of a prestigious list—or does not, allowing the book to settle onto the mystery backlist, competing there with those by powerful series authors for shelf life. A conservative cultural critic wails because undergraduates at Ivy League schools are reading this mystery novel instead of *Death Comes for the Archbishop*, or maybe the novel remains immune from carping of various sorts and becomes first a "coterie," then a "cult," and finally a "mainstream" literary item.

Genre novels that make the jump to literature are often marketed aggressively, providing a rough map to the literary by being contrasted against their nonliterary cousins back in the world of genre fiction. The novels of Patrick O'Brian are a good example. First published in the United States by Lippincott in the early 1970s, with kitschy cover art and pulpy pages, O'Brian's Aubrey/Maturin novels were originally marketed as a routine entry in the wooden-ships and woodener-characters Nelson's Navy genre, a tiny but vigorous subgenre of literature of the sea. Repackaged by Norton in the 1990s, O'Brian's series now appears as a uniform set of exquisitely produced trade paperbacks, their collectability as a series highlighted while the cover blurbs suggest that the novels within have much more in common with Joseph Conrad than they do with Horatio Hornblower.[1] O'Brian wrote in 1995 of this sea change: "Recently I heard (not without a complacent simper) that the best bookshop in America had moved my books across the aisle from Fiction to Literature. It would be a foolish affectation to pretend that the change does not please me or that I do not find a moderately heavy purse more agreeable than one so light that the first breath of crisis would blow it away; but I can place my hand on my heart—both hands, and spread them wide—and assert that it does not affect my writing in any way at all" ("Just a Phase" 3). O'Brian is sharp here about two things: that the shift from fiction to literature can occur without anything changing in the texts themselves and that writing serious literature is not always a guarantee of authorial penury.

The formula for conferring literary status on a genre novel is exemplified by commentary on O'Brian and can be seen repeated in many other genres and authors. The genre as a whole is derided as vulgar or written-out, whereas the example at hand is said to have gone past generic limitations and to have become original, unique, and unpredictable in its literary complexity. Such a move is also risky. Making the work sound too strange alienates genre fans; reaching out to highbrow readers may insult the core readership that has made an author popular. Relying too much on the external trappings of the genre, in terms of art, series identification, and catchphrases, misses an opportunity to interest the "intellectual" reader—as these readers seem to be imagined by the back covers of books, at any rate.

O'Brian notes that his novels have merely been repackaged as literary. There are some experiments in genre fiction, however, that deliberately transcend the formulas of series or archetype and risk breaking a compact with an author's earlier readers. For Raymond Chandler's readers, *The Big Sleep* and *Farewell, My Lovely* established the Philip Marlowe novel; *The Long Goodbye* violated that compact. One senses that *The Long Goodbye* did not violate the compact as much as Chandler would have wanted, for Marlowe fans expanded their horizon of expectations to include *The Long Goodbye* without the repudiation that might have signaled a successful break with a series formula and a leap into the literary. The same impulse is present in Ian Fleming's *Spy Who Loved Me*, a rewriting of the James Bond novel from the point of view of one of the female characters so often silenced and objectified in those novels. This experiment proved to be too much for Hollywood, where only the title of *The Spy Who Loved Me* survived in the routine Roger Moore vehicle.

There are genre authors who seek to remake their entire authorial image rather than heighten the literary profile of their typical work—hence the common pattern of killing, retiring, or otherwise disposing of the series hero: Holmes, Maigret, Bond.[2] Having retired the genre hero, an author is free to write a "serious" novel, as Simenon did with *Le Testament Donadieu* or John LeCarre, putting Smiley on hiatus, did with *The Naïve and Sentimental Lover*. There are analogies in baseball fiction; Mark Harris, after three Henry Wiggen novels in four years (1953-56), sent Henry on a long leave of absence while he wrote nonbaseball fiction, reviving him only for *It Looked Like For Ever* in 1979. The four Wiggen novels are sometimes called a "tetralogy," but they might be better characterized as a series obeying the familiar impulse to break off and move the texts' image over to serious non-genre fiction—as well as the gravitational force a successful series continues to exert even when the series is officially over. Like Jules Maigret, Henry Wiggen proves to be difficult to retire.

Henry Wiggen is virtually the only series hero in adult baseball fiction. Being in a series is almost the definition of being in a genre, because a series implies predictability and formula, the very way we recognize types and kinds. Series publication also forms the most visible link between children's fiction and adult genre fiction, both of which thrive on series. For many reasons, most readers do not perceive baseball fiction as a genre with the same status as detective, espionage, science fiction, or even Nelson's Navy novels. Baseball fiction is a relatively small genre, of course, and it frequently intersects with other genres, especially mystery. Nevertheless a basic primary bibliography of baseball novels would include hundreds of books. Sports fiction in general has a primary bibliography of several hundred texts, many of which are in print at any given time. Yet bookstores do not have sports fiction sections. They have large nonfiction sports sections, where sports novels are sometimes revealingly shelved—although no bookstore manager would want to shelve mysteries in true crime or Westerns in history. The baseball novel is always in danger of disappearing into other genres, a danger I suspect it embraces.

People who play key roles in defining the genre do not see themselves as baseball novelists or as reviewers of baseball novels. Virtually every major baseball novelist is someone who has written only one baseball novel: Philip Roth, Robert Coover, Irwin Shaw, Bernard Malamud, William Kennedy, Don DeLillo, and Michael Shaara are obvious examples. This group is not a bad syllabus for a course in American postmodern fiction, although it may be an excessively white male one. Other examples of the one-baseball-novel author include lesser-known but critically esteemed writers such as Tony Ardizzone, Brendan Boyd, Lamar Herrin, David Carkeet, and Jerome Charyn. The exceptions, Mark Harris and W. P. Kinsella, have published several books of baseball fiction, but the bulk of each author's work is decidedly outside the genre. Most baseball novels give the impression of having been written to get an obsession out of the author's system (Coover's *Universal Baseball Association* or Roth's *Great American Novel*) or the impression of a tour de force in a genre that the author will master once and then back away from (DeLillo's novella "Pafko at the Wall").

Since novelists do not define themselves as "baseball novelists," reviewers of baseball novels are therefore *not* baseball novelists. Baseball novels are published as general fiction and reviewed by the people—general novelists—who review all sorts of nongenre "generic" novels (notice: the generic novel does not belong to any genre). Therefore the genre consciousness that reviewers of science fiction have (for instance) is lacking in most reviews of baseball fiction. It is not, as I have said, a huge genre to begin with. If in your career as a critic you run into a baseball story once in every two or three hundred novels that you read, the idea of a baseball novel will seem, well, *novel;* it will convey the originality that gives any work of literature a special value. At most for general reviewers the genre background for a new baseball novel consists of a couple of texts, usually *Bang the Drum Slowly* and *The Natural.*

The back cover of the August House paperback edition of Rick Norman's *Fielder's Choice* illustrates the point. The Little Rock publishing house promotes the novel with a sampling of critical praise. Kinsella's opinion that it is "this spring's brightest piece of baseball fiction" is featured, but it is balanced by reviews that downplay the genre. *The Plain Dealer* suggests that you will love the book "whether you love baseball more than life itself or would rather watch paint dry"; the *Library Journal* claims that "this is less a baseball story than a story of growing up in difficult times." Several of the critical excerpts do not mention baseball at all, stressing instead the novel's language, its historical detail, or its southernness. This cover is a typical example of how publishers try to sell a genre novel as something more than just a genre novel; what makes the example significant is that this is the way *all* baseball novels are sold. Some genre novels can be sold by making them seem to be the hardcore essence, the "real thing." This ploy is successful when used on mysteries or science fiction, but it is absent from the marketing of baseball fiction.

Lack of genre consciousness goes back to the beginning of "serious" baseball fiction and is almost a condition for its birth. The reception of adult baseball fiction begins with John J. Maloney's review of *The Natural* in the *New York Herald Tribune Book Review* for August 24, 1952.[3] Maloney drew the first line in the sand. He set apart the genre of serious adult baseball fiction, which at the time consisted basically of the one book he was reviewing, from the genre of children's' stories and the associated genre of lowbrow fiction: "Sooner or later, I suppose, some one of our generation had to attempt to write a serious novel about baseball. Certainly those of us who are addicts and are not hopelessly illiterate had long yearned for something a cut or two above the Frank Merriwell sort of pap that gets serialized in some of our more widely circulated magazines." The figure recurs in other discussions of genre fiction— the nonliterary as "pap," "pabulum," baby food. *The Natural* is food for people with their permanent teeth. This distinction is crucial for the status of the novel even though Maloney's is a negative review. He finds the novel "avant-garde" and off-putting, "saddled . . . with all the trappings of the post-Kafka school." It is *bad* literature, for Maloney, but it is *literature.* And that is all that matters.

Only eight months later Herbert Kupferberg could say this in the *Herald Tribune:* "Baseball being such a fascinating sport and sports reporting being such a lively art (at least in theory) it is surprising that so few baseball novels, aside from the juveniles, get written. Except for Ring Lardner's wonderful 'You Know Me Al,' what baseball story can a fan conscientiously recommend?" Of course Kupferberg might not have known of the existence of *The Natural*, and no one at the *Herald Tribune* was under any obligation to get him to consider it. He might not have "recommended" it in any case, but the result is the same. Mark Harris's *Southpaw*, the text being reviewed, becomes in turn the sole adult exception to a juvenile genre. Kupferberg's review is positive ("a clean single to the outfield" ["Trials and Triumphs"]) although somewhat condescending; where Maloney found *The Natural* to be adult to a fault, Kupferberg thinks that *The Southpaw* relies a little too much on familiar kids' formulas: "Does it sound just a little like the old Baseball Joe juveniles?"[4]

In terms of baseball fiction's reception, those are fighting words. It is better for a text to make the cut and become serious general fiction (which is after all nearly always underappreciated by its first reviewers) than to be appreciated only too well and remain locked in a childish genre. Reviews ever after would insist that a literary baseball novel will appeal mainly to readers who do not know baseball. Kupferberg would call *The Year the Yankees Lost the Pennant* "good news to people who can't tell a ball from a strike but who can appreciate a novel that is as fanciful as 'Faust' and a lot funnier" ("Meet Joe Boyd"). The comparison to Goethe is far more powerful than a comparison, even a positive one, to Malamud or Harris.

Do adult baseball novels tend not to follow a predictable formula? Are they really novels that stand out as original and are only incidentally connected to the games' rituals? These reviewers and publicists would be justified if there were nothing connecting one baseball novel to another but the mention of baseball. A rundown of the basic plots of some baseball novels is in order. In most baseball novels the reader follows a team and one or more of its players through a season's play. In *Bang the Drum Slowly* the Mammoths come through adversities to win the World Series, which they win also in the first Mammoth novel, *The Southpaw*. In *Sometimes You See It Coming* the team wins the World Series. In *The Greatest Slump of All Time* they win the World Series. In *The Dreyfus Affair* they lose the World Series, quite a plot twist; Lefcourt's novel is more in the tradition of *The Natural*, where they lose the pennant-clinching game (of course in the film of *The Natural* they win that game, as they win the clinching game in the films *Angels in the Outfield* [both versions], *Rookie of the Year*, and many others). In "Pafko at the Wall" the Giants win the pennant ("The Giants win the pennant!"). In *It Happens Every Spring* the team wins the World Series. In Brendan Boyd's *Blue Ruin* and other Black Sox novels they lose the World Series, but then they were *trying* to lose that World Series, so I suppose, in a twisted way, they win the World Series. In Paul Molloy's *Pennant for the Kremlin* the team loses the World Series; in H. Allen Smith's *Rhubarb* they win the World Series; and in James McManus's *Chin Music* the city of Chicago is destroyed by nuclear weapons *during* the World Series—rather a satisfying outcome after one has read through several dozen other baseball novels.

One can establish a plot archetype for the baseball novel. A team seems to be headed for failure(s) both on and off the field, finds inspiration, blends as a unit, and wins the Big Game for the championship. However unrealistically, the championship in a baseball novel tends to be decided by a single game on the last day of the season. These plots derive directly from young adult series baseball fiction. In John R. Tunis's *Kid from Tomkinsville* the Dodgers win the pennant, and then, in the sequel, *World Series*, wouldn't you know it, they win the World Series. The team is rebuilt in *Keystone Kids*, wins the pennant in *Rookie of the Year*, wins the pennant in *The Kid Comes Back*, wins the pennant in *Highpockets*, loses the World Series in *Young Razzle* (though here one's attention is transferred to a player on the Yankees team that beats them), and wins the pennant in the last of the series, *Schoolboy Johnson*.

In virtually every young adult baseball title a team blends its talents, overcomes conflict and despair, and wins the Big Game. The pattern resonates through adult novels of major-league baseball, minor-league baseball, college baseball, and imaginary baseball (as in Celia Cohen's *Smokey O*, where the Delaware Blue Diamonds win the title in a speculative "Women's Baseball League") into Ellen Cooney's *All the Way Home*, where a group of women in small-town New England shed various individual feelings of purposelessness to come together as a softball team and win the Big Game. (Think too of the film *A League of Their Own*, where the big series, the Big Game, the big inning, the big at-bat, the big pitch, and the big slide keep deferring the conclusion in an almost campy way.) The Big Game archetype is intensified in magical realist baseball novels such as Kinsella's *Iowa Baseball Confederacy*, where the Big Game goes on for forty days and forty nights in Big Inning, Iowa.

Nonetheless the Big Game archetype is one that adult fiction, striving not to seem formulaic, either masks or presents somewhat disingenuously as original. Sometimes the baseball novel recognizes the Big Game archetype only to present it as part of the natural rhythm of narrative itself, as Ricky Falls notes in *Sometimes You See It Coming*: "The last inning of the last game of the World Series. The fastest, meanest pitcher against the best hitter in the game. There was no way you could avoid it in any good story" (K. Baker 316). There are in fact many ways of avoiding it, but to present a plot line as unavoidable can be (as it is here) a way of disguising a deliberate choice of formula as mandatory. If we cannot avoid the last inning of the World Series, then all that seemed trite becomes a setting for originality; all that is optional in the story becomes part of the background without which it cannot exist.

Whereas formula is masked or denied in adult baseball fiction, it is presented with unashamed enthusiasm in juvenile baseball fiction. Young adult baseball novels are built aggressively around the formulas of series writing, and their authors (or corporate author-functions) are identified unabashedly with the recurrences of series writing. Gary Carter, Matt Christopher, the Southside Sluggers, the High Fives, and the various Christian sports series all belong to a genre that is vital, self-aware, and competing for shelf space against other kinds of series while fostering skilled consumers, young readers who develop brand and genre loyalties through these texts.

The adult baseball novel must mask its archetypes precisely because the juvenile novel does so little to hide them. When a reviewer or a publisher assures an adult reader that a baseball novel is much more than mere sports fiction, the assurance means that the novel in question is not a kids' story. Literariness is a guarantee against juvenility in fields far beyond sports literature. Jane Tompkins draws the following distinction between children's and adult Westerns, for instance:

Children's serials, as you might expect, emphasize the hoped for mutuality of the horse-rider arrangement. . . . In adult Westerns it is different. The horse is not a friend won through nurture and gentle suasion, but an occasion for proving the hero's superior strength and cunning. Where some television shows and most B Westerns . . . imagine a peaceable kingdom where all beings gratefully accept their roles after a few bad characters have been expelled, A Westerns posit a kingdom of force and conflict, where humans and animals, men and women, bosses and underlings vie for dominance and define themselves by competing with each other. (100)

Especially important here is how Tompkins seamlessly connects kids' Westerns with TV Westerns and B movies, the culturally low end of the genre. Children are cultural lowbrows, and lowbrows are cultural children.

The adult/child conflict is intensified in sports literature. For one thing, serious adult sports fiction is historically an outgrowth of children's stories (Oriard, *Dreaming of Heroes*), a pattern not true of romance or the detective story (although to some extent true of the Western, with its similar origins in dime novels). Consequently, although young adult romance or mystery, as back formations from their adult genres, can work without embarrassment as transitional forms of reading taste for the reader who will continue to follow the genre into adulthood, the adult sports story tries to set itself against juvenile reading tastes. Within the larger context of sport itself, a taste for sporting events is always potentially suspect as childish (or worse, adolescent). Especially in baseball, one of the most agonizing dynamics of fanhood is the conflict between the childishness and innocence of the game and the aging of spectator and player alike. Aging people watch a children's game and want to see it played by those who are morally children, not prey to the same responsibilities or ambitions that afflict adults.

Virginia Woolf was only half-joking (if that much) when she said that *Middlemarch* was the first English novel written for grown-up people. Woolf's history of serious fiction begins when the novel becomes fully adult. Classics can become classic by making their precursors into children—a process quite different from the Oedipal slaying of a parent-precursor in literary history according to Harold Bloom. The literary work says "I am for grown-ups. Put away childish books and read me." For this demand to be effective, the reader must have a sense of the patterns and formulas of juvenile books. A work achieves adulthood by transgressing—through distortion, reversal, exaggeration, or trespass—the codes of the juvenile. Conversely one way to downgrade a group of texts is to read them primarily as children's literature. D. H. Lawrence realized that juvenilizing was the main barrier to British critics' serious treatment of American texts: "We like to think of the old-fashioned American classics as children's books. Just childishness, on our part. The old American art-speech contains an alien quality, which belongs to the American continent and to nowhere else. But, of course, so long as we insist on reading the books as children's tales, we miss all that" (7). Lawrence himself does not embrace American literature *as* childish, however; he only insists that adult critics are more fully adult for treating American literature seriously.

The serious art of the present moment is often serious by contrast to the childishness of the past. Hardy (Thomas, not Andy) makes Dickens seem childish, and Joyce makes Hardy seem childish. Roseanne is more adult than Donna Reed was. Sam Shepard and Karen Finley are more seriously grown up than were William Inge or Frank Gilroy, but the appeal of Inge or Gilroy was based on their being more successfully adult, for their generation, than Susan Glaspell or Thornton Wilder were. To develop adult artistic tastes, one must embrace the complicated, the troubled, the tangled, the historically unique—all the things that are opposed (if perhaps only rhetorically and from the adult's perspective) to the formula and sameness of children's tastes.

Baseball literature, which becomes literature by flaunting how it cannot be reduced to genre, represents a larger dynamic in the construction of the literary. If baseball fiction is a genre that would not be a genre, literature itself may be the kind of text that refuses to be placed as a "kind of" text. Originality and avant-gardism are typical of literature. Originality as a marker of high artistic status has possibly been eroded by postmodern parodies, but it is more robust than one might think. Certainly values like originality, autonomy, and the sui generis flourished in 1950s New Criticism (at about the time when the adult baseball novel was being established). If a text constructs an autonomous world, it is the finer New Critical object. If one masks the connections of "the world of *Hamlet*" to the "worlds" of fifty other plays by seeing it as unique, one establishes a scale on which the best works are those that most effectively create their own genres and refuse to be put into a category.[5]

Almost fifty years after the height of New Criticism, some readers may be convinced that no status called "literary" exists—that someone has banished it from critical discourse. Broadly, the question "What is literary?" in the 1990s might be answered by academic critics according to largely external criteria. What is literary, we might think, is what some social force—a syllabus, a book club, William Bennett—*says* is literary. Forces of power, desire, emulation, and the need for cultural capital would conspire to produce a category of the literary even if nothing like what we call literature had ever been written.

Arguments for a categoryless category of literature nevertheless abound in postmodern criticism (as well as in definitions of the postmodern itself as something that avoids categories). These arguments have a detailed rhetoric. Theories of what is literary are effective because they are far more than mere reading lists; they are strategies of thought that train people to distinguish between the literary and the subliterary. The social transmission of literature as a value depends on convincing a lot of inquisitive people to read in broadly similar ways while at the same time reading critically and eruditely. It takes considerable effort to bring about even a general alignment of reading tastes and pleasures. A theory of the literary is far from being just an apology for tastes that have been formed by market forces or ideological pressures. Answers to the question "What is literature?" themselves form tastes and future critical judgments.

Readers, once convinced of the justification for calling certain texts "literary," then become competent individually to identify literature. Literary discrimination is not a swearing of allegiance to a set canon but a process one can repeat on a set of unfamiliar subjects. You have to be able to try it at home; it is not just for experts on a closed track. Literary taste, formed in school and in independent study, is slightly different from fashions in clothes or tastes in popular music, although it is in no way free from the kinds of institutions that channel tastes for those things. Partly for this reason the literary depends (like baseball) on classic style—old leather, green baize, restrained lighting, good wood, and fountain pens being the literary analogues to worn mitts, natural turf, day games, wooden bats, and the wordsmith's manual typewriter.[6] Readers of fine literature take comfort too in the projection that their current favorites will be the next century's classics—just as today's rookie of the year may be tomorrow's hall of famer.

Central to literary values is discrimination against the nonliterary rather than detection of the literary. This process operates negatively, against a wider indiscriminate world of interaction with texts. Here again the contrast between the adult and the child is crucial, because children are encouraged—by libraries, schools, and public television—to read absolutely anything, to read for the sake of reading rather than to choose what they read carefully.[7] Educated adults are encouraged to be picky about what they read or at least to be ashamed when they do not live up to highly discriminating standards. University education in literature—which is largely the process I am considering here—works by encouraging discrimination when one's formative experiences have (in the late twentieth-century United States) encouraged one to be as indiscriminate as possible. It is an exclusionary and difficult training that works on few who receive it, convincing those few in turn of the exceptionality of true literary taste—as the object is unique, so is each truly discriminating reader.

Literature is a core value, engaging the most important things in life. It is also a classic value, engaging them in the timeless manner in which generation after conservative generation has engaged them. Hence a continuously reproduced value is the *book*, itself an arbitrary but venerable way of producing a text in a form that people will respect.[8] This principle of timelessness also explains the odd sterility of much conservative discourse that insists that literature must address vitally important issues, because in conservative formulations literature can be good only if it keeps on addressing vital issues in the most utterly abstract fashion. In this moist hazy center of abstraction, literature is supposed to keep us going on about such questions as "What is the good life?" These questions are either rendered moot by how most folks have to live their *real* lives or so definitively answered in advance that the literary work becomes a hall of mirrors for reading the same judgments reproduced in infinite regression.

Literature at the present moment is defined by theorists as an escape from the categories of genre. It is so theorized by Robert Alter, whose scholarly work of moving the Bible from the genre of scripture to that of literature has been enormously influential in the academic study of the Western tradition as a whole. In *The Pleasures of Reading in an Ideological Age* Alter addresses the definition of literature. "It should be evident that the distinctive resources of literary language do not work like a simple on-off switch, marking this as literary and that as not. A piece of philosophic or historical writing, a legal opinion, the exposition of a psychological theory, could exhibit some or even many of the characteristics of literary language. . . . But it is only the literary text that as a matter of intrinsic purpose marshals all these resources for the construction of a world" (48). Note here how literature is defined by discrimination, by naming genres that must not participate in the literary. Note too the circle that Alter begins to draw, a circle centered on fiction ("the construction of a world") but seen as the general basis of all art. Only the literary text can fulfill this function, but the literary text and its definition are tautologically related; presumably a text that starts in a lower, more limited genre would achieve literariness at the moment when it crossed over a line and created a world.

How a reader perceives that line is less clear, but Alter's definition portrays literature as being defined by "literary language." This is not an entire tautology, if one has defined literary language (as Alter has):

> If any purposeful ordering of language implies some intention of communication, literature is remarkable for its densely layered communication, its capacity to open up multifarious connections and multiple interpretations to the recipient of the communication, and for the pleasure it produces in making the instrument of communication a satisfying aesthetic object—or more precisely, the pleasure it gives us as we experience the nice interplay between the verbal aesthetic form and the complex meanings conveyed. It is on these grounds that it is valued as literature. (28)

Pleasure, as the title of Alter's book indicates, is the extra quality that separates the literary text from similar genres like legal or medical opinions (which involve detailed communication and a high degree of interpretation by readers). Alter further qualifies pleasure as *aesthetic* pleasure, presumably to include texts that give no actual pleasure in any common sense of the term, like *Paradise Regained* or the novels of Joyce Carol Oates.

Nonetheless even aesthetic pleasure can be as subjective a quality as erotic or gustatory pleasure. Alter needs to fence pleasure, first inside intentional communication, next inside complex meaning, and then inside texts with objectively many meanings. Alter's theoretical statement is an example of the "nice interplay" he requires from literature itself. Alter longs for a pleasure that can be communicated to those willing to be trained to tell the good from the bad. It is a pleasure of refinement and the refinement of pleasure.

Alter's "pleasure" is located, as his examples (Balzac, Dickens, Melville, James) show, in the big nineteenth-century novel—or perhaps in biblical narrative as seen through the corrective lens of the nineteenth-century novel. In fact his theory seems designed to fit these novels; that fact does not disqualify it but merely shows that like Poe's "Philosophy of Composition" of "The Raven," it probably was not arrived at deductively. There nevertheless is a sense in which Alter's preference for the novel must be hidden inside an argument about literariness that sees novels as the books that are least reducible to formula. In this regard—though not explicitly—Alter echoes Mikhail Bakhtin, whose work has done as much to place the novel at the heart of literary study as has that of any modern theorist.

In Bakhtin's organic metaphor, "the generic skeleton of the novel is still far from having hardened, and we cannot foresee all its plastic possibilities" (3). The novel is a focus for Bakhtin's own central aesthetic theory, the genre he prefers because it is least a genre. In "Epic and Novel" Bakhtin opposes novel to "fossilized" genres—largely to epic but also to lyric, tragedy, and other genres that can be composed according to set formulas. The novel has no formulas. It is engaged with the present and open to possibilities of a future: "The novel comes into contact with the spontaneity of the inconclusive present; this is what keeps the genre from congealing. The novelist is drawn toward everything that is not yet completed" (27). In these viscous metaphors Bakhtin argues that the novel is more full of vital fluid than are other genres.

Bakhtin also sees the novel as a latecomer: "All these genres, or in any case their defining features, are considerably older than written language and the book, and to the present day they retain their ancient oral and auditory characteristics. Of all the major genres only the novel is younger than writing and the book; it alone is organically receptive to new forms of mute perception, that is, to reading" (3). Bakhtin invokes the novel as young, still growing, still plastic, but I think that the specific metaphors here mask potential opposites. The novel is a latecomer, but not therefore for Bakhtin an upstart. Instead it is the final and permanent flowering of literary evolution—and therefore the fully mature genre in a scheme where older genres are limited, crude, and insufficiently sophisticated about the real world.

In short other genres are implicitly *childish* by contrast to the novel.[9] As the most fully literary genre (literally, because it is the only genre to grow out of books rather than out of preliterary art forms), the novel is also the most fully grown-up of genres. As such, in a familiar pattern, it is the genre that is least a genre: "the novel has no canon of its own, as do other genres; only individual examples of the novel are historically active, not a generic canon as such" (3). The novel has great power here. It takes precedence over less vital genres and can replenish itself and remain permanently ahead of the curve of future literary history. If the novel cannot be shoehorned into a category, then any work a critic wants to promote can be called a "novel" and move into the undefined center of the literary universe.[10] The novel is then to the rest of art as America (for cultural nationalists) is to the rest of the world.

I have been arguing that literature is both core and margin, core because for its theorists it is the most valuable art form and margin because it is so frequently seen as avoiding the center, or as forming a new circumference around art and life. Eugenio Bolongaro intensifies this problem of center and margin in his essay "From Literariness to Genre." Bolongaro sees literariness as an Aristotelian mean. He sees language as extending from a pole of pure instrumentality to one of pure play. He locates the literary at the mean between these two poles; texts that hold play in perfect tension with concrete usefulness are the most perfectly literary. For Bolongaro, "The 'literariness' of a text is defined by its approach to cognition. A text is literary when it attempts to occupy the center (a space, not a point) of the cognitive spectrum constituted by the trajectories of instrumental communication and ludic 'freedom'" (281). Bolongaro's map is similar to Alter's: language communicates, and language that both communicates and gives pleasure (if it is appropriate to connect "pleasure" and "play") is fully literary. This is a satisfying approach to some of the problems of genre theory, but its very success alerts one to how it is put together. Once again the balance between communication and play, akin to other balances such as function and pleasure, realism and fantasy, and content and form, values the realistic novel at the expense of, for example, lyric (too playful) and autobiography (too communicative). More problematic still, however, is the metaphoric device of conceiving of communication and play as opposites. Such a formulation seems to foreclose certain avenues of thought about language and texts from the start.

Most basically play is opposite not to communication but to *work*, suggesting that for Bolongaro communication is the equivalent of language at work. Work and play are uneasy opposites, however—as they are throughout baseball fiction—each always threatening to become the other (as in the phrase "professional sport" itself). If play is a function, how does it "work"? If *play* is an antonym for *communication*, is nothing communicated in play? Play then seems to become something for solipsists, not something one could do with others. And what is the space at the center of a continuum between communication and play? Especially since the terms are *not* necessarily or logically opposite, the central ground that Bolongaro claims for the mean between them becomes, rather disturbingly, a margin in its own right, a borderland between uneasily adjacent realms of language. The literary, although profoundly central, becomes a borderland trader between a realm governed by logical market exchange in language (communication) and wanton disregard of market realities (play)—although also, and intriguingly for my purposes here, at a potential border between adult communication and childhood play. I do not mean to suggest that Bolongaro intends to portray the literary as a perpetual adolescent, however. In playing around I have possibly missed his point, but that is the way of language.

One could and should argue that Robert Alter's liberal humanism and Bolongaro's Aristotelianism are small components of current thought about the literary. Poststructuralist thought may have pushed the literary so far toward the ludic that the literary may now more comfortably be seen as inherently antigeneric and anticommunicative. This hypothesis—which I think is fairly near correct—only continues to define a poststructural literary as a site for continuous transgression of genre—in other words, the very place where Alter's humanist, realist approach places it.

Of course Literature with a capital *L*—belles lettres or, most practically, the content of the sophomore survey—is the category against which much poststructuralist theory places the texts it finds most interesting, and the category of "interesting" (note the tag words of many conference papers, "I am interested in," as the effective content of the argument) frequently is decidedly *not* what is literary. Nowadays it is often likely to be medical case studies, prime-time soap operas, or children's baseball stories. With its name unexpressed, the interesting goes by provisional names, most often cycling back to a virtual synonym for the literary: the textual.

Jonathan Culler, in his essay "Towards a Theory of Non-Genre Literature" (1975), makes an important statement at the beginnings of a coherent "poststructuralism" in American academic criticism. Culler apparently rejects the idea of communication that has undergirded thought about the literary from Aristotle through Auerbach to Alter: "The essence of literature is not representation, not a communicative transparency, but an opacity, a resistance to recuperation which exercises sensibility and intelligence. Just as we would stop playing games if we could master them completely, so our interest in literature depends on what Geoffrey Hartman calls 'the differential relation of form to consciousness,' the tension between writing and reading" (258). Culler approaches Alter's object from the other extreme. Alter begins in communication and ends in pleasure; Culler begins in lack of communication and ends in . . . pleasure. For Alter, this realm was literature; for Culler, it is the text: "The text is a region in which characters are placed in relation to one another and inaugurate 'a play of meaning.' The job of literary theory is to specify the forms of this game: the procedures used to defer meaning, and the procedures of recuperation" (258). The text defers meaning and loses surface meaning altogether. It instead presents an opaque surface, ostensibly one of play rather than one of communication. The value of the text, the amount of interest it holds, is defined by the amount of resistance it offers to "recuperation," which might be further glossed as solution of a mastered code. The text is the difficult, the not-for-children, the best-left-to-experts. For all that, the text is in its highest form a *game*, a game at which the critic is present in a role that resembles nothing so much as that of the ultimate sportswriter. If life is like literature and sport is like life, then literature is like sport.

Crucial in Culler's influential theorizing is not, for my purposes, its conjunction with writing about sports. Culler's larger purpose in "Towards a Theory of Non-Genre Literature" is just that—to conceive of a literature beyond the constraints of genre, a literature in which one might suspect the central text, given Culler's interest in Flaubert, will be *Madame Bovary*. For Culler, the essence of literature is to exist at the point of the greatest tension and uncertainty. Whether conceived as center or as margin, this place will be where we cannot reduce the text to a type. We no longer have interest in texts that are solved games, texts exemplified by ritual incantation, liturgy, hymn—or nursery rhyme, song, kids' infield chatter, texts so childish that they communicate nothing.

Information theory defines communication as information, and information is "a statistical measure of uncertainty" (Hayles 270). Whatever cannot be reduced to formula constitutes the information in a communication. The great postmodern theorist of genre is Gérard Genette, and it may be argued that Genette's work aims at reducing noise to formula, at classifying "the procedures used to defer meaning" in order to clear a space at the middle (or margin) for pure literature seen as pure information. Perhaps Genette would see this exercise as akin to Peer Gynt's with the onion—the cleared space being the void—but one cannot be sure. What is clear is that Genette's theorizing has given rise in turn to the search for texts that transcend his schemes. This is precisely Jacques Derrida's project in "The Law of Genre" (1980), where Derrida critiques Genette by referring to a central text that seems not to fit any known genre, Maurice Blanchot's *Folie du jour: Un récit!* (Today's folly: An account?). Blanchot's text is so incomprehensible that Derrida himself concludes "It would be folly to draw any sort of general conclusion here" (80). Fool that I am, I conclude that the space cleared *for* Blanchot's text—whether or not that text itself is the grail of the quest for the literary—is the space of the void, where the text moves beyond genre, the space I have already identified as the fullest embrace of the present and the new, the greatest producer of difficulty and pleasure, the greatest tension between work and play, the quality of lacking qualities: the quality, in a word, of literature.

Literature is for both Alter and Derrida a difficult undertaking, one to be approached as soberly and earnestly as possible—although for Alter his work is his pleasure and for Derrida his play is his work. True play is ritual and rhythmic, of a childlike simplicity; work, even the work of reading playfully, resists rhythm and its seductions. In either case, humanist or postmodern, the pleasure one gets from literary study (or from the study of what one will not call literature) is a pleasure sanctioned by intellectual effort—the insistence that Culler, for instance, shares most strikingly and most thoroughly with Alter. For all the hand-wringing among conservative culture warriors over the esoteric difficulty of humanist scholarship, it seems clear that theories along both sides of the divide agree on the basic issue of difficulty, presenting two elitisms that are sides of the same coin. For either academic theory, it must be hard to be good.

Above all else the study of literature (or not literature) must never be easy. "Easy Does It Not" is in fact the title of an early theoretical piece by Mark Harris on the relation between baseball fiction and general fiction. For Harris, writing à propos *A Ticket for a Seamstitch*, literature requires heroic effort from the writer and an equally heroic effort from the reader. "The novelist in search of his own best self . . . persuades himself that his defiance of the temptation to increase personal comfort at the sacrifice of craft assures him the distant reward of fame. . . . He may live to hear, as Faulkner has, the praise of a generation which has discovered that his seeming difficulty is in fact the inevitable result of his ambition to express a difficult idea" (xvi). Harris gives full points only for a high degree of difficulty. "I will talk baby talk to babies and dog talk to dogs, but I cannot tell you in baby talk or dog talk of the excitement of being a human being in a world so wondrous with hope and sorrow and loyalty and defeat and anguish and delight" (xix). Effort is a grown-up attribute; effort consecrates both the text and the reading experience. Easy reading and easy writing are child's play.

Put aside for a moment the observable fact that no reading or writing experiences are harder-won than those of children composing or interpreting their first texts; Harris's aesthetic hinges, like a manager's judgment of ballplayers, on an unobservable moral supplement. If one finds his words inspiring, one must ask whether it cost him an effort to write them. If one is not inspired, is it because those words were composed in a facile way?

"Easy Does It Not" is in part a narrative of Harris's own tribulations as he was writing *A Ticket for a Seamstitch*. He tells of how *Life* magazine first commissioned and then declined to publish the work, substituting a piece of fiction by William Brinkley. Harris savages Brinkley's prose for its flaccid reliance on clichés and its easy-reading-level quality. In fact it is bad prose by almost anyone's reckoning. Harris testifies that, by contrast, *Ticket* cost him enormous, barely compensated pains in its composition and in its marketing to publishers. He describes how he had to fight for his vision, to scratch to feed his family as the story was taking shape. By his own aesthetic standards, *A Ticket for a Seamstitch*, per word, is therefore one of the best works of literature ever written.

One can never know, of course, whether William Brinkley's work on his dreadful novel cost him even more effort than Harris's on his good one. It is a criterion of merit familiar to baseball fans: player A makes the hard plays look easy, and player B makes the easy ones look difficult. How (unless testimonials are appended to every text) is one ever to know whether a text was truly easy or hard to write? Is it easy to make the easy look hard? And from the reader's perspective, can the easy by definition never be good?

Harris's theory of the author's effort and the corresponding theory of the reader's effort are powerful. Their diametric opposites are just as powerful, however. The work that seems to indicate that its author has labored mightily is valuable, but so is the work that seems effortless; in a further deepening of the problem, it is often the seemingly effortless work that is really (or purportedly) the hardest. As William Butler Yeats said: "A line will take us hours maybe; / Yet if it does not seem a moment's thought, / Our stitching and unstitching has been naught" (28). The impression of effort can be created easily sometimes, and the impression of ease can take great effort. No textual pretension to ease *or* effort, and no reader's testimony to the ease or effort of a reading experience, can ever free itself from the suspicion that it masks its direct opposite.

Robert Alter contends that literary study must be intensely in earnest:

> In both criticism and debates over curriculum, one encounters an insistence that daily newspapers, pulp fiction, private diaries, clinical case studies, and imaginative literature belong on one level, that any distinctions among them are dictated chiefly by ideology. One need not argue for an attitude of unreserved adulation toward literature, but without some form of passionate engagement in literary works, without a sense of deep pleasure in the experience of reading, the whole enterprise of teaching and writing about literature quickly becomes pointless. (11)

Literature, as one might guess from Alter's title, exists somewhere as free from ideology as from genre. Even if there were places where ideology could not reach, however, Alter's view would be troubling—and revealing. His two main assertions are not at all logically connected to his ostensible issue, the generic boundaries of the literary. He says that one must be profoundly engaged with literature and that this profound engagement occurs in the teaching of literature. To any people who have contemplated modeling themselves on Chaucer's Clerk—essentially any English majors who have taken the British Survey, that is—these assertions may seem to be so self-evident as almost to lack meaning. But they convey a profound ideology.

The rhetoric of passionate engagement is at the same time a rhetoric of *dis*passionate engagement. It is Culler's exercise of "sensibility and intelligence." Alter clearly if somewhat illogically implies that one cannot engage passionately with pulp fiction (in the pre- and likely also now the post-Tarantino senses), that one cannot develop a sense of deep pleasure in the reading of private diaries—or that if one did, such passion would be misdirected, would be a guilty or forbidden passion. In particular, I think, passionate engagement with what Alter elsewhere calls "downright bad literature" (47) is both a sign of bad taste and a symptom of addiction. Addictions, as we know from Eli Kapp's gambling problems in *The Celebrant*, are destructive. They can even be un-American.

Both bad taste and addiction—if not un-American behavior—are part of childishness. Any parent who has watched a Care Bears movie five or six times in a row can testify that children's tastes are notoriously indiscriminate and fierce. In particular a reading taste that is not just insensitive to literary merit but obsessively so defines how kids enjoy stories. The extent to which an innocuous text can become an *idée fixe* as bedtime story or car trip pacifier, demanded over and over again with a sense of variorum detail positively Hinmanesque in its attentiveness, is a remarkable feature of how children relate to narrative.

Bad taste and addictive behavior are also what fans of genre fiction have in common with children. Addiction as bad taste is a key factor in how literary tastes are defined. The literary work is one that can be—must be—approached with completely voluntary readerly attention. Literature is not just something that one can stop at any time; it is emphatically something that one should never take up casually to begin with. Genre fiction, by contrast, is recreational—bad enough—but also a positively unhealthy indulgence. Cycles of reading genre fiction are like all cycles of addiction: it is bad for me, but I cannot help myself; I know how it is going to end, but I keep reading anyway; I know I am going to become mentally flabby (and will have to go to the library and do fifteen reps of Walter Pater), but it tastes so good.

Is genre fiction instrumental or playful? In Alter's analysis it scarcely matters. In fact it is off the chart in both directions; genre fiction passes both poles of Bolongaro's continuum. As opiate of the people (as in the corporate-quietist work of John Grisham) or as aggressive therapy meant to make a reactionary out of you (as in

Tom Clancy or sub-Clancy military romances), genre fiction is direct political communication. But it has direct clinical indications, too. As the pill that will get you through turbulence at 30,000 feet or will keep you calm in the dentist's waiting room, genre fiction is outperformed by few sedatives. It even has the same amnesiac quality as some painkillers, for it becomes difficult to remember, and finally irrelevant, which Maigrets or which Dick Francis novels one has read. Genre fiction probably ranks second in sales only to caffeine among over-the-counter antidepressants.

At the same time, what could be more playful than genre fiction? Detective novels are puzzles, Westerns are cowboys and Indians, romances and medical thrillers are "playing doctor," and science fiction is setting up little plastic spacemen on the floor and flying them in little plastic rocket ships to the planet Dining Room Table. Sport fiction, too, however grudgingly, ends up being about playing games.

The line between serious literature and genre fiction is primarily one between will and addiction. Other less moralizing distinctions have their own problems. If pleasure is the criterion of literature, for instance, then genre fiction gives only the false pleasure of the addict. If violation of the text's decorum defines literature, then genre fiction is the place off both ends of the chart where the ludic meets the instrumental and explodes, like a terrorist bomb over the Super Bowl (one of genre fiction's favorite sites). What could be (or has been, as in the work of Umberto Eco, Marshall Blonsky, Jane Tompkins, and others) more interesting for poststructural analysis? Genre fiction is the tiniest of steps away from the highbrow avant-garde, the step from *The Mousetrap* to *The Real Inspector Hound*; the difference is in whether you are addicted. We can stop watching *The Real Inspector Hound* any time we want (and we have), but the West End is in the grip of a maddening illness from which it can never free itself, doomed to rehearse the detection of its own guilt over and over and over again forever.

The popular psychology of the 1990s reduces all dysfunctionalities to addictions, seeing the cure for all problems as an exercise of the will that will free the individual from addiction. A list of addictions in one self-help book includes "alcohol, prescription drugs, nonprescription drugs, illegal drugs, food, television, sex, work, spending, stress, jogging, reading, speed/danger, nicotine, caffeine, relationships, power, sleep, gambling, cults" (Friel and Friel 32).

Reading? The reader (and ominously, the professional reader) must go through a checklist to see whether a reading addiction is at the heart of his or her dysfunctionality (35–36). Do you think about reading, talk about it, look forward to it (curling up with a good book); do you read more and more as you develop a tolerance for it; do you experience white-knuckle abstinence when you try to go a day without reading (or ration yourself, ten pages a day, a nickel in the jar for every page you read); are you moody when you withdraw? Do you stash books by the bed, in the bathroom, and in the car? Do you have blackouts (what was that conversation you started while I was reading Roger Martin du Gard)? Do you do things under the influence of literature that you would never have done prior to your addiction?

Literary education is a therapy designed to reintegrate the reader's personality and cure it of its unreasonable addictions and dependencies. The hostility of literary educators toward cultural studies can be likened to that of the medical establishment toward alternative practitioners (something it resembles politically as well). A century and more of the painstaking establishment of a doctrine, by the American Medical Association or the Modern Language Association (MLA), is under continual and sometimes critical threat from those who will undermine its way of seeing its own part of the universe. Far worse in the case of the MLA, the patients appear to be taking over the hospital.

The primary distinction between voluntary tastes and involuntary addictions depends on underlying pairs with the general pattern volition/instinct, choice/addiction, human/nonhuman (machine or animal), initiative/automation, entrepreneurship/socialism, free will/determinism. A good reader thus might display a freely chosen, highly developed (in elective courses, of course) taste for Proust, and a bad reader (the good reader's mother-in-law?) might show an ignorant, falsely conscious, morally reprehensible inability to keep from reading Danielle Steel. Nothing could be clearer than the gulf between those two texts or the utter opposition of the two tastes—or could it? Because if Danielle Steel is an over-the-counter drug, Proust may be merely her designer equivalent. As Eve Sedgwick puts it, "I am now able to prescribe 'Proust' to my friends in erotic or professional crisis or in, for that matter, personal grief with the same bland confidence as I do a teaspoon of sugar (must be swallowed quickly) to those suffering from hiccups" (*Epistemology of the Closet* 241). Hold on—

maybe Proust is a kind of nonaddictive cosmetic pharmaceutical of the literary world, the guilt-free reading experience. Is Proust addictive? Is reading Proust voluntary? Open Proust and one finds a description of

> la volonté qui est le serviteur persévérant et immuable de nos personnalités successives; cachée dans l'ombre, dédaignée, inlassablement fidèle, travaillant sans cesse, et sans soucier des variations de notre moi, à ce qu'il ne manque jamais du nécessaire. . . . Elle est aussi invariable que l'intelligence et la sensibilité sont changeantes, mais comme elle est silencieuse, ne donne pas ses raisons, elle semble presque inexistante; c'est sa ferme détermination que suivent les autres parties de notre moi, mais sans l'apercevoir tandis qu'elles distinguent nettement leurs propres incertitudes. [*A l'ombre des jeunes filles en fleurs* 262]

> [that will which is the persevering and unalterable servant of our successive personalities; hidden away in the shadow, despised, downtrodden, untiringly faithful, toiling incessantly, and with no thought for the variability of the self, its master, to ensure that the master may never lack what he requires. . . . It is as invariable as the intelligence and the sensibility are fickle, but since it is silent, gives no account of its actions, it seems almost non-existent; it is by its dogged determination that the other constituent parts of our personality are led, but without seeing it, whereas they distinguish clearly all their own uncertainties.] (*Within a Budding Grove* 930)

When one reaches the heart of the literary canon and reads the work that above all other novels carries the mystique of literariness and requires the most willpower to master, one comes to the place where the will *(la volonté)* is the most automatic part of the personality. Here the voluntary choices of the individual *(l'intelligence et la sensibilité)* are the most subject to whim and caprice. The firmest distinction in the definition of literature is demolished in the text that most defines the literary.

For much of the midtwentieth century the opposition of literary to nonliterary seemed from within academic English departments to be as silent as the operations of Proust's will. The basic work of academic critics was seen as unrelated to taste; they were to develop interpretations of literary texts.[11] Therefore one of the major 1970s upheavals in academic literary study was caused by Stanley Fish's "Interpreting the *Variorum*," which introduced the notion of "interpretive community." According to Fish, "Interpretive communities

are made up of those who share interpretive strategies not for reading (in the conventional sense) but for writing texts, for constituting
their properties and assigning their intentions. In other words, these
strategies exist prior to the act of reading and therefore determine
the shape of what is read rather than, as is usually assumed, the
other way around. . . . Interpretive communities are no more stable
than texts because interpretive strategies are not natural or universal, but learned" (327–28). Fish's ideas have been widely feared (because they point so cheerfully to the instability of textual meaning)
and widely influential, because they frame in a cogent way what
should have seemed so obvious: reading is something living individuals do in social groups, not an automatic decoding of texts. In fact
Fish shares a central literary value with mainstream promoters of
the value of voluntary responsibility in reading: "what utterers do,"
says Fish, "is give hearers and readers the opportunity to make
meanings (and texts)" (328), instead of merely decoding fixed utter-
ances with a standard key.

The threat of Fish is that his ideas tend to seep, as he encourages
them to do, into realms more politically charged than the interpretation of *Lycidas*—specifically, into law and religion. If I assert the
textual instability of "the grim wolf with privy paw," I am likely to
shock no one at all. My assertion about the instability of a text in
one sphere tends to call into question the stability of texts in others,
however; the next thing you know, I will be wondering about the
First Amendment. In fact the entire question of the interpretive
community may have been controversial in literary studies for only
a few years, till its effects boiled over into politics, where they
continue to ferment today. The notion of an interpretive community in literary criticism has become part of the wisdom of the
profession, underpinning a common or garden variety of deconstruction that is the standard close-reading strategy of 1990s interpretive communities.

What has gone far less examined, even in the canon debates from
1985 to 1995, is how Fish's basic structural argument can focus
thought about what literary study does. If one takes "Interpreting
the *Variorum*" and substitutes the word *taste-making* for *interpretive* at every point, one comes much closer to describing how academic critics do most of their work, both in publications and in the
classroom. For Fish, the question of taste—how he chooses an object
for interpretation—is not interesting. In this essay, as in much of his

early work, his text is Milton; Milton's greatness is a given. It would in fact seem obtuse to talk about creating a *taste* for Milton as opposed to struggling over the proper *interpretation* of Milton. Milton is at once both the poet so unapproachably great that fashions in taste cannot affect him and the poet so impenetrable to most undergraduates that no one ever really *likes* reading him. Nevertheless the stability even of Milton is as ephemeral as the stability of interpretation—or rather, as stable as the groups of people who uphold the towering status of Milton.

We cannot change the Constitution except by piecemeal amendment, and we cannot change the Bible except by geologically slow textual emendation. The communities that surround these texts do not allow otherwise. We can change literary canons from semester to semester, however. Moreover a central battleground of the canon wars is not simply the substitution of Ellen Glasgow for Hemingway or Sui Sin Far for Dreiser or Zitkala-Sa for Sherwood Anderson. The central battleground is the formation of reading tastes, of getting people to *like* various kinds of texts and to *dislike* or disdain others. People are not centrally worried about including texts by one flavor of author in the place of once-familiar texts by authors of another or even (to color this abstraction) the empowerment of women readers/writers and readers/writers of color instead of white men. The central anxiety is that the canon wars will replace a cultural category of appreciating "good" literature, which only the elect can manage, with a cultural category of just plain reading books, which anyone can do.

I do not mean in these statements to underplay the enormous significance that race and gender have to debates over the canon, and still less do I wish to reduce such debates (as John Guillory perhaps does in *Cultural Capital*) to Marxist or neo-Marxist analyses of class and the commodification of literature. In fact, in an American context where we can take commodification for granted, the debates over the literary and the nonliterary take a form that is not amenable to strictly Marxist analysis, except as this analysis is simply reductive. Literature is cultural capital in that possessing the key to literature (in the form of a well-developed taste for the literary) is another of the lines between classes in the United States. The issues and the human dramas of the production and reproduction of such cultural capital are often irreducible to a material base, except in the least "interesting" of ways.

How does one certify that one possesses literary taste, after all? A bumper sticker that says "I'd rather be reading Jane Austen"? Membership in a club that sends one the One Hundred Greatest Books for $39.95 apiece, one every few weeks? Subscriptions to the *Times Literary Supplement* and the *New York Review*? A degree in English? Having read every novel of Dickens and being fairly diffident about it because Dickens is really for children? Having read every novel of Raymond Chandler—but also every novel of John D. McDonald and Sara Paretsky? Owning a shelf of leather-bound antique books (which may be printed in a language one does not understand)? Or perhaps by knowing that certain authors or genres constitute literature, even though one may never read them? In this last way cultural capital can be upheld by those who do not read "good" books at all, those who know that Hemingway and Faulkner are the greatest modern novelists, for instance, and who proceed right on with their addiction to Victoria Holt, just as you may know full well that celeriac and arugula can provide all your vitamins, but you just could not resist that box of Ho-Hos for dinner.

A literary education, that brew of teaching and study that Robert Alter places at the heart of the survival of literature itself, is not centrally made up of critical thinking or of learning to interpret. One must learn to read a cultural map drawn by a taste-making community. A belief in great literature is ultimately a community's ratification of its own adulthood and of its seeing certain cultural endeavors as childish.

In one sense this concluding chapter is my own guarantee that this book, *Making the Team*, is not "just about baseball," my childhood and childlike delight, that it addresses far more adult theoretical issues—and in turn that these issues are not "just" about the themes or characteristics of genre fiction itself but about big cultural matters in general. While I have been writing this book, the comments I have gotten from people to whom I have described it have taken the form "But I didn't know there *was* any baseball literature" or sometimes "Well, there are books about baseball, but would anyone think they were good literature?" If I refer to a course I teach on baseball writing, I hear, "Can you get college credit for *that*?" I would get far more slack if I were teaching a course on the Connecticut Wits (the late eighteenth-century poets, not the Red Sox AA club). And I would get more still if I were teaching Zora Neale Hurston. But I have the sheer bad taste to teach Hank Aaron's autobiography written with Lonnie Wheeler (which says no less about America than do Hurston's stories and is "well written"). I thereby threaten nonacademic and academic audiences alike and invite their contempt and their anxiety. For me, this is a grass-roots example of the cultural work of genre fiction: it makes people embarrassed to like something.

Nor am I merely encountering (and complaining about and defending against) something trivial. The literary is constructed against many genres—functional and instrumental texts, children's books, and genre fiction—that include some of the most politically controversial expressions in modern society. The construction of the literary as a category beyond genre is meant to isolate literature as apolitical. The most inflammatory of the nonliterary fictional genres is pornography, and the most incisive commentary on the cultural work of pornography, as in the work of Catharine MacKinnon, invests a great deal in the literary as a countercategory to the pornographic.

MacKinnon's *Only Words* assumes that pornographic texts and images do effective cultural work: "What pornography does, it does in the real world, not only in the mind" (15). MacKinnon relentlessly breaks down the idea that there is a world of expression isolated from a world of action. Her opponents are free-speech absolutists who see all words and images as belonging to a realm of free speech and their expression as an inalienable right. For the absolutists, speech is separate in kind from actions that invite legislative and police regulation. "First Amendment absolutism did not begin in obscenity cases, but it is in explaining why obscenity should be protected speech, and how it cannot be distinguished from art and literature, that much of the work of absolutism has been done, taking as its point of departure and arrival the position that whatever is expressive should be constitutionally protected. In pornography, absolutism found, gained, and consolidated its ground and hit its emotional nerve" (89). For MacKinnon, the distinction between pornography, which acts, and art and literature, which apparently do not act at all, is nearly as absolute as the absolutists' division of speech from action. She is more anxious to preserve a category of the literary (and therefore fearful of the argument that regulation of pornography will censor art) than she is anxious to make her central case that all expression is a kind of action—so anxious, in fact, that she leaves her definition of literature completely unexamined. The idea of literature is so important that it must be protected even where it seems irrelevant to the highly ideological arguments of a legal and political theorist like MacKinnon.

Yet what distinguishes Nicholson Baker's *Vox* or *Fermata* from pulp pornography? (Well, *nothing* distinguishes Nicholson Baker's *Vox* or *Fermata* from pulp pornography except that the writer has a familiar *New Yorker* byline and a major publisher. Next question.) What distinguishes Kathy Acker's work from pornography? Colleen Kennedy poses the question of Acker's typical mode of simulated pornography: "The simulation *is* reality. It does not 'cover up,' but is indistinguishable from what is posited as covered. . . . Pornography written by women ultimately renders them victims of it" (175). Acker's work is recognizably feminist and postmodern, however; it *seems* to be deeply antipornographic. One might fairly ask in turn what separates Acker's simulated (because self-authored) pornographic passages from Andrea Dworkin's actual (but quoted, nonself-authored) citations of pornographic passages in *Pornography: Men Possessing Women*?

I am hardly going to suggest ways of deciding this issue in a book about baseball fiction, but I want to suggest that arguments over the lines one draws or does not draw between literature and not literature are far from academic concerns. They may be more vital than anything literary critics have argued about for a very long time.

Notes

1. The dust jacket of the first edition of O'Brian's *Post Captain* shows a scene, found nowhere in the novel itself, in which a dashing sea officer defends a woman on the deck of a ship, his sword drawn and a boarding party approaching. On the back of the jacket is this blurb, from the *Chattanooga Times* review of *Master and Commander*: "Comes now another wonderful story of the British Navy fighting Boney and the Spaniards that brings to mind, as every good naval novel must, the immortal Hornblower series." In the 1970s Lippincott had been glad to use the Hornblower comparison in their jacket blurbs.

2. Walter Mosley, author of the popular Easy Rawlins mysteries, which have recently moved onto the cusp between genre fiction and literature, finds it necessary to forestall readers' fears that he may be tiring of his series hero: "I'm not going to kill off Easy—not for a while. I want him to become old" (quoted in "Mosley's Moves").

3. By coincidence Sylvia Stallings reviewed Patrick O'Brian's first novel, *Testimonies*, in the same issue. The authors' careers would diverge wildly before reconverging as literature. *Testimonies* is a work of general fiction, a regional novel of love and family set in Wales. O'Brian would become known almost solely as a genre novelist and Malamud almost solely as a writer of general fiction.

4. Kupferberg would later review Douglass Wallop's *Year the Yankees Lost the Pennant* for the *New York Herald Tribune* (Sept. 12, 1954) without referring back to *The Southpaw*. One contemporary reviewer who did connect *The Southpaw* back to *The Natural* was Harry Sylvester, in his pieces for the *New York Times Book Review* (Aug. 24, 1952, and April 12, 1953).

5. See Maynard Mack's classic (and wonderful) essay "The World of Hamlet."

6. See Nicholson Baker's "Books as Furniture" for an extended analysis of this phenomenon. Baker actually reads the books that mail-order catalog companies use as props in their advertisements.

7. Literature sometimes includes representations of these indiscriminate antiliterary reading tastes. Here is Florentino Ariza in Gabriel García Márquez's *El amor en los tiempos del cólera:* "Había aprendido a llorar con su madre leyendo a los poetas locales que se vendían en plazas y portales en folletos de a dos centavos. Pero al mismo tiempo era capaz de recitar de memoria la poesía castellana más selecta del Siglo del Oro. En general leía todo lo que le cayera en las manos, y en el orden en que le caía, hasta el extremo de que mucho después de aquellos duros años de su primer amor, cuando no era joven, había de leer desde la primera página hasta la última los veinte tomos del Tesoro de la Juventud, el cátalogo completo de los clásicos Garnier Hnos., traducidos, y las obras más fáciles que publicaba don Vincente Blasco Ibáñez en la colección *Promoteo*" (103; "He had learned to cry with his mother as they read the pamphlets by local poets that were sold in plazas and arcades for two centavos each. But at the same time he was able to recite from memory the most exquisite Castilian poetry of the Golden Age. In general, he read everything that fell into his hands in the order in which it fell, so that long after those hard years of his first love, when he was no longer young, he would read from first page to last the twenty volumes of the Young People's Treasury, the complete catalogue of the Garnier Bros. Classics in translation, and the simplest works that Don Vincente Blasco Ibáñez published in the Prometeo collection [*Love in the Time of Cholera* 75]). Although the text makes fun of Florentino Ariza's inability to distinguish literature from tripe, this same indiscriminateness forms his character and his love of letters and therefore sets the whole direction of the novel's plot. *El amor en los tiempos del cólera* is literary and antiliterary at once, both romance novel and serious fiction. It is literary

because it is antiliterary. It achieves maximum self-consciousness of the role of readers' tastes in the construction (in all senses) of texts.

8. This book you are reading participates cheerfully in this dynamic, for its author's professional benefit. For more on the cultural status of the printed book, see Ralph Cohen, "Do Postmodern Genres Exist?"

9. For the Bakhtinian antagonism toward non-novelistic genres, see Mark Jeffreys, "Ideologies of Lyric."

10. It can be argued that E. V. Rieu's key theoretical achievement in beginning the series of Penguin classics with his 1950 translation of the Iliad was to present the great Western epic as a modern novel, in novelistic prose and mass-market paperback form. Even the epic must become the novel to remain central.

11. For the triumph of interpretation in America, see David Shumway, *Creating American Civilization*, 191–218.

Works Cited

Aaron, Henry, with Lonnie Wheeler. *I Had a Hammer: The Hank Aaron Story.* New York: HarperCollins, 1991.

Ahearn, Kerry. "'Et in Arcadia Excrementum': Pastoral, Kitsch, and Philip Roth's *The Great American Novel.*" *Aethlon* 11, no. 1 (1993): 1-14.

Alexander, Charles C. *John McGraw.* New York: Penguin, 1989.

Alter, Robert. *The Pleasures of Reading in an Ideological Age.* New York: Simon and Schuster, 1989.

Ambrose, Stephen E. *Nixon: The Education of a Politician, 1913-1962.* New York: Simon and Schuster, 1987.

Asinof, Eliot. *Man on Spikes.* New York: McGraw-Hill, 1955.

Augustine. *Confessions.* Ed. W. H. D. Rouse, with translation by William Watts. Loeb Classical Library. Cambridge, Mass.: Harvard University Press, 1989.

Baker, Kevin. *Sometimes You See It Coming.* New York: Crown, 1993.

Baker, Nicholson. "Books as Furniture." *The New Yorker,* June 12, 1995, pp. 84-92.

Bakhtin, M. M. "Epic and Novel: Toward a Methodology for the Study of the Novel." In *The Dialogic Imagination,* trans. Michael Holquist and Caryl Emerson, 3-40. Austin: University of Texas Press, 1981.

Berman, Neil. "Coover's *Universal Baseball Association:* Play as Personalized Myth." *Modern Fiction Studies* 24 (1978): 209-22.

Bishop, Michael. *Brittle Innings.* New York: Bantam, 1994.

Bledsoe, Lucy Jane. "State of Grace." In *Women on Women 2,* ed. Naomi Holoch and Joan Nestle, 232-54. New York: Plume, 1993.

Bloom, Harold. *The Anxiety of Influence.* New York: Oxford University Press, 1973.

Bolongaro, Eugenio. "From Literariness to Genre: Establishing the Foundations for a Theory of Literary Genres." *Genre* 25 (1992): 277-313.

Boyd, Brendan. *Blue Ruin: A Novel of the 1919 World Series.* New York: HarperCollins, 1993.

Broun, Heywood. *The Sun Field.* New York: Putnam's, 1923.

Candelaria, Cordelia. *Seeking the Perfect Game: Baseball in American Literature.* New York: Greenwood, 1989.

Carkeet, David. *The Greatest Slump of All Time.* New York: Penguin, 1985.

Carlson, Ron. "Zanduce at Second." *Harper's,* May 1994, pp. 71-80.

Cleese, John, and Connie Booth. *The Complete Fawlty Towers.* New York: Pantheon, 1988.

Cohen, Celia. *Smokey O: A Romance.* Tallahassee, Fla.: Naiad, 1994.

Cohen, Ralph. "Do Postmodern Genres Exist?" In *Postmodern Genres,* ed. Marjorie Perloff, 11-27. Norman: University of Oklahoma Press, 1989.

Cooney, Ellen. *All the Way Home.* New York: Putnam's, 1984.

Coover, Robert. *The Universal Baseball Association, Inc., J. Henry Waugh, Prop.* New York: Plume, 1971.

Culler, Jonathan. "Towards a Theory of Non-Genre Literature." In *Surfiction: Fiction Now . . . and Tomorrow,* ed. Raymond Federman, 255-62. Chicago: Swallow, 1975.

Davies, Valentine. *It Happens Every Spring.* New York: Farrar, 1949.

DeLillo, Don. "Pafko at the Wall." *Harper's,* October 1992, pp. 35-70.

Derrida, Jacques. "The Law of Genre," trans. Avital Ronell. *Critical Inquiry* 7 (1980): 55-81.

———. "Structure, Sign and Play in the Discourse of the Human Sciences." In *Modern Criticism and Theory: A Reader,* ed. David Lodge, 108-23. London: Longman, 1988.

De Vries, Julian. *The Strike-Out King.* Cleveland: World, 1948.

Dworkin, Andrea. *Pornography: Men Possessing Women.* New York: Perigee, 1981.

Eagleton, Terry. "Capitalism, Modernism and Postmodernism." In *Modern Criticism and Theory: A Reader,* ed. David Lodge, 385-98. London: Longman, 1988.

Eskenazi, Gerald. *The Lip: A Biography of Leo Durocher.* New York: Morrow, 1993.

Fetterley, Judith. *The Resisting Reader: A Feminist Approach to American Fiction.* Bloomington: Indiana University Press, 1981.

Fiedler, Leslie. "Come Back to the Raft Ag'in, Huck Honey" (1948). In Mark Twain, *The Adventures of Huckleberry Finn,* Norton Critical Edition, 2d ed., 413-20. New York: Norton, 1977.

Fish, Stanley. "Interpreting the *Variorum.*" In *Modern Criticism and Theory: A Reader,* ed. David Lodge, 311-29. London: Longman, 1988.

Fraser, Steven, ed. *The Bell Curve Wars.* New York: Basic, 1995.

Friel, John, and Linda Friel. *Adult Children: The Secrets of Dysfunctional Families.* Deerfield Beach, Fla.: Health Communications, 1988.

García Márquez, Gabriel. *El amor en los tiempos del cólera.* Madrid: Mondadori, 1989.

———. *Love in the Time of Cholera.* Trans. Edith Grossman. New York: Penguin, 1989.

Gardner, Howard. "Cracking Open the IQ Box." In *The Bell Curve Wars,* ed. Steven Fraser, 23-35. New York: Basic, 1995.

Giff, Patricia Reilly. *Left-Handed Shortstop.* Illustrated by Leslie Morrill. New York: Delacorte, 1980.

Goldstein, Warren. *Playing for Keeps: A History of Early Baseball.* Ithaca, N.Y.: Cornell University Press, 1989.

Gorman, S. S. *Home Run Stretch.* New York: Minstrel, 1991.

Gorsuch, Richard L. *Factor Analysis.* 2d ed. Hillsdale, N.J.: Erlbaum, 1983.

Gould, Stephen Jay. "Curveball." In *The Bell Curve Wars,* ed. Steven Fraser, 11–22. New York: Basic, 1995.

———. *The Mismeasure of Man.* New York: Norton, 1981.

———. *Wonderful Life: The Burgess Shale and the Nature of History.* New York: Norton, 1989.

Greenberg, Eric Rolfe. *The Celebrant.* New York: Penguin, 1986.

Grey, Zane. *The Short-Stop.* New York: Grosset, 1909.

Guillory, John. *Cultural Capital: The Problem of Literary Canon Formation.* Chicago: University of Chicago Press, 1993.

Hammett, Dashiell. *The Maltese Falcon.* New York: Vintage, 1989.

Haraway, Donna. *Primate Visions: Gender, Race and Nature in the World of Modern Science.* New York: Routledge, 1989.

Harris, Mark. *Bang the Drum Slowly, by Henry W. Wiggen, Certain of His Enthusiasms Restrained by Mark Harris.* Lincoln: University of Nebraska Press, 1984 [1956].

———. "Easy Does It Not." In *A Ticket for a Seamstitch. Henry W. Wiggen but Polished for the Printer by Mark Harris,* vii–xix. Lincoln: University of Nebraska Press, 1984 [1956].

———. *It Looked Like For Ever.* Lincoln: University of Nebraska Press, 1989 [1979].

———. *The Southpaw by Henry W. Wiggen. Punctuation Freely Inserted and Spelling Greatly Improved by Mark Harris.* Indianapolis: Bobbs-Merrill, 1953.

———. *A Ticket for a Seamstitch. Henry W. Wiggen but Polished for the Printer by Mark Harris.* Lincoln: University of Nebraska Press, 1984 [1956].

Hayles, N. Katharine. *Chaos Bound: Orderly Disorder in Contemporary Literature and Science.* Ithaca, N.Y.: Cornell University Press, 1990.

Herrnstein, Richard J., and Charles Murray. *The Bell Curve: Intelligence and Class Structure in American Life.* New York: Free Press, 1994.

Homer. *The Iliad.* Trans. E. V. Rieu. Harmondsworth, Middlesex: Penguin, 1950.

James, Bill. *The Bill James Baseball Abstract, 1982.* New York: Ballantine, 1982.

———. *The Bill James Historical Baseball Abstract.* New York: Villard, 1986.

Jefferson, Thomas. *Notes on the State of Virginia.* Ed. William Peden. New York: Norton, 1954.

Jeffreys, Mark. "Ideologies of Lyric: A Problem of Genre in Contemporary Anglophone Poetics." *Publications of the Modern Language Association* 110 (1995): 196–205.

Kelly, Robert E. *Baseball's Best: Hall of Fame Pretenders Active in the Eighties.* Jefferson, N.C.: McFarland, 1988.

Kennedy, Colleen. "Simulating Sex and Imagining Mothers." *American Literary History* 4 (1992): 165-85.

King, Martin Luther, Jr. "I Have a Dream." In *The Heath Anthology of American Literature,* 2d ed., ed. Paul Lauter et al., 2 vols., 2:2483-86. Lexington, Mass.: Heath, 1994.

Kinsella, W. P. *The Iowa Baseball Confederacy.* New York: Ballantine, 1987.

———. *Shoeless Joe.* New York: Ballantine, 1990.

Klinkowitz, Jerry. "Philip Roth's Anti-Baseball Novel." *Western Humanities Review* 47, no. 1 (1993): 30-40.

Kupferberg, Herbert. "Meet Joe Boyd, Who Sold His Soul and Raised His Batting Average." *New York Herald Tribune Book Review,* September 12, 1954, p. 1.

———. "Trials and Triumphs of a Rookie Pitcher." *New York Herald Tribune Book Review,* April 12, 1953, p. 18.

Lacan, Jacques. "The Insistence of the Letter in the Unconscious." In *Modern Criticism and Theory: A Reader,* ed. David Lodge, 80-106. London: Longman, 1988. .

Laird, A. W. *Ranking Baseball's Elite: An Analysis Derived from Player Statistics, 1893-1987.* Jefferson, N.C.: McFarland, 1990.

Lardner, Ring. *Lose with a Smile.* New York: Scribner's, 1933.

———. *You Know Me Al.* Urbana: University of Illinois Press, 1992 [1914].

Lawrence, D. H. *Studies in Classic American Literature.* Harmondsworth, Middlesex: Penguin, 1971.

Lefcourt, Peter. *The Dreyfus Affair: A Love Story.* New York: HarperPerennial, 1993.

Levinson, Marilyn. *And Don't Bring Jeremy.* Illustrated by Diane de Groat. New York: Holt, 1985.

Lewin, Roger. "Evolution's New Heretics." *Natural History,* May 1996, pp. 12-17.

Litvak, Joseph. "Discipline, Spectacle, and Melancholia in and around the Gay Studies Classroom." In *Pedagogy: The Question of Impersonation,* ed. Jane Gallop, 19-27. Bloomington: Indiana University Press, 1995.

Lord, Bette Bao. *In the Year of the Boar and Jackie Robinson.* Illustrated by Marc Simont. New York: HarperTrophy, 1986.

Mack, Maynard. "The World of Hamlet." *Yale Review* 41 (1952): 502-23.

MacKinnon, Catharine A. *Only Words.* Cambridge, Mass.: Harvard University Press, 1993.

Mailer, Norman. *Marilyn.* New York: Grosset, 1973.

Malamud, Bernard. *The Natural.* New York: Noonday, 1990.

Maloney, John J. "Baseball as Folk-Myth." *New York Herald Tribune Book Review,* August 24, 1952, p. 8.

McManus, James. *Chin Music.* New York: Crown, 1985.

Messenger, Christian K. *Sport and the Spirit of Play in Contemporary American Fiction.* New York: Columbia University Press, 1990.

Minkowitz, Donna. "A New Enterprise." *The Advocate* 687/688 (Aug. 22, 1995): 64–78.

Minoso, Minnie, with Herb Fagen. *Just Call Me Minnie*. Champaign, Ill.: Sagamore, 1994.

Molloy, Paul. *A Pennant for the Kremlin*. Garden City, N.Y.: Doubleday, 1964.

Moore, Marianne. *The Complete Poems of Marianne Moore*. New York: Penguin, 1982.

"Mosley's Moves." *The New Yorker*, August 7, 1995, p. 27.

Mount, Nicholas J. "'Are the Green Fields Gone?': Pastoralism in the Baseball Novel." *Aethlon* 11, no. 1 (1993): 61–77.

Myers, Walter Dean. *Me, Mop, and the Moondance Kid*. Illustrated by Rodney Pate. New York: Delacorte, 1988.

Norman, Rick. *Fielder's Choice*. Little Rock: August House, 1991.

O'Brian, Patrick. "Just a Phase I'm Going Through?" *The Patrick O'Brian Newsletter*, March 1995, pp. 1, 3.

———. *Post Captain*. Philadelphia: Lippincott, 1972.

O'Connor, Gerry. "Bernard Malamud's *The Natural*: 'The Worst There Ever Was in the Game.'" *Arete* 3, no. 2 (1986): 37–42.

Official Baseball Rules. N.p.: The Sporting News, 1989.

Oriard, Michael. *Dreaming of Heroes: American Sports Fiction, 1868–1980*. Chicago: Nelson-Hall, 1982.

———. *Reading Football: How the Popular Press Created an American Spectacle*. Chapel Hill: University of North Carolina Press, 1993.

Portnoy, Mindy Avra. *Matzah Ball: A Passover Story*. Rockville, Md.: Kar-Ben, 1994.

Proust, Marcel. *A l'ombre des jeunes filles en fleurs*. Deuxième partie. Paris: GF-Flammarion, 1987.

———. *Within a Budding Grove*, trans. C. K. Scott Moncrief and Terence Kilmartin. In *Remembrance of Things Past*, 3 vols., 1:465–1018. New York: Random House, 1981.

Quigley, Martin. *Today's Game*. New York: Viking, 1965.

Rahv, Philip. "Paleface and Redskin." *Kenyon Review* 1, no. 3 (1939): 251–56.

Rey, Margret, and Alan J. Shalleck. *Curious George Plays Baseball*. Boston: Houghton Mifflin, 1986.

Rosen, R. D. *Strike Three You're Dead*. New York: Walker, 1984.

Ruth, George Herman. *Babe Ruth's Own Book of Baseball*. Lincoln: University of Nebraska Press, 1992 [1928].

Sedgwick, Eve Kosofsky. *Between Men: English Literature and Male Homosocial Desire*. New York: Columbia University Press, 1992 [1985].

———. *Epistemology of the Closet*. Berkeley: University of California Press, 1990.

Seuss, Dr. [pseud.]. *The Cat in the Hat Comes Back*. New York: Beginner, 1986.

Seymour, Harold. *Baseball: The People's Game*. New York: Oxford University Press, 1990.

Shaara, Michael. *For Love of the Game*. New York: Carroll, 1991.

Shumway, David R. *Creating American Civilization: A Genealogy of American Literature as an Academic Discipline*. Minneapolis: University of Minnesota Press, 1994.

Slote, Alfred. *Hang Tough, Paul Mather*. New York: HarperTrophy, 1985.

Smith, H. Allen. *Rhubarb*. Garden City, N.Y.: Doubleday, 1946.

Solomon, Eric. "Jews, Baseball, and the American Novel." *Arete* 1, no. 2 (1984): 43–66.

Stallings, Sylvia. "Love Forborne and Guarded in Silence." *New York Herald Tribune Book Review*, August 24, 1952, p. 4.

Sullivan, Dean A. *Early Innings: A Documentary History of Baseball, 1825–1908*. Lincoln: University of Nebraska Press, 1995.

Sylvester, Harry. "Touching All Bases." *New York Times Book Review*, April 12, 1953, p. 5.

———. "With Greatest of Ease." *New York Times Book Review*, August 24, 1952, p. 5.

Thorn, John, and Pete Palmer, eds. *Total Baseball*. CD-ROM. Creative Multimedia, 1994.

Tompkins, Jane. *West of Everything: The Inner Life of Westerns*. New York: Oxford University Press, 1992.

Tunis, John R. *Highpockets*. New York: Morrow, n.d. [1948].

———. *Keystone Kids*. San Diego: Harcourt, 1990 [1943].

———. *The Kid Comes Back*. New York: Beech Tree, 1993 [1946].

———. *The Kid from Tomkinsville*. San Diego: Harcourt, 1987 [1940].

———. *Rookie of the Year*. San Diego: Harcourt, 1990 [1944].

———. *Schoolboy Johnson*. New York: Morrow, 1991 [1958].

———. *World Series*. San Diego: Harcourt, 1987 [1941].

———. *Young Razzle*. New York: Morrow, n.d. [1949].

Wallop, Douglass. *The Year the Yankees Lost the Pennant*. New York: Norton, 1954.

Wasserman, Earl R. "*The Natural:* Malamud's World Ceres." In *Bernard Malamud*, ed. Harold Bloom, 47–64. New York: Chelsea House, 1986.

Westbrook, Deeanne. *Ground Rules: Baseball and Myth*. Urbana: University of Illinois Press, 1996.

Wineapple, Brenda. "Robert Coover's Playing Fields." *The Iowa Review* 10, no. 3 (1979): 66–74.

Wolfe, Alan. "Has There Been a Cognitive Revolution in America? The Flawed Sociology of *The Bell Curve*." In *The Bell Curve Wars*, ed. Steven Fraser, 109–23. New York: Basic, 1995.

Yeats, William Butler. *Selected Poems and Two Plays*. New York: Collier, 1966.

Young, Iris Marion. *Justice and the Politics of Difference*. Princeton, N.J.: Princeton University Press, 1990.

Young, Michael. *The Rise of the Meritocracy, 1870–2033: An Essay on Education and Equality*. Baltimore: Penguin, 1961 [1958].

Index

TIMOTHY MORRIS is a fan of the Texas Rangers and lives in Arlington, Texas, with his wife, Margaret, and son, Fran, who are fans of the New York Yankees. He is the author of *Becoming Canonical in American Poetry* (University of Illinois Press, 1995) and articles in *Studies in American Fiction, ATQ, Arizona Quarterly, Aethlon,* and other journals.

People of Prowess: Sport, Leisure, and Labor in Early Anglo-America
  Nancy L. Struna

The New American Sport History: Recent Approaches and Perspectives
  Edited by S. W. Pope

Making the Team: The Cultural Work of Baseball Fiction *Timothy Morris*

Reprint Editions

The Nazi Olympics *Richard D. Mandell*

Sports in the Western World (Second Edition) *William J. Baker*